COVENTRY
THE HIDDEN HISTORY

COVENTRY
THE HIDDEN HISTORY

IAIN SODEN

The History Press

In the name of Jesus Christ
Lord and Saviour

First published 2005

Reprinted in 2013 by
The History Press
The Mill, Brimscombe Port,
Stroud, Gloucestershire, GL5 2QG
www.thehistorypress.co.uk

© Iain Soden, 2013

The right of Iain Soden to be identified as the Author
of this work has been asserted in accordance with the
Copyrights, Designs and Patents Act 1988.

British Library Cataloguing in Publication Data.
A catalogue record for this book is available from the British Library.

ISBN 978 0 7524 3345 5

Typesetting and origination by
Tempus Publishing Limited
Printed and bound by TJ International Ltd, Padstow, Cornwall

Contents

Preface

The City of Coventry is around a thousand years old. Its transformation from a small, Late Saxon village from the ninth or tenth centuries to an urban centre in the thirteenth was total, if not always rapid and spectacular. In terms of wealth and consequent taxation it is reckoned by historians that in 1377 Coventry ranked, on the basis of a national Poll Tax index, as the fourth city in the kingdom, after London, Bristol and York. At this period it was approaching the height of its influence. Its regional predominance gave rise to a proud governing class and a self-belief which led to civic pride on a grand scale. The city fathers walled in the city and contained its archaeology. The city possessed a wool and woollen cloth export trade which had few parallels and such wealth meant that the city attracted the best craftsmen, offering the most expensive skills and producing the finest of buildings and goods during the late fourteenth and fifteenth centuries. By then seven monastic orders came to settle in the city or its immediate vicinity: Benedictine, Cistercian, Knights Templar (later Hospitaller), Franciscan, Carmelite and Carthusian. It was considered for an eighth, Austin Friars. All drew on the burgeoning wealth of the medieval city while giving back a spiritual and cultural dimension which today can only be recovered through field archaeology and the complementary study of documents of all kinds.

The dramatic decline which overtook the city from the early sixteenth century was all the more disastrous since it stood in stark contrast to the wealth which had gone before. The Dissolution of the Monasteries meant that within four months between October 1538 and January 1539 the heart of the medieval city stopped beating and its trade network was wiped out with such thoroughness that the already depleted economy stood little chance of recovery for at least a generation. In the event it was much slower. The city was still considered a stately sight on the eve of the Civil War, but the city of 1642 was perhaps a pale economic shadow of its pre-1539 self. However, the city which emerged from the Civil War, swollen with war-ravaged refugees and prisoners of war, was bursting at the seams. After apparent release from the burdens of war, the Restoration of the monarchy in 1660 led to the city's further woes as the Crown strove to rid a potentially rebellious Coventry of its defences. In 1662 the medieval walls, so long a symbol of status, were made indefensible and the stone carted away. The one-time jewel of the Midlands, bereft of its monasteries, four of its seven spires, and now its walls, was reduced to little more than a market town, still governed like a city but with revenues a fraction of previous levels. The end of the medieval period in Coventry was marked by national events which had dire local consequences.

While John Speed's map of the city in 1610 (*1*), shows the medieval city with huge open wounds where the monasteries had stood, a map by Samuel Bradford

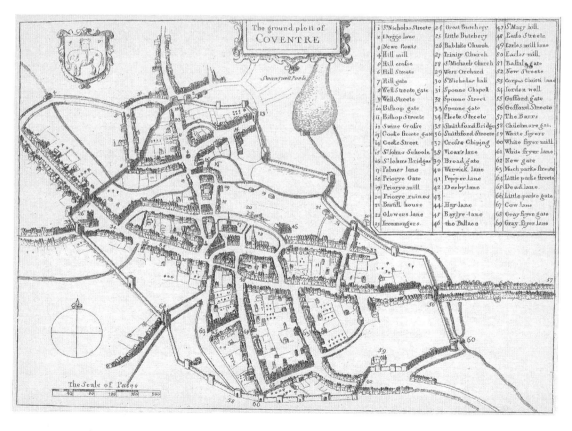

1 Map of Coventry by John Speed 1610. *From a print of 1870*

of 1748 indicates little had changed since 1610. No one had been able to expand the comparatively stagnant and ailing city across the former defences and great gaps yawned across the former monastic precincts. It was only with the rise of the silk ribbon and watch trades that Coventry again began to enjoy a place in the mercantile life of the country.

The everyday events in the lives of individual citizens in any generation, triumphs and disasters, big and small, all leave their mark on the physical remains of the old city. New buildings, demolition, redevelopment, extensions, fires, war, growing businesses, businesses failing; all have vestiges in archaeology, producing a physical document of constant change to be read whenever the opportunity arises for excavation. The walled city of Coventry comprises a third of a square mile of deeply stratified archaeology. Its dependent villages, the modern suburbs, which from 1451 constituted the County of the City of Coventry, cover a further 38 square miles: a lot of archaeology (2).

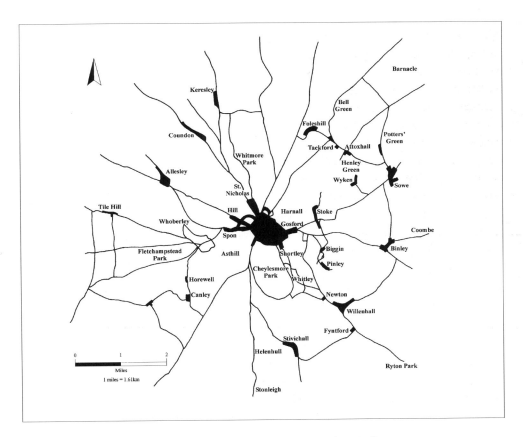

2 The roads, villages and hamlets around the medieval city. *Jacqueline Harding*

Some may wish to see a chronological layout in a book of archaeology and history. However, the archaeology of Coventry does not present itself so readily. I have set out the various aspects thematically rather than chronologically since there is really no single event which sensibly breaks up the medieval period in Coventry. Its strategic position throughout the period means that while it certainly suffered when the rest of the country suffered, and triumphed when the rest of the country triumphed, it nevertheless had an undeniable ability to recover from disaster and adapt to change. While there was certainly a physical Norman Coventry and a Plantagenet, pre-plague and post-plague periods, a Tudor and a Post-Dissolution, none of these periods betoken changes present and discernible on a city-wide scale in the physical archaeological record. There is continuity everywhere. The city never languished as a whole; it just kept growing until the sixteenth century; until the medieval world finally passed from the whole stage of English history in a spectacular economic slide from around 1500 and in the bloody throes of religious and civil strife between 1539 and 1651. Only then was there an ending of sorts and new, faltering beginnings.

Systematic archaeology in Coventry is relatively new. Although there was fieldwork carried out before and just after the Second World War, it was small-scale and haphazard, with no concerted approach. Its use by historians has often been widespread but is arguably misguided. Archaeology has only played a growing part of the city's changing landscape since the 1960s. The pace of redevelopment quickened from the 1980s and national approaches changed markedly in 1990 with the introduction of Government Planning Policy Guidance Note 16. This enabled the local planning authority, Coventry City Council, in common with the rest of the country, to require prospective developers to make suitable provision to either preserve significant archaeological deposits beneath new developments using largely sympathetic foundation designs, or else to fund the professional excavation of those deposits. The increase in sites has been almost exponential. This system works for the most part and now covers not just the city centre but also the innumerable sites of known historic significance which lie in today's suburbs. Thus medieval villages, hamlets, manor houses and moats are all included and the sites mapped. Their historic landscape setting is also becoming better understood through the city's new and pioneering Historic Environment Record. Since 2003 Coventry has enjoyed its own distinct place in the English Heritage-sponsored West Midlands Regional Research Framework for Archaeology, separate from both the historic and contemporary counties within which it stands, as befits its singular development and history. This includes both an Assessment of the Resource and the Research Framework within which fieldwork will be carried out over the next generation.

I hope that amongst these pages I have been able to place the archaeological discoveries of the last 50 years into a historical framework and at the same time illustrate aspects of Coventry's history with the highlights of archaeological breakthroughs, many of which rarely see the light of day beyond learned but obscure journals (all archaeologists are to blame for this, me included). The sites represented here are the most revealing of those which have been investigated and the results analysed. They contribute most to the bigger picture. Some, excavated but yet to be analysed, can only add to the already rich array. The future will widen our view further.

Archaeologists come and go. I have been fortunate to spend a large portion of my career so far close to one archaeologist in particular, Margaret Rylatt. Most of the excavations with which I have been involved have also entailed her input and encouragement, however much her role was constrained by irksome local authority administration (which she so often spared me). She has also been my link to the largely unwritten work of the antiquarian John Shelton, who was almost the only antiquarian presence during Coventry's great rebuilding of the 1930s, '40s and '50s, and whose biography she co-wrote.

Beyond Coventry I have also had the privilege to have directed extensive excavations in half a dozen of England's other fine historic towns and cities, particularly on monastic sites. I have also travelled widely across Europe, seeking relevant archaeological context. I hope that this has enabled me to see the relative value of Coventry's urban and suburban archaeology in a wider arena. Some of the ideas I proffer here are inevitably borne out of these wider studies, both archaeological and historical.

Throughout this book archaeology and history mingle, hopefully seamlessly, since my own background covers both. As disciplines, archaeology and history should not be separated since they are simply complementary tools for the study of the same past. I make no apologies for using history to provide context for the results of excavations and use excavations to challenge accepted history. Archaeology and history are always in parallel, but they do, on occasions, appear to be in tension, since they do not necessarily throw light upon the same processes, sequences and events. Just as historical documents are not always truthful, can be downright forgeries, or describe wishful thinking or proposals never carried out, so archaeology can be misinterpreted by over-confident or inexperienced archaeologists because of inadequate dating or insufficient evidence. Rarely is evidence unequivocal and an element of interpretation almost always creeps in. Too many archaeologists wish their site to be the biggest, the best or the most important of its type and talk it up in these terms. In reality, it rarely is; many can be simply mundane. Thus interpretation should not be pushed too far, nor any site's importance overstated. Such are the chinks in the armour of both archaeologist and historian alike.

Coventry has seen many antiquarians and archaeologists in the century between around 1860 and 1960. I owe a debt to them all for the work they did. In my own time there have been many others whose sojourn in Coventry, however long or brief, has left its mark both on the city and on me: Adrian and Christine Adams, Colin Baddeley, Albert Barnett, John Bateman, Bunny Best, Alan Birch, Marion Carlick, Ray Cartwright, Brent Coates, Myk Flitcroft, Bill Ford, Val Goode, Alan Hannan, John Haslam, Tom Heyes, Tony Howard, Terry Leonard, Barry Lewis, Bernard and Joan Oakley, Jim Owen, Steve Parry, Mark Redknap, Keith Scott, Bob Thompson, Paul Thompson, Paul and Charmian Woodfield, Ray Wallwork and Peter E. Woodward. Some, I have been (and remain) privileged to know personally, others I know only from their work; sadly, some are now dead. Many have been leading lights in the Coventry and District Archaeological Society, whose work since the 1960s has been an indispensable cornerstone of fieldwork in the city.

This book is about my home city. I was born, raised and schooled in Coventry. Since University, I have been privileged to hold various professional archaeological posts in the Herbert Art Gallery and Museum and the Planning Department of the City which has been home to many generations of my family. Today I am a contractor, with my own archaeological business (www.isheritage.co.uk). As a small child I sought to be an archaeologist and to live my dream. However, it would not have been possible without the support of some fantastic teachers, colleagues and companions whose encouragement, advice, help, cajoling and friendship have been principal factors in my education, which I hope will continue until the day I too become a piece of archaeology. I owe so much to my parents, my wife and sons, whose support has never wavered. To Ted Norrish, for the foundations of my Latin and Greek, but who also nurtured my self-belief in the Pindos Mountains. To Margaret Rylatt, so long a colleague but always my friend and mentor. Her presence was ever a spur. The many teachers and colleagues who have challenged me over the years, particularly Trevor Anderson, the late Philip Barker, Paul Blinkhorn, John Cherry, John Cole, Glyn Coppack, George Demidowicz, J. Edward Dickinson, Oliver Dickinson, Brian Dix, Rod Dunnett, David Gaimster, Roberta Gilchrist, Stephen Hill, John Hunt, the late John Hurst, Stanley Ireland, Simon Johnson, Helen Keeley, Martin Locock, Paul Mason, Maureen Mellor, Steve Moorhouse, Richard K. Morris, Beverley Nenk, Nick Palmer, Steve Parry, Jeff Perry, Joe Prentice, Stephanie Ratkai, Peter Rhodes, the late Mike Stokes, Jeremy Thomas, Roger White, Anna Wilson and Gavin Townend.

I am very grateful also to a number of individuals in particular who offered me great help with archives, particularly Michael Hinman, David Rimmer and Susan Worrall (Coventry Archivists, past and present), Dom Luc Fauchon, sometime Archivist of La Grande Chartreuse, Grenoble and Fr Ninian Arbuckle, Archivist of the Franciscan International Study Centre, Canterbury. I am also indebted to the staff of the National Archives, Kew, Warwickshire and Lichfield

Record Offices, Birmingham City Archives, and those of the Shakespeare Birthplace Trust, Stratford-upon-Avon.

The list of people who have found themselves at the mercy of my every whim while excavating gets longer with each passing year. Unfortunately, my memory gets shorter. They all have my thanks and sympathy. In an age where multiple careers characterise many working lives, some are archaeologists for only a short period. However brief our working association, I record my gratitude to exceptional colleagues whose own contributions to Coventry's archaeology at any one time have inadvertently benefited me, in particular: Sophie Barrington, Diana Bernard, Jenny Butterworth, Vanessa Clarke, Richard Cuttler, Bryn Gethin, Tim Hallam, Jacqueline Harding, Mark Holmes, Harriet Anne Jacklin, Chris Jones, Barry Lewis, Danny McAree, Alex Thorne and Jo Wainwright.

My thanks to George, Stephanie and Steve, who have helped in providing comments and checking the text of this book; to Jacqui and Harriet, in providing drawings far better than I can manage; and to Barry and Danny for photographs which have admirably filled the gaps in my own records. All photographs in this volume are by the author unless otherwise stated. Doubtless, despite my own efforts and the strivings of others on my behalf, there will still be some of my own, quirky errors, for which I apologise. The perfect record does not exist.

While I enjoy the Coventry-kid's privilege of an insider's view of the city, I am acutely aware that archaeology can be a wonderfully neutral thing and it is pertinent to all who live in, work in or merely visit a place. For the most part archaeology deals with buildings, artefacts, past landscapes – manifestations of environments long past. But most of all it is about people and they don't change. Thus archaeology can enjoy an immensely wide appeal, crossing borders, ignoring race, devoid of politics. On occasions when archaeology has been used to justify a contemporary cause, or legitimise the ownership of a single group's history, it has brought only discredit to the discipline. In our present fluid society few of the 300,000 or so Coventrians in the early twenty-first century can claim distant ancestry in Coventry. The number who remember the city before the Blitz of 1940 inevitably dwindles.

Therefore this book is written with both the archaeologist in mind and the thousands of people who have stopped to gaze at the remains uncovered in the welter of redevelopment since the 1960s, or chanced upon their reporting in the local press. Whether you can claim distant Coventry ancestry, or arrived only yesterday; whatever your origin, this is your heritage, your culture, your city.

1

Life on the streets

'A citie very commodiously seated, large, sweet and neat, fortified with strong walls and set out with right goodly houses.' Dr Philemon Holland 1551-1636

Dr Philemon Holland, teaching at the Old Grammar School, wrote of a city already 500 years old. His was a city of timber-framed houses, with a street layout long since fossilised. This was, however, the product of a long process in which some street frontages had crept back and forth, at one time pressed for space, at another enjoying relative wide open space. The archaeology of the city's streets is as diverse as their number. It is also a story which needs to be unpicked from the morass of heavily redeveloped frontages which have characterised the post-war city.

BEGINNINGS

The Coventry which emerged from relative Saxon and Norman obscurity was ideally placed to exploit both its location at the centre of a unified kingdom and an abundance of natural resources which existed in the region. It was, however, probably quite small and inward-looking, its homesteads grouped around the minster church endowed by Leofric and Godiva in the early eleventh century. The immense manor of Coventry appears to have been owned in its entirety by Godiva herself, in whose name it was administered. Her death at around the time of the Norman Conquest and the consequent estate's passage to the Crown made it an ideal estate to be re-assigned to a new Norman overlord, a transition from the Saxon for which there is no evidence of bloodshed or serious rankle. The new overlords were the Earls of Chester, who followed their peers' lead elsewhere and established a castle. The contemporary transfer to Coventry of the Chester Bishopric ensured that Coventry was following the same pattern of Norman conquest by wholesale replacement of existing institutions with new ones of a continental flavour, with church and state inter-twined. If ever it were needed, there was the threat of force to back them up.

There had, in fact, been occupation in the area now known as Coventry for at least a thousand years, but it bore no resemblance to the character and fantastic growth which the early medieval period would witness. An Iron Age settlement of some 14 round-houses at Canley represents the earliest evidence for occupation so far proven (probably third century BC to first century AD, excavated by the University of Warwick in 2002). The Lunt Roman fort at nearby Baginton was occupied briefly in the first century AD and reoccupied for an even shorter time in the third when a military presence was thought necessary, while its nearby civilian settlement seems to have been continuously occupied. The enclosure ditch of a second-century Romano-British farmstead has been found at Willenhall (Eastern Bypass excavations 1987) and at Walsgrave (Cross-Point cinema site 1991), while the first recorded 'modern' archaeological find in the city was made in the form of a late fourth-century coin hoard near the Foleshill Road as far back as 1793.

Like the Roman and prehistoric periods before, Saxon remains from Coventry are few, not least because their relatively ephemeral nature means that the growth of a medieval city and the spread of its post-medieval and modern successors have very successfully smothered and truncated the earlier remains. For this reason Coventry is not generally a profitable place to research midland Saxon towns. It remains surrounded, however, by a former Saxon landscape in which names are key characteristics. It is very likely that many of the villages which today constitute the city's suburbs owe their beginnings to Saxon farmers, sometime between the fifth and the eighth centuries. Their Old English names alone fit good patterns of Saxon origins, such as the numerous -ley word-endings signifying the clearings in the woodland in Keres-ley, Alles-ley, Can-ley and Bin-ley. The -hall names are redolent of administrative capacities and centres of local power: Stivichall, Attoxhall and Willenhall. Other lesser areas signify an Anglo-Scandinavian (Viking) presence, on the frontier of the Danelaw as agreed by treaty in 886. In Canley can be found Gunneputtes from the Old Scandinavian (and modern) personal name Gunnar, with related Norse name-derived fields, while as late as 1279 can be found in the Hundred Rolls significant numbers of residents with Anglo-Scandinavian names such as Tostig and Thurstan intermingled with the majority Saxo-Norman. Settlements around the city still resonate with Norse name endings like Rug-by, Prince-thorpe, liberally intermingled with the Saxon endings of -ton and -burgh. Seemingly the area had been a frontier melting-pot for some time.

To date the nearest excavated early-to-middle Saxon remains are those of a sixth-century pagan cremation-cemetery beneath Baginton Airport in the 1930s, which seems to betoken a near-continuity of occupation from Roman to early Saxon in the area, but without any Coventry focus. While this may appear isolated, there is probably other such settlement-related evidence in Coventry yet to be found, possibly connected with the later, medieval foci, such as the 'suburb' of St Nicholas, whose original settlement name is entirely unknown but whose church of the same dedication at the corner of Sandy Lane and St Nicholas' Street is reputed to have been in existence as early as 1003. The site has periodically produced human remains since the nineteenth century.

In the city itself, pre-Conquest evidence is entirely linked to the most densely occupied part of the centre. Most comes from excavations around the Cathedral and Benedictine Priory of St Mary (1999-2003), where a medieval cut-and-fill approach to construction on the hill slope had truncated some remains but buried others. A stone window- or arch-head was found there which is carved exactly like that from the tower of All Saints' Church, Earl's Barton (Northamptonshire, eleventh century), while a fragment of Saxon cross-shaft bearing interlace decoration was earlier pulled from below Trinity Street. A Viking-style riding stirrup and a contemporary iron axe-head are from the same Priory area, near the River Sherbourne, as are numerous late Saxon floor and wall-tiles.

From the excavations of the Priory comes the only evidence of a pre-Conquest structure. Beneath the north arcade of the Romanesque Cathedral nave lay a relatively nondescript patch of sandstone rubble, bonded in a distinctive greenish lime mortar. It described an arc along one well-cut edge but had been otherwise truncated by one of the twelfth-century arcade piers of the Cathedral. A skeleton buried beneath the arcade pier was dated by Radiocarbon calibration to 1160, helping date the arcade, while below the arc of masonry was residual human bone in a grave subjected to the same scrutiny. The Radiocarbon-date of AD 875 shows that there has been Christian burial on the site since the ninth century. A second early body in the cloister was also tested in this way and a date in the tenth century confirmed the pre-Conquest presence. Of a small number of Saxon coins which have surfaced over the years, a gold coin of 886 (Alfred the Great), was spectacular evidence of the ninth-century focus.

Whether the early structure was part of the purported Godivan minster church or the even more anecdotal ninth-century nunnery of St Osburga is, in many ways, not in the purview of archaeology. Over the years too many myths and legends have sprung up around the supposed founders and benefactors of these early establishments for any new find to be treated with anything but healthy circumspection. Leofric and Godiva's legend was a political pawn for the Benedictine institution in the medieval period and the nature of real archaeological remains should not be sullied by too close an association with persons whose lives are shrouded in myths, not provable by archaeological means. It is enough for the archaeologist simply to agree that certainly they existed and exercised some authority in the eleventh-century Midlands generally and in Coventry specifically, but no more. Even a hypothetical discovery of the Cathedral's twin chapels containing tombs (as a medieval historian purported) named as those of Leofric and Godiva would need to be viewed with considerable scepticism since 'ownership' of a long-lived Christian tradition and patronage became politically desirable in the medieval period and forgery was commonplace in order to legitimise claims to lineage and social and political standing.

EMERGENCE

That early medieval Coventry emerged in the twelfth century as a minor centre of Anglo-Norman power is without doubt, although once more archaeology can do little to settle argument about what was the exact balance of power since administration leaves little trace in the ground except where boundaries – the limits of power, jurisdiction, or ownership – are physically marked, by castle, church, wall, fence and ditch. The earliest phases of medieval Coventry, like their late Saxon predecessors, are largely ephemeral and truncated, lost under the expansion which characterised the city's rapid rise to prominence in the thirteenth to fourteenth centuries (3). Archaeology has, however, found no evidence for wholesale and forcible substitution of Saxon occupation with Norman, such as happened, for instance, when the castle bailey was laid out at Norwich. Similarly there appears to have been no creation of a meticulously-planned 'French Borough', such as at Norwich or Northampton. Coventry's transition seems to have been more peaceful and perhaps reflects a lack of urgency felt towards this well-placed but then under-developed town. Early finds suggest its focus was the open market place, where now Broadgate and Ironmonger Row lie, joined early on by other encroachments, Potter Row, Glover Row, Spicerstoke and other mercantile gatherings.

Dominated by the twin bastions of Benedictine Priory (Abbey until *c.*1100 when the Cathedral was created) and Castle, the early direction which the town was to take was a decision vested in the partisan attitudes of Bishop, Prior and Earl of Chester and the personal ambitions and tensions enjoyed by this powerful triumvirate. In 1250 the de Montalt Earls sold their claim to the manor to the Prior, but only with an annual rental payment of over £800 to them and later the Crown as eventual heir to the Earldom. By the fourteenth century the Bishop had moved his seat to the other half of the double See at Lichfield,

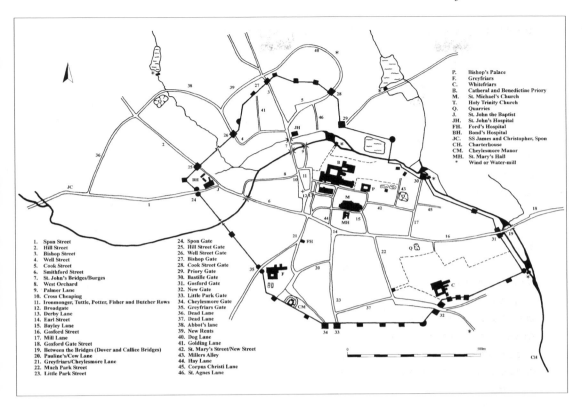

P.   Bishop's Palace
F.   Greyfriars
C.   Whitefriars
B.   Cathedral and Benedictine Priory
M.   St. Michael's Church
T.   Holy Trinity Church
Q.   Quarries
J.   St. John the Baptist
JH.   St. John's Hospital
FH.   Ford's Hospital
BH.   Bond's Hospital
JC.   SS James and Christopher, Spon
CH.   Charterhouse
CM.   Cheylesmore Manor
MH.   St. Mary's Hall
*   Wind or Water-mill

1. Spon Street
2. Hill Street
3. Bishop Street
4. Well Street
5. Cook Street
6. Smithford Street
7. St. John's Bridges/Burges
8. West Orchard
9. Palmer Lane
10. Cross Cheaping
11. Ironmonger, Tuttle, Potter, Fisher and Butcher Rows
12. Broadgate
13. Derby Lane
14. Earl Street
15. Bayley Lane
16. Gosford Street
17. Mill Lane
18. Gosford Gate Street
19. Between the Bridges (Dover and Callice Bridges)
20. Pauline's/Cow Lane
21. Greyfriars/Cheylesmore Lane
22. Much Park Street
23. Little Park Street

24. Spon Gate
25. Hill Street Gate
26. Well Street Gate
27. Bishop Gate
28. Cook Street Gate
29. Priory Gate
30. Bastille Gate
31. Gosford Gate
32. New Gate
33. Little Park Gate
34. Cheylesmore Gate
35. Greyfriars Gate
36. Dead Lane
37. Dead Lane
38. Abbot's lane
39. New Rents
40. Dog Lane
41. Golding Lane
42. St. Mary's Street/New Street
43. Millers Alley
44. Hay Lane
45. Corpus Christi Lane
46. St. Agnes Lane

3 The late medieval city streets and late medieval town wall. *Jacqueline Harding*

although he and the others continued to exercise considerable rivalry for the city's burgeoning wealth.

For most of the period *c.*1100-1250 one of the biggest bars to the development of the city was the fortunes of these individuals. Their mode of government, in line with the rest of Anglo-Norman society, was feudal; based upon a seemingly simple hierarchy of allegiances. In practice it led to land restrictions, protectionism and a search for patronage which might produce personal alliances on the one hand, but personal enmities on the other. In terms of the changing topography of the fledgling town, this meant that the present parishes of St Michael and Holy Trinity on the ground mimic an earlier civic distinction between Earl and Prior, whose personal spiritual lives were enhanced by their respective parish churches, apparently enough to serve the comparatively small numbers of people in the town. Likewise the south side of the city butted upon the personal estate of the Earl in the form of Cheylesmore Park. Around the park lay the park-pale, a massive ditch and bank, topped by a hedge. The ditch, known as the Hyrsum-ditch or 'obedience' ditch was a physical constraint upon the southward expansion of the town and it was only a relaxation of its role, sometime in the thirteenth century, which enabled the creation and growth of Much and Little Park Streets as viable thoroughfares. Prior to that, goods bound for London probably had to go further east and turn down a street later relegated to the status of a mere lane, Whitefriars Lane, to head south alongside the edge of the park on what is still known as London Road. This great ditch, later more often called the Red Ditch or the Town Ditch (not to be confused with the later defences), ran from east of Greyfriars Lane almost to Whitefriars Street, parallel with the line of High Street– Earl Street–Jordan Well, before turning south at each end. It was seen in section in 1974 during the construction of Civic Centre 4 and again in 1980 when the Law Courts were built. At several metres deep and wide, it was a considerable barrier and even when increasingly used as a town sewer and culverted over some of its length by the end of the fourteenth century, it still remained in the public psyche and documents continue to refer to it into the eighteenth century.

By the end of the medieval period, the traveller John Leland would write of Coventry in *c*.1543: 'There be dyvours fayre suburbs without the waulls of Coventry'. They became typical medieval ribbon-developments, spreading along the principal routes into the city. However it was not always so and the unwalled Anglo-Norman town was, for some time well into the thirteenth century and possibly later, a very separate entity from the outlying hamlets which began life as Gooseford, Sponna, St Nicholas, Hull and Arnhale.

In three places it has been seen just how tightly concentrated was the Anglo-Norman nucleus of the town. At 114-5 Gosford Street (1987), Cheylesmore Manor (1992) and even as far in as 7-10 Much Park Street (1970), the infilled remains of pronounced twelfth-century ridge-and-furrow cultivation have been found lying beneath the buildings in each case. At 114-5 Gosford Street, the location (beneath the rear of the property) and the north-south alignment mean that there would have been insufficient room to turn a team of oxen in the space between there and the street. Thus not only can there have been no frontage building there in the twelfth century, it is likely that the roadway too had not yet materialised as a permanent way and was perhaps no more than an occasional track beaten down along a causeway embankment between fields to the Goose-Ford; fair game for any farmer who wished to maximise his cropping area. Here too the last share-cut of the plough lay in the furrow, and the ox-team's hoof prints were preserved in the heavy clay of the ridge-sides as they dragged the plough north under what is today the 'Whitefriars' public house, a building itself tree-ring dated to the 1350s.

However, there were certainly buildings in the vicinity before 1350, but which post-dated the ridge-and-furrow cultivation, since there were twelfth- to thirteenth-century rubbish pits cut into the infilled furrows and the ridge sides, but their proximity to the roadside suggests that any frontage was for quite some time discontinuous, there being apparently no great press for space. It seems that the city at its eastern end would have enjoyed a sort of medieval green belt between it and its satellite neighbour at Gosford. Recent (1995, 2003, 2006) fieldwork off Far Gosford Street and Whitefriars Street, and other excavated evidence from adjacent plots (1995 and 2004) confirms the dearth of domestic occupation in the twelfth century but notes an expansion beginning in the thirteenth, including widespread evidence for metalworking, stone-quarrying and specialist horticulture. The evidence from 114-115 Gosford Street suggests that expansion took quite some time to gather pace and be turned into hard development all along the street where neighbouring plots seem to have been put to very different uses.

If the eastward expansion of the town towards Gosford took some time, it seems part of a measured pattern mirrored on the west where there was a similar lack of urgency. Excavations took place at the rear of 121-4 Spon Street, historically part of Spon End or Spon Causeway at the corner with Barras Lane, known in the medieval period as Dead Lane; one of a number to share that name. The plot in question became known as Swan Terrace and is today a restored group of late medieval cottages. Before the development of their characteristic long, sinuous rear plots in 1992, archaeological excavations uncovered the ditches which had originally marked out the rear plots. Material found within their basal fills dated them to the mid-thirteenth century, roughly contemporary with the evidence for the earliest eastward expansion towards Gosford. The buildings of 121-4 can be traced to 1410 when they were Priory property, while four previous owners were attested at that date. If each previous ownership had lasted a generation of *c.*30 years, then the property would date to *c.*1290; history and archaeology in almost perfect harmony!

BOOM TOWN

The continuous occupation of Coventry's street frontages for more than 800 years means that little remains of its earliest domestic buildings. They were almost certainly of timber, from the post-holes which characterise those scant remains smothered by later structures. Some buildings made increasing use of the excellent local sandstone from the thirteenth century onwards, and a particular style developed in which a timber house of two or (more rarely) three storeys would be built over a vaulted stone 'tavern' or cellar. Some particular examples, such as the White Cellar tenement, which stood on the east corner of Much

Park Street and Earl Street, are distinguished by their title in early deeds. Others make brief spectacular appearances in records. Kelly's Directory for 1850 records that:

> In 1820 the west side of Broadgate was pulled down, together with several houses on Smithford Street (north side). In excavating the foundations of the site of the old Broadgate, the cellaring exhibited some fine specimens of massive stone arches ....

4 The fourteenth-century Stone House, Much Park Street, interior

On Much Park Street stands an example of one similar house, which eschewed most timber elements and was built entirely of stone (*4*). Related fourteenth-century stone vaults still survive on Bayley Lane, under the 1950s shops on Earl Street and under the Coventry and Halifax Building Societies in High Street. Many more, probably bereft of their vaulted ceilings, lie as yet undiscovered on these streets, on Bishop Street, Cross Cheaping, Smithford Street and many others.

A fourteenth-century cellar on Bayley Lane was actually set back from the historic street frontage, apparently behind the building which people would see as they walked along the street. This would not be remarkable except that in 1995 a roughly contemporary cellar was exposed in a similar position behind The Phoenix public house (then the Sir Colin Campbell). It was dated to the period 1380-1410, the heyday of such cellars in the city, but had been unroofed and filled in during the nineteenth century. The location of these cellars, almost shoe-horned in, might suggest that as a status symbol they were sought after, but that their construction might be too disruptive to dig under existing buildings. One example of such disruption actually being contemplated was a fifteenth-century application to the Holy Trinity Guild by one of their tenants in Hill Street, who wished to dig a tavern *under* his shop. It is certain this was to be of stone since his request states that he already had the masons standing by. Such a construction, as the base for a contemporary rear wing, however, might be less disruptive.

Understanding of the word 'cellar' has become coloured by the thousands of Victorian houses which lie over such structures in our towns and cities. In fact many medieval cellars were not totally buried but had windows on one or more sides. That under the corner of Bayley Lane actually had a large four-light north-facing window which looked out on the former St Michael's churchyard and New Street. It was blocked probably when Priory Street was built in the 1840s (then called Edward Street, after the new-born Prince of Wales, Edward VII). Such a window would have allowed some natural light in while its northerly aspect meant that with no direct sun, temperatures could be kept low if needed. Conversely, the cellar behind The Phoenix/Sir Colin Campbell in Gosford Street contained a west window; on that plot was evidence of non-ferrous metalworking, so a west window would allow work to go on indoors, even in bad weather, late into the afternoon, making use of the last of the afternoon light. It would also ventilate the cellar if it was being used for work, rather than storage. Access to such cellars might be from inside the building above, such as at Gosford Street or also from outside, as at the Stone House in Much Park Street or at the Bayley Lane cellar where two entrances are present. Another Bayley Lane cellar was excavated in 1988 on the west side of the street, where it had been dug into the fill of a former quarry; the tenement was known at that time as 'the delph'. Here there was no evidence for windows per se, but only for narrow slits which barely let in light but might still have served as ventilation (5). It is likely that in this particular location such slits looked directly into the neighbour's yard, so there may have been precious little light to admit anyway. That the neighbour may have run a foundry (John Foundur), with all the noise and noxious fumes this entailed, may have precluded further development. Both the excavated cellar and numerous waste metal moulds attest this potentially uneasy juxtaposition.

Of course not all buildings were cellared; perhaps only 20 per cent at most. The vast majority began life as timbered structures of single or two storeys in the thirteenth century. Most known from excavations seem to have been redeveloped, perhaps in the later thirteenth or fourteenth centuries, some involving initial

5 Remains of the cellar in 'the delph', Bayley Lane, 1988. Note the narrowest of windows

subdivision, but generally most by wholesale rebuilding in the fourteenth or fifteenth centuries (when the cellared examples are mostly conceived). The rarest plots are those on which no medieval cellar was constructed and no later Victorian cellar dug, with minimal Victorian foundations. Since, by the nineteenth century, most plots had fossilised with the legal boundaries seen today, Victorian foundations, on strips of iron-hard, brick-laced concrete were dug directly into the identically-aligned foundations of their predecessors; archaeologically they have been very destructive.

Such a situation arose at Derby Lane. Also known in the medieval period as Tirryston Lane, possibly from the thirteenth-century Tirry family of Coventry who lived nearby, much of the east side of the lane was excavated archaeologically in 1982–84. The site was regularly broken up into compartments by

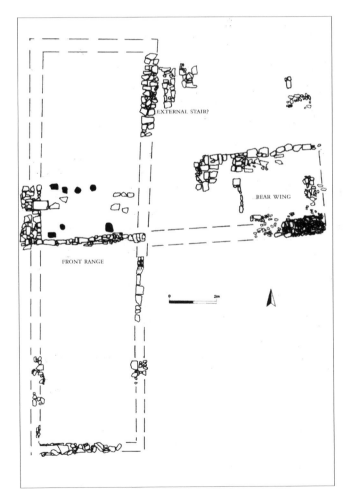

EXTERNAL STAIR?

REAR WING

FRONT RANGE

0   2m

6 Thirteenth- to fourteenth-century stone buildings excavated on Derby Lane, 1982–84. Probably a hall and chamber behind shops, a common Coventry arrangement

the foundations of the nineteenth- and twentieth-century buildings which had succeeded their medieval counterparts. In almost every case these more modern foundations had truncated large portions of the medieval buildings. However, a reconstruction from surviving dwarf walls points to a large, thirteenth-century, stone-founded tenement shop with a rear wing, later subdivided before being swept away in the late medieval period by new buildings (*6*). This is not an uncommon arrangement in the city. The west side of the Lane, down to the plateau of Broadgate (itself partly excavated in 1974-5), had been graded almost down to the natural geology just after the Second World War, such that no medieval building remains survived at all, but only deeply cut pits and ditches. The route of Derby Lane no longer exists, subsumed under the Cathedral Lanes development in the early 1990s. The deepest features remain beneath it.

The archaeological record of artefacts from ordinary houses is remarkably diverse. It suggests a wide range of activities which were pursued in the city's homes at any one period of the 500 or so years which constitute the medieval period. However, the situation is complicated by the fact that very few of the excavated house plots of the city can be said to exclusively reflect a solely domestic environment and likewise very few reflect a purely industrial or a mercantile function. Thus at Derby Lane the same tenement produced evidence for domestic weaving (spindlewhorls), recreation (bone dice and tuning pegs) and industry (recycling of bronze for metalworking). A similar mix derived from the back of 24 Bayley Lane where the artefacts included a very large, complete metalworking crucible, wholly encrusted with melted copper impurities (1990). More often than not the owner or tenant of any one messuage, tenement or cottage (the three most common documented types of house description in this industrious city) combined one or more function which, when lying cheek-by-jowl in the narrow confines of the street frontage, mingle indiscriminately. It is likely that the vertical divisions of cellar, ground floor and jettied first (and sometimes second) floors retained the best such divisions which, of course, do not survive in the archaeological record and are to be found only in exceptional very late sixteenth- or seventeenth-century probate inventories and a few rare surviving buildings, such as are still found in Bayley Lane (*7* and *8*) or Spon Street, some moved wholesale in the 1970s from Much Park Street.

Recreation was perhaps not as structured as it is today but there was much spectacle to enjoy. The regular processions and mystery plays for which Coventry became well known, drew huge, often unruly crowds at religious festivals, prompting the Benedictine Prior in 1421 to call for a special watch to be mounted for crowd-control. Bowls became a very popular pastime in late medieval Coventry and numerous Bowling Greens are known from documents. In 1518 raucous bowlers in Shortley were arraigned before the authorities for disturbing

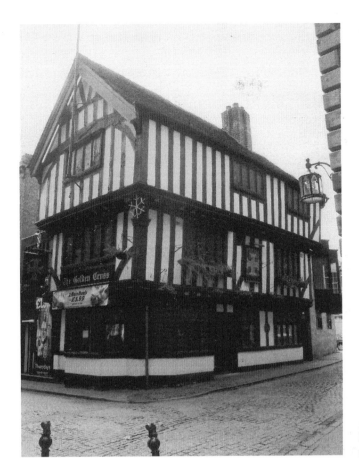

7 The Golden Cross Inn,
Hay Lane; arguably the site of
a Royal Mint

the monks at the Charterhouse with their games just beyond their precinct wall, so noisy had they become. In 2002 what is probably a wooden bowling ball was found in a waterlogged section of the town ditch adjacent to Bond's Hospital. To judge from the numerous dice and gaming counters found in excavations, draughts- or backgammon-type games and gambling were regular pastimes. So was cheating, since a high proportion of bone dice are weighted by way of their slightly irregular shape or are set out incorrectly (all opposed sides should add up to seven). Bone whistles and tuning pegs from stringed instruments attest simple musical pleasures on the street and in the churches, while for those with more earthy desires, just outside the city in Radford lay 'Fuckers' Fields', presumably akin to medieval Northampton and Banbury's 'Gropecunt Lane'! The Radford name was first coined by the Benedictine Priory in 1410, who preferred to call it Closegrove, attributing its less savoury title to 'The Laity'. It seems that amidst the ubiquitous industry there was always time and space to play.

8 22 Bayley Lane, an exceptional
timber-framed survival

Of the frontage sites substantially excavated in Coventry, 7–10 and 122–
23 Much Park Street still offer the best sequence to date, despite their being
excavated over 30 years ago, although much of what the excavators then had
to say now lies in a context better-informed by three decades of subsequent
fieldwork. Here the sequence was traceable through 800 years from open field to
nineteenth-century court-style housing. The added value of these sites is that the
ancient houses which were taken down, opening the plots for excavation, were
thereafter painstakingly re-erected in the Spon Street Townscape Scheme, begun
under the architect Freddie Charles. While the wholesale dismantling of rare
surviving timber-framed Wealden-type buildings was at the time experimental
and subsequently highly controversial, it must now be seen as a move which
almost certainly guaranteed their longer-term survival just as at open air
museums such as Avoncroft (Worcestershire) and Singleton (Sussex).

Perhaps what startles most about the Much Park Street houses is the amount of redevelopment a single plot can stand. Here the excavators defined nine periods of development on the ground. The houses which survived to be dismantled and re-erected only appeared in about the sixteenth century, more than half way through the sequence. Their sites had already been redeveloped twice.

Numbers 122-3 Much Park Street had already contained timber structures perhaps as early as the twelfth century, although they may not have comprised 'habitable' accommodation at that stage, but merely workshops and yards. It was only in the thirteenth century that the first proper signs of buildings appeared, with cobbled floors and an alleyway connecting a rear yard to the street. Curiously the building was then scrapped and was given over to metalworking hearths in a move reflected by so many other sites in the city. Non-ferrous metalworking in the thirteenth century seems to be a massively increasing sphere of activity, seemingly disproportionate to the demand. In addition to those at Much Park Street 1970-74, metalworking crucibles or hearths have been found in thirteenth- to fourteenth-century levels in a significant proportion of city centre frontage excavations since 1970 (Broadgate 1974-75, Derby Lane 1982-84, Much Park Street 1986, Bayley Lane 1988, Hay Lane 1990, Whitefriars Street 1995, 2003, 2004). At 122-3 Much Park Street the metalworking was swept away as quickly as it had begun and a four-square stone-founded building was erected to mimic the plot and layout of its timber predecessor in about *c*.1300. It comprised conjoined front and rear blocks, the rear one heated by a central hearth, and therefore presumably open to the roof. The two were linked to the street and rear yard by the same transverse alley which had been laid out in the thirteenth century. Thereafter changes appear to have been related entirely to the timber-framed superstructure which was completely renewed at the end of the medieval period. Subsequent changes in the accommodation showed simply an increasing need to make the existing accommodation more commodious. The everyday central domestic hearth was only moved to the sides of rooms to form a fireplace with the spread of chimneys and the widespread use of brick in the seventeenth century in Coventry. This of course had the benefit of being able to create multiple flues to feed into one stack and with it the ability to heat upper floors. Previously chimneys had been of stone and restricted by cost to the better houses. Early wall-mounted fireplaces and accompanying stone chimneys of the thirteenth and fourteenth centuries are known only from the city's monastic houses, Cheylesmore Manor and the Stone House on Much Park Street. Fragments of a chimney found in excavations on the west side of Bayley Lane in 1988 may have come from the adjacent Drapery, a site of great wealth and kudos.

One curiosity about 122-3 is that the frontage line was very fluid. While the earliest workshops stretched back from the street, the first buildings seem to have been placed some way back, behind the area used for industry. This suggests that the workmanship was designed to be on show to all who came up the street from the direction of London. Only later, when the industrial aspect of the plot receded, did the buildings spread forward to the pavement area (and Coventry's principal streets were paved from the late thirteenth century). This pattern can be paralleled in Winchester but is in contrast to Northampton and Norwich where twelfth-century building frontages (in parts dominated by Norman re-planning) often lay hard up against the kerb. A number of later plots, both excavated and containing standing historic buildings, are divided into equal front block and rear block, suggesting an earlier front/back division which might have begun in this fashion. That some of the excavated fourteenth century cellars (Bayley Lane, Whitefriars Street etc) also lie well behind the eventual frontage might be a further suggestion that this was a widespread trend and not just a matter of expediency.

At 7-10 Much Park Street later cellarage had cut up the early archaeology considerably to both front and rear but here, in contrast to the west side of the street, the early period contained the ridge-and-furrow cultivation evidence. There was also some evidence that the street had undergone a period of destruction, with widespread deposits of burning in the thirteenth century, for which there is no contemporary documentary evidence. Holy Trinity Church is known to have burnt down in the mid- thirteenth century but it is far from clear whether its demise was part of a wider conflagration or whether it was an isolated fire, which must have been all too common in a city filled with furnaces, hearths and kilns of one industry or another. Perhaps a benefit of placing houses behind front yards was that the industries of those yards, containing furnaces and kilns, were more accessible from the street for firefighting purposes.

HIERARCHIES

Despite the recovery of vast quantities of pottery, animal bone and other finds, it is often difficult to judge the relative wealth of different parts of the town. There was certainly a documented mercantile pecking order, with the clothiers and wool merchants at the top (preferring Earl Street, Much Park Street, Bayley Lane and Gosford Street) and the rather smelly tanners, barkers and dubbers at the bottom (eventually squeezed out to Hill Street, Spon Street and Well Street). Occasional higher-status properties are discernible from the finds, such as very rare specialist horticultural pottery from Whitefriars Street (i.e. Gosford Street; 2004). Nevertheless the spectrum between rich and poor was a wide one and there was hardly a trade which did not at some stage pride itself upon its products and galvanise to form a mutually protective guild which fostered an entrepreneurial spirit within a framework of social and religious conformity.

In assessing relative wealth it is useful to be able to achieve something akin to a price index to which all consumers had to adhere, since most had access to the same markets and shared a broadly similar aspiration to status. Very few prices are known for everyday personal commodities at source but some indication survives of the value placed on certain items when they were the object of theft and turned up in court proceedings. In archaeological terms home security seems a common concern to judge by the numbers of locks, barrel-padlocks and keys which are regularly excavated. While the value of stolen goods in these circumstances may be overstated by the plaintiff, in a sort of over-egged insurance claim, they are likely to be relatively consistently overstated. Thus in the short period 1377-97 can be found the following range of goods being stolen and the subject of a court-claim, either in the Gaol Delivery Rolls, the Cheylesmore Court Rolls or the Rolls of the Sessions of the Peace:

Cloth
A bed sheet 16d
Another sheet 6d
A blanket 6s 8d
Shirt 6d
A sleeveless tunic 4s
Two cloaks 20s *(from the Prior's chamber); the felons, two visiting Irishmen, were hanged for this theft*
4lb wool 12d

Metals
A piece of silver tableware 16s
Silver cup £1
3oz of broken silver 5s
two silver spoons 2s
A lamp 22d
Skillet (frying pan) 3d
3lb wax 3s
A rosary 6s 8d

Livestock
Horse £3 6s
Horse £1

Horse with saddle and bridle 16s
Ox 13s 4d
Two chickens 3d

Arms
Sword 6s 8d
Hauberk £1
Dagger 18d *(Curiously all murderers and assailants had the value of their weapon recorded!)*

The average annual rent lay in the range of 12d for the most basic cottage such as on Hill Street to £1 for the largest capital messuage, a principal residence, such as might be found on Earl Street. Sharing of premises was common and poor families might inhabit as little as one bay of one house, which could be bought, sold and, on occasion, even physically dismantled and re-erected elsewhere by new owners. Rents changed very little in value over many generations and it was only the real threat of economic collapse in the early sixteenth century which changed this state of affairs in the city. With a peasant income of perhaps only £1 a year, and between 25 per cent and 50 per cent of this expended on food, there was often very little to spare. To rise up the social ladder was the aspiration of many, but the trappings of wealth were not cheap. For any contemplating work in the city, there was often a stark choice between rural poverty, which meant regular meals but few luxuries, or urban wealth, which meant access to goods but total reliance on others for their food surplus.

The items which found their way into the Gaol Delivery Rolls and the Rolls of the Sessions of the Peace constitute a glimpse into a very unlawful society indeed. These accounts, combined with the Coventry Assize Roll of 1221 make disturbing reading. They are filled with murder, rape, arson and theft at levels which far outweigh modern experience, especially given the comparatively low population of Coventry at this period, *c.*4000-5000. From one generation to another the city was a very violent place indeed, from a drunken man arrested for firing his bow indiscriminately through the darkened streets at night to a monk of Coombe Abbey and a shepherd being found dead in their sheep-fold in Binley. Perhaps most violent was the discovery of a house in Stoneleigh in which five women were found murdered. In each case the verdict was murder but the perpetrator was long gone. In the days before reliable methods of police detection, there was rarely a hope of catching the felon, unless in the act. For those who were caught, there was the Gaol Hall at the corner of Bayley Lane and Cuckoo Lane, set up under Queen Isabella in 1344, or the Bishop's Prison.

Previously there had been the de Montalt prison at the castle, mentioned in the Pleas of the Crown in 1247 (possibly the last reference to the castle before it was dismantled), when someone escaped and shut himself in St Michael's. However there was no accepted system of prison terms and the commonest punishments were either the payment of a fine or capital punishment, with little between. Gallows or gibbets stood in Binley, Keresley, Canley and Gosford, while beheadings were carried out at the conduit-head in Smithford Street. Someone escaping justice might flee to a church, claiming asylum, but their only real choice thereafter was to 'abjure the realm', effectively give up all rights to English citizenship and make straight for a port of the court's choosing: banishment by another name.

Without a system of punishments to fit crimes, street justice was common, exacerbated by the fact that everyone had a right to bear arms; numerous knives, daggers and leather scabbards have been found in excavation, most recently in 1990 on the corner of Bayley Lane and Hay Lane, where an early thirteenth-century scabbard was found in the castle ditch infill (*11*). Two historical episodes stand out as typical of the lawless nature of the city:

1377 John Atte Yate, John Selby, John Bocher and Henry de Eyton, glovers, lay in wait by night outside the King's Gate at Cheylesmore for Walter de Eton, King's Parker. Walter, thoroughly beaten up, enjoyed the satisfaction of seeing his assailants fined, but no more.

1380 The constables swear on oath that Thomas de Whateley, mason, murdered John de Lyveden, mason. Later they gave evidence that William de Needham, Clement Mason and William de Darley aided and abetted in the act and that they also beat up another, Wendleburgh by name, so that he was in fear for his life. They were fined for this apparent workers' quarrel. Miscreants and victims alike were all stonemasons working in the city. The perpetrators had apparently moved on by the time the case came to court since it was heard before the Kings Bench at Reading.

Very little seems to have stood in the way of the growing city in the thirteenth and fourteenth centuries. The new place name-related surnames which appear in the city's documentary record of the thirteenth century betoken an influx of people from the villages and the Midlands countryside, perhaps drawn by the promise of rich pickings in the city. Certainly there was a great deal of money to be made, but the city would always equally be home to a landless poor whose only recourse was to the altruism of the church and the growing number of monasteries.

For the poor, housing was a more basic matter. Some trades rarely made much money and their very nature meant that the practitioners were banished to the outer margins of settlement, just as soon as the authorities could galvanise into action to have their smelly practices restricted within the city. Thus beyond the city gates of Hill Street and Well Street (both beyond the later Bond Street) lay dozens of houses whose occupants plied noisome leather trades as tanners, barkers, and dubbers and were joined by fullers who worked with cloth at Hill (Nauls) Mill (9). The houses described in documents here suggest the establishment in the fourteenth century of 'Rows', blocks of terraced, box-framed cottages which appear in documents in blocks of four and five and survive until the sixteenth or seventeenth centuries, when many were converted into barns. One or two survived to be drawn in the nineteenth century, but most were not of sufficient build quality to last more than a couple of hundred years and the nature of marginal occupation meant that they did not attract either wealthy tenants or investment. Two rentals, by the Crown in 1545 and the city in 1650, suggest that the streets hereabouts were populated by many poor, containing a

9 Fifteenth-century suburban houses *c*.1800, Upper Well Street, just outside the wall on the north side. *Birmingham City Archives, Aylesford Collection; Volume 1: Country Seats and Castles fol 176*

high proportion of widows, traditionally bereft of income and dependent upon others. One such typical block of five can be traced at the upper end of Hill Street at the corner with Nauls Mill Lane from the late fourteenth century in both Priory and Holy Trinity Guild records until 1545. They are distinguished by their corner plot and the fact that they originally had a stone quarry just behind them. Later references to the former block of five, knocked together into a barn of five bays, ensure that their downward slide can also be seen until they disappear totally in the seventeenth century.

Tanning never ceased in this area, since the Radford Brook, flowing midway between Hill and Well Streets, continued to be the source of water for the industry. Sufficient other industries existed alongside the leather trades to ensure they remained essentially viable suburbs but they did experience some of the worst economic conditions the sixteenth and seventeenth centuries could throw at them and by 1650 the formerly packed frontages depicted by John Speed in 1610 were, at best, discontinuous; at worst empty.

DECLINE

The last century of the medieval period is fraught with difficulty archaeologically, and historians have long debated the extent to which the city, the region and the majority of towns in England were suffering. A survey of 1522 states that there were 525 empty properties within the city. Even the Benedictine Priory suffered and their Pittancer, Brother John Boydon, was charged with negligence in his office in 1521 since the number of empty Priory tenements had increased so much. The charge was meaningless, his office was suffering like everywhere else and there was widespread poverty and economic difficulty. While there were such problems in many of our towns at this period, Coventry seems to have suffered acutely. More specific signs of this can be seen in the records of the Holy Trinity Guild between 1524 and 1532–35 when the Guild felt it necessary to drastically reduce the rents on both its city and suburban properties. With so many empty properties in which tenants might choose to squat if necessary, the need to keep sitting (and paying) tenants was paramount to avoid a massive loss of income. The records in many cases can be used to trace individual properties from a rental of 1485 through to those of the period 1524–35 and on to the Dissolution of the Guilds and Chantries in 1545, which generated its own rental. Theirs presents a story of economic stagnation (on the whole the rents never picked up) with the suburban margins of the city being increasingly run-down. There is archaeological evidence of numerous cottages in Hill Street and Well Street (excavations in 2002–3) beginning to be lost at this period, in many cases on frontages not being replaced until the nineteenth century, corroborated by a glance at historic maps. John Leland, in passing through *c.*1543, may have done no more than view the exterior of empty cottages, just as John Speed's map of the city in 1610 may show unbroken suburban street frontages, but no distinction can be seen between tenanted and derelict properties.

Wholesale suburban destruction occurred during the Civil War, primarily to remove those buildings which blocked the defenders' view from the city walls and which might afford shelter to an approaching enemy. These took place outside most of the gates. At Hill Street it is clear that such demolition removed almost the last of what was there. John Speed's map shows the north/east side of the extramural suburb as unbroken frontage in 1610; Samuel Bradford's map of 1748 depicts a totally empty frontage. Many documents of that period relate plots where Mr X's cottage or Widow Y's tenement 'once stood'. Others refer to blocks of four or five bays of 'barning, once cottages'. This was a very run-down suburban landscape by 1650.

Ironically, just as one or more suburbs may have been barometers of the city's decline, another, at Far Gosford Street, may have been on the up. Excavations at the rear of 121-4 in 2003 showed that the sixteenth-century listed buildings of this address related to a sequence of rubbish disposal which actually began at that date. There was no evidence of earlier rubbish pits on the site. This might suggest that this plot at least was unoccupied before the late sixteenth century; its infilling at that date might be seen as going against the flow of the city's economic fortunes.

RUBBISH DISPOSAL

One aspect of the archaeology of domestic plots which is common to both the intramural plots and the extramural suburbs is the disposal of waste. On every plot can be found the pits into which generations of Coventrians dumped their rubbish. Some were so deeply dug that their bases even survive deeper than Victorian cellars. At Bayley Lane (1988) the archaeological deposits and intercutting pits lay 3m thick, while the castle ditch under the west side of Hay Lane (seen in 1990 beneath a 3m-deep Second World War static water tank) still lies undamaged beneath the cellars of 'Newtz', the public house which stands there. The pits and rubbish-filled deposits provide the best cross-section of the finds and artefacts which signify the lives and aspirations of the people of medieval Coventry. They provide insight into the industries, commerce and domestic lives of 15 generations of medieval citizens.

Some equally large medieval cities, such as Norwich, acquired more systematic rubbish disposal during the late medieval period. This was largely due to the increasing organisation which was effected by the city authorities, meeting a growing population's needs (Coventry in 1500 is reckoned by the historian Charles Pythian-Adams to have had a population of between 8000 and 9000). The result of increased civic rubbish disposal is a comparative dearth of rubbish pits of the fifteenth, sixteenth and seventeenth centuries, when compared with those of earlier centuries, the rubbish being taken out of the city and dumped as manuring in the outlying fields or in old quarries in a forerunner of today's landfill system. Coventry's archaeology is something of an enigma in this matter. While some sites clearly indicate a drop-off in levels of pit-digging and rubbish disposal in the late medieval period (such as Derby Lane 1982-4), others very close by (Broadgate 1974-5) reflect new heights of rubbish-dumping in pits. A significant proportion of the pits excavated in Broadgate were dug at this late date, and they contained some of the best sixteenth- to seventeenth-century material anywhere in the city. At St Mary's Cathedral Priory (1999-2000) there was widespread evidence of later sixteenth-century butchers dumping their waste, not into pits, but with no fuss onto the west end of the cathedral ruins, together with documentary evidence for their consequent arraignment before the authorities for the health hazard and mess they were creating (supporting a pack of feral dogs in the process). Some people were clearly able to take advantage of some form of rubbish disposal since it was during the late medieval period that Graffery Muckhill appeared. This took its name from the Franciscan Friary, the Greyfriars, and was simply a dumping place on what is now Greyfriars Green, just a stone's throw from Greyfriars Gate. A similar deposit was remarked upon by the antiquarian William Andrews at Gosford Green when it was flattened out in the 1880s. Andrews had also commented in his diary on the vast quantities of tanning waste (cattle horn cores and skulls) to be seen near Well Street. Clearly if rubbish was taken out of the city, it was not taken far.

Sewage disposal was always a problem in the city's close confines. For the city's monasteries there was good sanitation and drainage, fed by water collected in cisterns and pump-houses. The latrines and main drain of St Mary's Cathedral Priory were excavated in 2001, running west to east below where Millennium Place now stands, but for most people open soil pits were the normal arrangement, an unsatisfactory system which persisted until the nineteenth century. Some of the better houses would have had garderobes or something akin to privies, as indicated by a medieval wooden toilet seat excavated on Bayley Lane in 1988, but for many there was just a night-soil jar and a pit in the yard into which to empty it. For those tenements which lay too close for even the dubious luxury of a soil pit, and for anyone who worked outside on the streets, there were a few public conveniences. One such block stood on Palmer Lane in the late medieval period and hung out across the River Sherbourne. Unappealingly situated next to a scalding house, for treating butchered animal skins to remove hair, this public toilet discharged directly upstream from the Priory, clearly unsatisfactory sanitation which gave rise to the Prior's repeated complaint about his mill stream being fouled by sewage, offal and other matter throughout the fifteenth century. This medieval public convenience can still be discerned on the city's 1851 Board of Health Map but had all but disappeared when the river was diverted into a new 3m-deep brick culvert in the 1930s.

The story of the city's former frontages is perhaps the most difficult aspect of the 1940 Blitz on the cityscape, followed by some unfortunate 1950s planning decisions, which were of their day. Many of the destructions were well-debated (Little Butcher Row/Trinity Street in 1935-7, had been publicly debated for a whole generation, beforehand) and were carried out in a climate of overall desire for a new Coventry which would not look back too much. The historic cities to which Coventry is often most unflatteringly compared (York and Chester for example) were simply not in the same industrial league, either in the 1930s or the 1950s. Nor even now. The much-maligned Coventry Inner Ring Road was already in the planning stage in 1942, directly following the Blitz. It would be many decades before such infrastructure was needed for most of our historic county towns, by which time attitudes had simply changed. Ironically, the rate of twentieth-century loss of Coventry's historic streets is directly proportional to Coventry's enduring economic standing.

With another round of redevelopment very much very much to the fore at the start of the twenty-first century, it must be asked which streets still hold archaeological potential. Many factors need to be taken into account, and these are now the preserve of Coventry City Council's Conservation and Archaeology Section. Its pioneering Historic Environment Record, funded by English Heritage and the City Council, is leading the way in the digital- and paper-reconstruction of the historic urban landscape. Preliminary work would seem to suggest that the very best intramural medieval street deposits are to be found in Bishop Street, Cook Street, Silver Street, Palmer Lane, The Burges–Cross Cheaping (east side), High Street, The Upper Precinct (for Smithford Street), Bayley Lane, Little Park Street, Much Park Street (east side), Greyfriars Lane–Salt Lane, Earl Street–Jordan Well, Gosford Street (south side). Only a few streets have actually been almost totally lost (Broadgate, the Butcher Rows, New Street, Cox Street (formerly [Earl's] Mill Lane), Much Park Street (west side), Gosford Street (north side) and West Orchard, for example, but then even they have buried short sections not beyond reach amidst the modern basements, services and former underpasses. Many smaller thoroughfares disappeared long before the twentieth century and themselves have only ever been retrievable through archaeology, such as Corpus Christi Lane (east of Cox Street), Catesby Lane (west of The

Burges), Maxstoke Lane (off West Orchard), Barelane (off Greyfriars Lane) St Agnes Lane and Angels Lane (adjacent to Cook Street), to name but a few examples. There is much to be done and much potential still to be realised.

Excavations in 2006 off Far Gosford Street show how the early suburbs contributed greatly to the economic life of the city. Here numerous phases of buildings were constructed between the eastern 'Dover' and 'Calais' Bridges over the Serbourne, just outside the walls. Evidence of dyeing, malting, and the discovery of a hoard of 38 silver pennies of the 1330s, beneath the floor of a house, show how precarious the economy might be for some individuals.

2

Fortress Coventry

'They filled all the land with these castles; and when the castles were built they filled them with devils and wicked men.' The Anglo-Saxon Chronicle for 1137

The arrival of Norman overlords brought with it new problems for the fledgling town of Coventry. In about 1100, the town benefited from a national move to transfer existing bishoprics from their old administrative Saxon centres to more prominent or strategic ones. Not known previously as a populous or particularly strategic place, Coventry may simply have been convenient since the new bishop and his administration came from Chester, a major frontier-post against the Welsh in the immediate post-Conquest period. Largely unsafe for all but the army, such far-flung unrest also accounted for the Bishop of Carlisle setting up his cathedral in Melbourne, Derbyshire! Thus, from Chester came a new Bishop with immediate plans for a Cathedral to replace the former Saxon minster endowed by the late Earl Leofric and Lady Godiva. Where the Norman Church went, however, the state soon followed and if the people lay in the grip of the Church, the Church lay in the grip of the new secular administration, not known for its light touch. Richard Earl of Chester or his successor, Ranulf de Gernons, were granted estates in Coventry and here was founded a castle at about the same time as the Cathedral was begun. With both Church and state present, Coventry assumed a new strategic position. This was bound to lead to trouble and it was not long in coming, as England spiralled into a civil war between the members of the Angevin royal house, the Dowager Empress Matilda and her son, King Stephen.

DOCUMENTATION

In 1144 the Earl of Tamworth, Robert Marmion II laid siege to Coventry Castle, apparently also kicking out the Benedictine community in order to fortify the unfinished Cathedral church, for which good excavated evidence survives and an act for which he received considerable condemnation. As Henry of Huntingdon put it *c.*1150:

> two of the nobles who had converted monasteries into fortifications, expelling the monks … Robert Marmion was one, who had committed this iniquity in the church of Coventry.

Later around 1200 the chronicler Roger of Hoveden wrote:

> they committed the offence in expelling the monks and turning the churches of God into castles and was punished … for Robert Marmion, a skilful warrior, had perversely acted thus towards the church of Coventry. Robert Marmion, while attacking the enemy, and in the very midst of a large body of his own men, was slain singly before that very monastery.

While the later, somewhat biased account of his attack was written in an age of partisan accounts, other chroniclers are agreed on the basic facts. Despite his own unorthodox methods and apparently consequential demise, Marmion's brief siege of the castle was successful and his troops took it for the King from Ranulf de Gernons, Earl of Chester, the Empress Matilda's supporter.

In 1147 the equally-biased *Gesta Stephani* (King Stephen's official history) records the lengths to which Earl Ranulf went, to wrest back the stronghold:

> And in front of Coventry Castle, to where the King's troops had withdrawn, the Earl himself fortified a castle and cleverly beat back their sallies into the surrounding land; until the King arrived in person surrounded by his bodyguard and brought in the supplies of which his garrison was in dire need. A number of times he fought off the Earl who had laid ambushes at awkward points on his way in. In the first engagement casualties were heavy and with some taken prisoner and others fleeing, the King fell back, also himself wounded there. However, recovering swiftly and with his strength returned he closed with the Earl. Many enemy were taken prisoner and their casualties were heavy; the earl himself fled the field in disgrace, barely escaping with his life. In the end the King received the surrender of the Earl's castle and demolished it.

This fast-paced and potentially confusing passage makes a number of points clear. Firstly, in 1147 the late Robert Marmion's troops still held the castle for the King, but were hanging on by the skin of their teeth. Secondly, Ranulf's preparations then included the raising of a nearby siege castle with an attendant blockade (a common occurrence such as at Dunster in 1139 or later at Huntingdon in 1174). Thirdly, the blockade was beaten by the arrival of the King himself with fresh troops, despite being harried by the rebel Earl. Fourthly, the siege was lifted forcibly but only after considerable bloodshed. Lastly, the siege castle was surrendered to the King and subsequently razed in short order as an adulterine (unauthorised) structure. Surprisingly, despite his prolonged opposition to the King, the Earls of Chester were granted their lands back in the peace which followed the deaths of both Matilda and Stephen in 1154. Henry II ushered in a period of relative peace in which the original castle would also dwindle from the landscape as the Earldom's focus shifted with events to the continent.

RECOVERING THE CASTLE

Archaeology's search for Coventry castle has been far from consistent and beset by more speculation than has been helpful. Some early antiquarians even placed it in Cheylesmore Park while most apparently were looking for something relatively insubstantial and larger features were often described as quarries. Documents more recently understood are clear, however, in that it lies between Broadgate on the west, the Benedictine Priory on the north, the Priory Street/Bayley Lane line to the east and Earl Street to the south. The names too are redolent of the castle's former existence. Early thirteenth-century documents state that properties on the north side of Earl Street, where today the Council House of 1916 stands, backed onto the disused castle defences. Bayley Lane takes its name from the castle bayley, while an early document records the name Broadgate as literally the *'porta lata,'* the broad or wide gate of the Earl's castle. It must, however, be stated that the description of a castle having a broad gate was a common medieval epithet for an entrance and was widely used in contemporary literature in the Anglo-Saxon, such as Layamon's Brut writing of St Albans *c.*1190.

While most commentators are agreed that the original castle was probably never of stone, but rather was a motte-and-bailey type, such as is seen nearby at its best at Brinklow (Warwickshire) or, to a lesser extent, at Allesley. Most have put the motte at its western end, close to Broadgate (*10*). This may be misleading since if that is where the Broad-Gate lay, than that should be the Bayley; the motte had no gate except to use as a redoubt in time of extreme danger. If a motte existed, it may equally have been further east from Broadgate. A ring-and-bailey is also a possibility, lacking a proper motte, such as is seen at Sulgrave and Long Buckby (Northamptonshire). Whichever sort it was, the levelling of

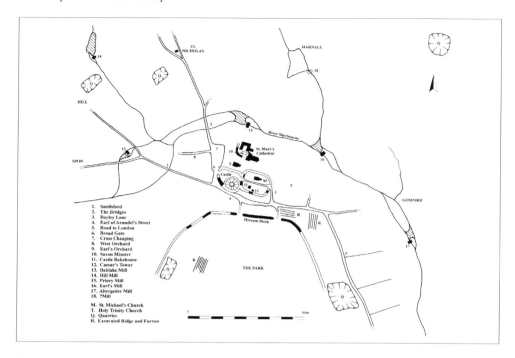

10 The twelfth-century castle and early town. *Jacqueline Harding*

its ramparts means that in an urban situation, only the deepest features, such as ditches, will probably have survived.

With hindsight the first hint at deeply buried remains came in the 1880s when the fifteenth-century spire of St Michael's church began to subside. Underpinning took place but not before it was pronounced to have been slipping into a deep ditch. In fact ditches have been the hallmark of modern archaeological research to locate the castle accurately and characterise its surviving elements. It is clear, however, that Robert Marmion's 1144 fortification of the Priory and Earl Ranulf's 1145-7 adulterine siege castle are immensely complicating (if archaeologically exciting) factors.

Major ditches have been found in excavation in the castle area since 1974. The key interpretative tool is which fortification to assign them to. At Broadgate in 1974 a section was cut across a massive rock-cut ditch measuring 6.5m (21ft) deep x 7.2m (23ft) wide. It lay at the south end of Broadgate close to the junction between Pepper Lane and the west side of the former Derby Lane. In it were found mid-twelfth to thirteenth-century finds indicating it was filled in possibly quite slowly. It turned a sharp corner but its apparent identification as a ditch (rather than a quarry), remains in question since during excavations on the adjacent Derby Lane (1982-4), there was no continuation across that site. There is no doubt however, that it was of the right date to have been related to the castle and that existing quarries might well have been pressed into service as part of the defences of any of the three known structures.

In 1988 the immensely deep excavations behind Drapers Hall, at the east end of Bayley Lane uncovered a possible castle ditch. Later medieval stone-lined pits and cellars had characterised the backfill of a deep rock-cut feature which was pronounced at the time of excavation in 1988 as the castle ditch, although only one side of this feature was exposed. However documentary research has since uncovered the early name of this plot, that of *stoneydelph*, the medieval word for a stone quarry (literally a delving or digging for stone). To some, this has surely debunked the original interpretation. However, as at Broadgate (where opposing sides were found), the use of former quarries as part of the defences would have been expedient and cannot be ruled out.

In 1990, the most reliable observation of a castle ditch was made. This involved the deep access afforded by the redevelopment of the former Hay Lane Baptist Chapel (bombed in November 1940 and turned into a temporary static water tank which lasted 50 years!). The chapel site was being prepared for the construction of a pub and the formerly lead-lined concrete base of this wartime emergency water supply was channelled for services and drains. At over 3m below the level of Hay Lane the chances of remains surviving were thought to be minimal. However, running north-south, parallel with the lane and aligned under the listed houses on the east side of the street, lay a massive ditch. Its sloping sides were evident as was a terminal at the north end of the plot where it met Bayley Lane (*10* and *12*). No other feature survived at this immense depth.

Seemingly the surviving ditch comprised only the lower portion of this massive feature. At a level 3m below the street it was still 9m (29ft) wide. It was packed with viscous, black, organically-rich silts with large amounts of rubbish, all of the twelfth or early thirteenth centuries. The finds included non-local pottery and a decorated leather scabbard for a dagger, one of the earliest so far found in the city (*11*).

At the same time, nearby excavations (in what is now called Castle Yard) were concentrated on the temptingly-named Castle Bakehouse, a name which can be traced as far back in documents to 1411. This plot, originally *Castelbachous*, contained, perhaps unsurprisingly, a sandstone building containing two large sandstone bread ovens, one of which still contained the thick charred deposit of bread-wheat left over from its last firing (*colour plate 1*). This last use of the ovens may have been disastrous since it is likely that the building burnt down, there being copious quantities of ash and charcoal covering everything, together with large numbers of scorched broken roof tiles. The curious thing about

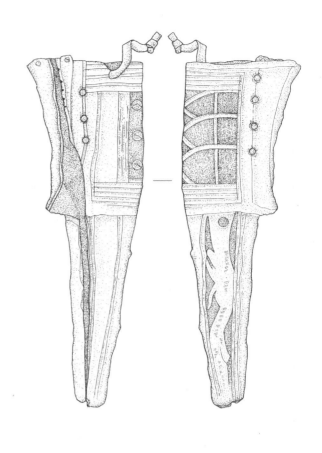

11 Early thirteenth-century
leather scabbard from the castle
ditch at the corner of Bayley
Lane and Hay Lane, 1990; length
200mm (8in). *Harriet Anne Jacklin*

the remains is that they post-date the castle's heyday by over a century, being
of mid-thirteenth-century date, and lasting into the fourteenth century. A
chronicler in 1642 records the fire which burnt the building down and alarmed
the city at that time. It was replaced by an open-sided structure, possibly an open
market hall-like edifice. This lasted until the end of the medieval period.

In 2000, excavations by Northamptonshire Archaeology on the site of the
nave of St Mary's Cathedral uncovered a large ditch cut north-south beneath the
western portion of the nave. It ran north under the north aisle (including one of
the aisle piers and the north wall of the church around the west claustral range)
while to the south it turned eastwards up the nave. Although the terracing which
characterised the Romanesque Cathedral's nave had truncated much of this
ditch, it nevertheless survived for a distance of over 10m (33ft) at 7.5m (24ft 8in)
wide and steeply-sided to almost 1.6m (5ft 3in) deep. Dug through the natural
clay into the sandstone bedrock beneath, the ditch was short-lived, being devoid

12 The modern site of the
Castle Bakehouse; behind are the
sixteenth-century rear wings of
Hay Lane properties. Under these
lies one of the twelfth-century
castle ditches

of silting, and was rapidly backfilled in the mid-twelfth century, containing only
a few finds. Against a background of the stories of twelfth and thirteenth-century
commentators, it seems likely that this ditch belongs to the siegeworks of Robert
Marmion when he fortified the as yet incomplete Priory and Cathedral Church
in 1144. On the basis of pottery recovered, the building work on the nave seems
to have resumed no earlier than 1150 although some settlement may have been
allowed (and desirable) before one of the stone piers of the Cathedral's north
arcade was set out within the fill of the ditch.

Thus, despite these few observations, the three aspects of castle fortification in
early medieval Coventry remain elusive, principally due to the depth at which
they survive, and the relative importance of the old, generally listed, buildings
which lie over the site, such as St Mary's Hall and St Michael's Church (the
'Old' Cathedral). It seems sensible to conclude that the original St Michael's, no
more than a single- or two-cell Norman church (such as at St Mary Magdalene,

Wyken) stood within the castle, for the Earl's own personal use. Its expansion in the thirteenth century (as suggested by its Early English south door onto the main castle thoroughfare, Bayley Lane) probably dates to a period after the redundancy of the castle, when its physical expansion would cause no problems. When the spire was built over a ditch in the early fifteenth century, the location of the castle defences was already a distant memory.

Documentary research has shown that in relation to Bayley Lane and Hay Lane, properties on neither street are subsidiary to the other, suggesting that they were laid out at the same time in the thirteenth century (*12*). Thus they appear, like the evidence for the surviving early St Michael's fabric, to have all dated to the period when the castle disappeared from the map, and constitute a new beginning, with 'burgage' plots, laid out to exploit the economic potential of the old castle site. Earl Hugh Kevelioc (Ranulf's son), acting between 1154 and 1181, clearly had not lost sight of his seat in Coventry when he extended the rights of his burgesses there, bringing them on a par with those at his other seat in Lincoln. He stated 'I prohibit and forbid my constables from taking them to plead for any cause to the castle'. How much was left after Stephen had 'demolished' it we may never know. Certainly the castle prison was still a prison as late as 1247, while the bakehouse was still known as such into the fifteenth century.

The Earls of Chester, suitably chastened by the family's bad experiences in the civil war, may have begun a process of urban regeneration at the same time as moving their seat to the more commodious apartments and fresh air of what rapidly became Cheylesmore Manor and Park. Coventry may simply never have been that important to them after the Civil War of 1137-54. After Earl Hugh died, the new Earl, Ranulf de Blondeville, was in 1186 married off by King Henry II to Constance of Britanny, widow of Prince Geoffrey, Duke of Britanny and brother to both the Princes Richard and John. Ranulf now found himself a royal son-in-law. Constance was pregnant with Geoffrey's child, Arthur, who was not only heir to the Dukedom by birth but who, in 1194 aged eight, was named by his uncle (now King) Richard as heir to the English throne, to Prince John's detriment. By this political marriage to the ambitious Constance, Ranulf was thrust to the forefront of politics and as Arthur's guardian he held the royal succession in his hands. It put him well into the political limelight and target for the young, ambitious Prince John. For most of the 1190s Ranulf played politics in France, between the court of the King of France and the Dukedom of Britanny. Constance died of leprosy in 1201 and soon after, the ill-starred youth Arthur was killed at the hands of John. The earls were in the thick of it as England lost Normandy inch by inch, and Ranulf's High Constable of Chester, Roger de Lacy, found himself commanding the ill-fated garrison at Château Gaillard when

13 Caesar's Tower, St Mary's Hall: arguably a survival of the twelfth-century castle; reconstructed after a Second World War bomb scored a direct hit

that almost impregnable castle fell to the King of France in 1204. For nearly 20 years the Chester holding at Coventry had been an irrelevant distraction. Ranulf became regent to the child Henry III but in 1224 fell foul of both the authorities and the Church. He was both excommunicated and deprived of the castles he held from the Crown, which included Coventry. His other English castles (such as Chartley, Staffordshire) were permanently tenanted at this time and it is in this period that Coventry Castle, probably anachronistic and poorly maintained, slips quietly from the already scant record. In Ranulf's later years, he moved his seat to Coventry to his newly-refurbished Cheylesmore Manor. He died in 1232 and the Coventry holdings were gradually dispersed, the manor passing eventually to the crown.

3

Benedictines

'As we know, the monastic order has been established in the church of Coventry, almost from the time of the first introduction of the Christian Faith into England.' Roger of Hoveden c.1201, quoting a papal letter of 1198.

The excavations of the Phoenix Initiative (1999-2003) have arguably provided more information about one of the city's monasteries than any other. Taking their initial lead from earlier, much smaller-scale work, the excavations successfully uncovered large portions of the medieval Cathedral of St Mary and the adjoining Benedictine Priory. A large portion of the remains found is now on spectacular public display off Priory Row and Millennium Place (*colour plate 2*).

The Benedictines arrived at the very end of the eleventh or the beginning of the twelfth century, possibly replacing earlier clerics or 'irregular' canons, who owed no allegiance to a monastic order. There is archaeological evidence for Christian burial on the Cathedral and Priory site going back to the third quarter of the ninth century (burials dated by radiocarbon calibration) and these may be the vestiges of those who lived and worked as part of the putative St Osgurg's Nunnery. This Saxon establishment, which seems to have survived into the eleventh century to be endowed by Earl Leofric and Countess Godiva, was probably a minster church (although some commentators prefer, quite plausibly, to see St Osburg's and the Godivan minster as separate churches, not the latter simply endowing the former). Remains which survived (much truncated) beneath the north aisle of the cathedral and the south alley of the Priory cloister may relate to the nunnery.

The remains of the minster church seem not to have survived long into the medieval period but were replaced by a new Cathedral which began to be built in the early twelfth century and continued, seemingly unabated, into the fourteenth century, with major interruptions when the monastery became embroiled in regional and national politics. In 1144 it was fortified as a base in the Civil War between King Stephen and the Empress Matilda and in 1189 the monks were ejected by the violent and acquisitive Bishop Hugh Nonant who, taking advantage of the change in kingship (Henry II/Richard I) and the near-permanent absence on Crusade and in France of the Earl of Chester, appropriated the sheriffdoms of Warwickshire and Staffordshire and, at first with impunity, proceeded to burn down their first claustral buildings. Thus a cathedral which was begun c.1100 at its east end in the Romanesque style, was only completed at its west end long after Nonant's death, in the Early English style c.1220, despite having reached as much as three-quarters completion in the Romanesque. The work was probably completed by a mason by the name of Reginald, whose lodge lay beyond the eastern end of the Cathedral and who died soon after the work's completion.

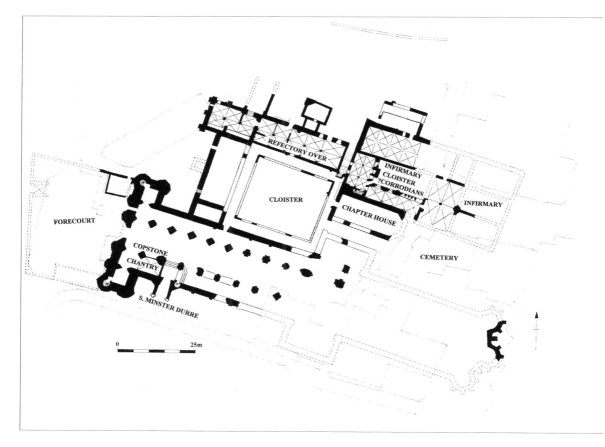

14 Plan of St Mary's Cathedral and Benedictine Priory from excavations, 1857–2002

Records show that his former lodge was demolished in 1224, partly to make way for the Bishop's Palace where Priory Street now runs past Coventry University.

The Cathedral itself was always largely a Romanesque church, with Early English and Gothic additions, some of which were added when the nave and north aisle may have been structurally compromised by its location, teetering on the edge of an earlier terrace which was designed for the earlier minster church, an altogether smaller foundation. The north arcade had to be set out twice before its construction proceeded to completion. The Priory conventual buildings, of which only the later, replacement structures survived to be excavated, lay to the north, downhill, themselves terraced into the hillslope, leaving spectacular ruins for the archaeologists to uncover in 1999-2002 (*14*).

The interrupted growth of the twelfth century was followed by economic difficulty in the thirteenth, but in the fourteenth century the predominance of the Benedictine house was unchallenged in Coventry, a state of affairs which continued, despite nationwide setbacks of famine, plague and the Wars of the Roses, to the Dissolution.

Like everywhere else the Benedictine Priory suffered from the plagues which struck all Europe from the middle of the fourteenth century. Settled in the heart of the city, their house was vulnerable and the close confines of the cloister made a monastery very unhealthy in time of plague. The Great Pestilence, known since Victorian times as 'The Black Death' struck first and most disastrously in 1349; then again in 1364. There are few references to it in documents of the time, so shocking was it and so busy were the survivors in eking out a living. It spread with astounding speed, it was apparently immune to climatic conditions, and it had a propensity to cross species, sometimes affecting livestock, as well as humans. In 1349, on the death of the Prior, William Irreys, from plague, the Benedictine Priory took stock of all it owned, a so-called 'extent of temporalities'. Chillingly it records, with no hint of emotion, that: 'there are two watermills, one at Radford and the other at Hill (*Nauls*) Mill and one windmill which were abandoned before the death of the same Prior for want of millers and no profit can be raised therefrom and which were wont to render before the pestilence 40s.' It goes on: 'in Radford, Exhall, Keresley Willenhall and Coundon, income is reduced since the majority of tenants are dead.' The same survey records that the Priory's cattle-grange at Whitmore Park was worthless in that year, presumably due to the loss of its herd.

At the heart of the estates, the monastery at its height was a warren of buildings arranged around the cloister. One commentator, Frederick Bliss Burbage, listed in 1957 the buildings within it as 'Chapter house, Prior's chamber, vaulted chamber, treasure house, muniment chamber, synodal chamber, herbary chamber, le seyn chamber (where the monks might eat red meat), the Princess's chamber (where Princess Mary stayed two days in 1526), cloisters, refectory, school and infirmary'. While this list omits some notable documented buildings (such as the priory prison, known in Diocesan documents from 1296) and others of immense value to archaeology (such as the latrines), it also overlooks what archaeology has revealed, the numerous cellars and undercrofts which lay beneath these named apartments, many of which may have been on the first or even second floors and of which precious little has survived. Other excavated rooms have no clear title (*15*). There were probably rooms or buildings which pertained to all the main offices within the house, namely Prior, Sub-Prior, Sacristan, Precentor, Treasurer, Cellarer, Penitenciar, Infirmarer, Steward, Pittancer, Succentor, Refectorer, Primus and Secundus Scolaris, Warden of the Lady Chapel and an office, known only from *c*.1520, that of Aqueductor, or water-manager.

15 The north-east undercrofts of the Benedictine Priory from the cloister yard, during excavation, 2001. These ruins are now conserved on public display beneath Youell House

While many of the rooms discussed above are standard manifestations of the Benedictine rule and life in the monastery, additional apartments are common. One such suite, today conserved for public view off Hill Top, with its warming-room style fireplace, may have been that set aside for corrodians. These were prominent pensioners whose high status and contribution to society, often at Court, meant that they were provided for in old age or during infirmity. Throughout the fourteenth century and into the fifteenth century State Papers (Close Rolls) make it clear that St Mary's received a constant stream of royal corrodians, sent by seven successive kings from Edward I to Henry VI, usually as recognition of their service. Some, to judge by their names and the offices from which they were retiring, may well have been of exceptional value to the house, and were not all necessarily the burden that some monasteries regarded them as (*author's italics*):

1301 Roger de Cestria, the King's Serjeant at Arms, 'who has long and faithfully served the
  King and was maimed in his service, so that he is unable to serve longer, and whom
  the King has caused to be sent to them and that they will find him for life the necessaries of
  life in food and clothing according to the requirements of his estate' (*it is tempting to regard his
  burial as that interpreted in a later chapter as a soldier's burial in the Copston Chantry (1299), with the
  skull bearing a partly-healed head injury*)

1303 Stephen Frere

1309 William at Halle

1309 Peter Maron (*also known as Marow/Marwe/Mary, dead before 1326*)

1312 Hugh de Titchmarsshe, Mason, 'who has long served the King, and will find him for
  life the necessaries of life according to his estate and a fitting chamber'

13xx Edmund le Fissher (*dead before 1326*)

1326 Peter le Paveour

1329 William de Londres, 'Yeoman of the King's Saucery'

1342 Nicholas de Bromfield, King's Sumpter, 'for his good service in the household'

1351 Reginald de Foxlee

13xx Juliana de Pembrugg (*Pembridge*), 'at the request of Queen Isabella'

1356 Agnes Augnet (*died 1369*), 'at the request of Queen Isabella'

1369 William Gamboun, 'Yeoman of the King's Chamber' (*dead by 1393*)

1393 John Wymbusshe, 'Yeoman of the King's Chamber, ...who rose in insurrection against
  the King in company of Thomas, late Earl of Kent'

1400 Matthew Swetman, Yeoman of the King's Chamber (*dead by 1417*)

1417 Richard Castelle

14xx William Gloucestre, Serjeant of the King's household (*dead by 1424*)

1424 John Gilbert

The likes of Peter le Paveour, arriving as Coventry's tiling industry was taking off, may have meant that the monastery benefited greatly from his expertise, as they would from the presence of the King's Mason, Hugh de Titchmarsshe. The former King's Sumpter would have been useful in keeping the Priory's accounts, while a yeoman of the King's Saucery would have ensured that entertaining at the monastery could draw on the latest styles of cuisine at Court. Such useful 'recruits' were certainly welcomed; witness the profession as a Benedictine of Richard Luff, ex-Mayor of Coventry, who by 1409 had risen to become Sub-prior. The presence of two women in the list means that the corrodian's apartments would, for reasons of monastic propriety, have to be accessed indirectly from the cloister. The excavated (2000-01) part-undercrofts of the north-east corner of the cloister would have been ideal for such a use; they would also have been

16 The collapsed fourteenth-century vault of the cellars beneath the Benedictine Priory's Refectory

close to the infirmary to the east and the other service-areas of the monastery to the west, where excavation revealed a line of collapsed undercroft vaults beneath the refectory, used for storage of all kinds of materials, entirely emptied at the Dissolution (*16*). The appearance in 1393 of a former political enemy of the Crown is a posting of expediency, since within a monastery, the corrodian was waited on and any visitors could be vetted. It could, for John Wymbusshe, have been a form of internal banishment or house-arrest.

The monks themselves were, at least in the early years, dominated by French recruits who, as a matter of expediency, gradually gave way to English monks. A list of 1409, relating the names of the full community of 26 monks, is dominated by locally-recruited monks and others known to be Coventrians or from the immediate area by their distinctive surnames, namely Luff, Coton, Warwick, Napton, Coventre, Maxstoke, Caldecote, Norton, Eton (Nuneaton), Clipston, Pakynton, Morton, Wolvey, Ashby and Stoke.

The Cathedral church contained wide open spaces and was used as neutral ground on which business could be transacted as well as being a place of worship (*colour plate 3*). Its nave was divided up into bands of tiling which marked out the main processional route towards the monastic screen near the crossing of the church. The nave aisles contained at least 10 chantry chapels from the fourteenth century and the spaces between the piers contained many tombs, of which 30 have been located in excavation. Many more lie beneath the nave. Civic and Guild processions into, out of, and through the church were a constant feature of the Cathedral in the late medieval period and the last tile floors, probably laid in the fourteenth century, proved to be some of the most worn ever seen in excavation in Coventry. For the most part, not only glaze, but also pattern had all but disappeared beneath the passage of feet (*colour plate 4*).

The Dissolution destroyed almost the whole house. Its location on the hillslope below the eponymous Priory Row protected those elements which lay in the lee of the hill, particularly the undercrofts or cellars, some of which are today on spectacular show to the public. However, for some six years the house languished while its future was hotly debated. During this time the lead from the other monastic houses was brought here and stacked for safe keeping. When the Cathedral and Priory roofs were added, the lead was said to have been worth £647, which equates to an astronomical 5,000 tons (at the 1539 price of 2s 6d per fother/19.5cwt). The process of Dissolution at St Mary's was clearly defined in the archaeological record. Unable to take carts south up the hill, north over the increasingly ruinous conventual buildings, the demolition gangs were forced to disembowel the church out through the main west door. Thus a ramp of clay and rubble was laid down over where the concentric arc of entrance steps had been. Carts sent down the ramp were backed between the arcade piers to collect the stone. Fully laden, their wheels cut deep ruts through the tiles and the mortar sub-floor into the clay and graves beneath. These heavily laden wheel-ruts could then be traced by the archaeologist across the increasingly wrecked floor to the ramp.

Within a short time looters, both official and vandal, took over and the church was ransacked. In the Copston chantry, where some chantry burials may have been moved to St Michael's church along with the documented transfer of the chantry's functions, a possible soldier's grave had been disturbed, producing a dagger and some fine bronze facemail. The robbers' pits were filled with domestic refuse and the whole nave inhabited by a pack of feral dogs. The nearby butchers of Butcher Row kept their flocks for fattening within the nave for some decades, and their waste fed the dogs, drawing criticism from the city authorities. The rubble of the Dissolution was strewn with hundreds of sheep leg bones. Five of the dogs came to a sudden end, crushed asleep in a huddled pack as the last standing bay collapsed suddenly at the end of the sixteenth century.

The Dissolution of the Benedictine Cathedral Priory affected the whole city's fortunes. As the pre-eminent landowner in the city and the surrounding suburbs and villages, the removal of the principal livelihood of masons, carpenters, tilers, and providers of every type left a yawning economic gap in the city's purse. It robbed the city of some of its finest art (*colour plate 5*). Land changed hands and plummeted in productivity since the flocks were no longer there for local consumption, sold off to speculators whose sphere was not centred on the city. Old trading networks disappeared overnight and the monastic provision for the urban poor evaporated. For Coventry the Dissolution was the beginning of the end of the medieval world.

4

Cistercians

'None of our monasteries is to be constructed in towns, castles or villages, but in places remote from human intercourse.' Cistercian general chapter 1134

In the 1150s, the second order of monks to arrive in the area settled within easy reach of Coventry, at Coombe and Stoneleigh Abbeys. Such was the rule and policy of the Cistercians, who had been in England since the 1120s. They strove to occupy land a stone's throw from population centres so that, although they might benefit from the ready benefaction which was to be had in towns and cities, they could settle far enough away for the seclusion of their site to offer them the peace and quiet of their strict rule. They also made a habit of accepting any piece of land which was offered to them, partly in an effort to ensure their early foundations did not suffer for lack of land. Often, however, this resulted in accepting nightmarish plots of land which were ill-considered for building and could on occasion be downright unhealthy. Such poor land resulted in Stoneleigh Abbey at first having two successive unsuitable sites and Coombe probably having to adapt its layout to the topography, in common with such as Tintern Abbey (Gloucestershire). The buildings were constructed quickly, since no monk was supposed to be even picked for the new house until the main buildings were complete, according to the Cistercian general chapter of 1134 (Ch 12). This must have been very inconvenient for both Stoneleigh and Coombe (*17*).

Although both Abbeys lay outside medieval Coventry – and still do lie beyond the modern city – their histories and archaeology are linked with the city since large portions of the villages around the city were owned by them. Today, many of these areas lie within the city bounds, such as Ernesford and Binley Granges and Primrose Hill Quarries (Coombe); Stivichall and Horewell Granges, together

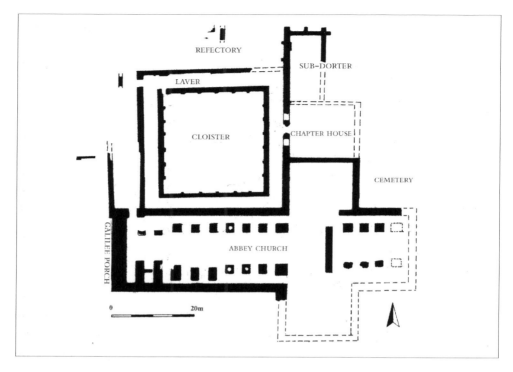

REFECTORY

SUB-DORTER

LAVER

CLOISTER

CHAPTER HOUSE

CEMETERY

GALILEE PORCH

ABBEY CHURCH

0   20m

17 Coombe Abbey from excavations, 1863-1994

with most of Flechamstead (Stoneleigh). In addition, Coombe Abbey park, from 1539 attached to Coombe as a stately home (now a hotel), is still administered by Coventry City Council as a popular place of recreation.

Excavations at Coombe Abbey began as long ago as 1863, when the father-and-son partnership of the Nesfields, architect and landscape gardener, set about transforming the ageing country house. While their redevelopment of the eastern half of Coombe Abbey represented simply the latest step in the regular reordering of living quarters which had evolved since 1539, their treatment of the south side of the house was drastic, effectively removing almost all traces of the archaeology of the monastic church. However, in an act for which modern archaeologists have reason to be thankful, the Nesfields carefully drew what they removed, recording to scale the plan of the nave and crossing of the twelfth-century Romanesque church of the Cistercians. This even included an opulent thirteenth-century mosaic tile floor, whose very existence ran counter to the edicts of the Cistercian general chapter from 1213 (Ch 1), unlike the layout of the church which otherwise reflects the simple austere lines which the order's greatest leader, St Bernard of Clairvaux, endorsed from the start, eschewing all ostentation. It appears to have been modelled upon the likes of Fontenay Abbey, a magnificently severe Cistercian house in France, completed in 1147 and a marvel of the Cistercians' austere interpretation of the French Romanesque style. The successes of the early continental houses formed the basis of the English layouts, down to details like the inclusion of a Galilee porch across the whole west end. Often of wood, the Coombe example appears to have been of stone.

Furthermore, the Nesfield designs for the eastern part of the house were so redolent of the remains they found there, both buried and standing, that they can be said to make more than a canting allusion to the enduring plan of the Cistercian claustral buildings. For many years it was unclear whether the so-called chapter house in Nesfield designs was the original facade or their own (it is the latter, a Victorian facsimile of the remains found *in situ* there).

Some work was done a century later but added little to Nesfield work until the conversion of the house into an hotel in 1991–5. Excavations and building analysis were both carried out in the process of conversion and there is now extensive evidence for the layout of the three other ranges which conform closely to a standard (but reversed) Cistercian plan (*17*). The Abbey's Cartulary makes it clear that the church and other buildings were built from stone quarried at Coombe's own quarry at Harnall (now Hillfields) at the top of Primrose Hill Street. It had been finished by 1224.

The monastery layout is set out using the monastic Romanesque architectural canon of 'One to the square root of two' (1:1.41). This relationship can be seen in numerous dimensions around the site, such as the length of nave to the length of the whole church, or the garth diagonal to the cloister diagonal.

In the east range the foundations of the north transept were exposed directly beneath the work of 1863, although a Nesfield creation of what amounts to an apse on the east of this side was clearly fanciful since no evidence for such was present in this area in 1994 when pipe-laying found monastic graves.

Nesfield's crisp chapter-house facsimile, which celebrates Romanesque detailing at its most elaborate and diverse (in an opulent manner most un-Cistercian-like), echoes the exact position of the original, which is confirmed by the presence of further graves just inside (now beneath the floor of the hotel reception) where the Abbots and perhaps other senior officials lie. Even the stair which characterised the Watergate building of Nesfield's design (now the south-east part of the hotel) closely mirrored the likely position of the monks' night-stair, leading down from their first-floor dormitory (dorter) directly into the north transept of the church. Access thus enabled them to process to the church to sing their night-time offices without having to go outside into the cloister, which, for much of its life until the late fifteenth century, would have been unglazed and probably also unlit at night.

North of the chapter house were exposed sandstone foundations buttressed on three sides (and therefore a projection beyond the cloister north range). This building is interpreted as the sub-dorter (*colour plate 6*). Although a bland title, which simply denotes that the building lay 'below the dormitory', the building was often put to use by the novices in the monastery. Evidence from the north range otherwise was almost non-existent, the area having been firstly truncated by early post-medieval foundations, and then heavily cellared in the 1860s by Nesfield. The north cloister alley, however, with its lavatorium (washing place) recess adjacent to the probable location of the refectory (central to the north range) stands relatively complete, along with both the fifteenth-century cloister arcade and the magnificently restrained oak-coffered cloister ceiling, originally covered only by a lean-to roof but in the seventeenth century turned into an under-shot beneath a fashionable long-gallery.

In the west range the cloister alley is almost complete, but lacking the original ceiling. Excavation and building analysis combined to trace half of the range which is traditionally associated with the lay brothers of a Cistercian Abbey. The later range contained cellars in its northern half, which may be redolent of the original Cistercian layout. Beneath the fifteenth-century cloister arcade at its south end lay reused blocks of the original twelfth-century arcade, built into the foundations. A blocked doorway still stood behind post-medieval panelling, mute reminder of the lay brothers' direct route into the nave of the church, separated from the Quire Monks to the east.

The conversion of the monastery into a grand house, principally from 1581, quickly denuded the medieval fabric and by the time the first surviving drawing was made in the 1650s, the buildings depicted are clearly those of a secular residence wrapped around three sides of an old cloister. The church had been totally lost from view and the monastic remains are almost indistinguishable from the secular, other than as architecture of fifteenth-century origin. Even after only a century they were unrecognisable as Cistercian and could easily have belonged to any order. Today the elaborate chapter house facade constitutes the entrance to Coombe Abbey Hotel, and guests checking in, enter over the graves of twelve generations of Abbots.

The site of Stoneleigh Abbey, by comparison, is further removed from the city and on its west side. Stoneleigh's link with Coventry's archaeology stems from the growth of the city from the fifteenth century. When Coventry was created 'County of the City of Coventry' in 1451, the new lands it encompassed included portions of hamlets which had previously fallen under Stoneleigh's purview, such as Horewell and Fletchamstead. The former was depopulated, probably partly by the Cistercians who wanted the land for sheep farming and set up a Grange there by 1291 (probably on land later redeveloped by Standard/Triumph Cars in the twentieth century and now a retail park). The latter was land leased by small farmers who worked for the Abbey until plague and rent arrears forced a wrangle over ownership rights in the fifteenth century. The winners were the Smith family of Coventry. Firstly John Smith in 1487 and then Henry Smith, his son, in 1496 threw out four fifths of the villagers of Fletchamstead (with no redress) and made a deer park out of it, also digging fish ponds. In 1504 Henry bought the rest of it directly from the Abbey and his park was complete. It was still in existence when Sir William Dugdale noted it in his county history a century and a half later. The state returns for depopulation for 1517-18 related of this episode:

> He imparked the land and then enlarged the said park with tenements and imparked them
> as well and enclosed them with palings and ditches ... he permitted the ruin of his own
> accord and converted those lands for the use of wild and other animals ... and on account
> of his use two ploughs were put out of action and twenty people lost their livelihoods and
> homes.

It was no more than other acquisitive and aggressive landlords were doing at the time but it brought to a premature end any firm Cistercian tenure on Coventry's western fringe, a generation or more before the Dissolution of the Monasteries.

In Coventry the last piece of Stoneleigh's land which they continued to hold until the Dissolution was the Grange of Kingshill or Helenhull. Today this is known as Stivichall Grange. While the eponymous house is of early seventeenth-century date, the home of the Gregory family of Stivichall, the Grange proper, surrounded by a moat, stood directly behind the house. It is today preserved under grass next to Stonebridge Highway; the moat is a gentle earthwork, mostly filled in and thus protected.

5

Franciscans

'O sorrow! O worse than sorrow! A tiresome plague! The Franciscans have arrived in England!' Florence of Worcester (a Benedictine), 1220s

By 1234 the Friars Minor, perhaps better known by the name Franciscans, had become the fourth monastic order to arrive in the Coventry area, following in the footsteps of the Benedictines, Cistercians and Knights Templar. Unlike the Cistercians and the Templars, however, their Rule intended that they should preach the Christian Gospel in the community from the outset. They owed their early patronage almost entirely to the impetus of Ranulf de Blondeville, Earl of Chester possibly as penance for his earlier excommunication in 1224. The house, known principally (in common with all the other houses of this order) as 'Greyfriars', was founded directly adjacent to the Chesters' manor house of Cheylesmore. The house appears to have contained some architectural masterpieces, of which the fourteenth-century spire survives (*colour plate 7*); a great deal of reconstruction is possible from contemporary sources (*18*)

RIGHTS TO BURIAL

No archaeological excavation has yet been seriously directed at this house to confirm the extensive documentary evidence. However, it is not only the surviving spire that makes this house remarkable. It is also notable for its burials. By the end of the medieval period the house contained a prestigious list of intramural interments which reads like a *Who's Who* of Coventry and Warwickshire's thirteenth- and fourteenth-century past. Attracting prestigious burials away from the Benedictines caused considerable rancour, as Florence of

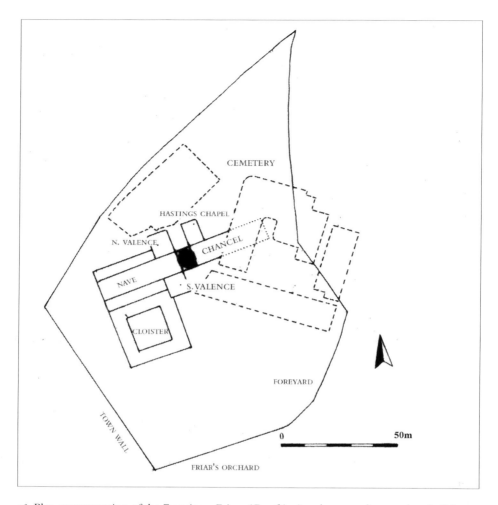

CEMETERY

HASTINGS CHAPEL

N. VALENCE

CHANCEL

NAVE

S. VALENCE

CLOISTER

FOREYARD

TOWN WALL

0   50m

FRIAR'S ORCHARD

18 Plan-reconstruction of the Franciscan Friary (Greyfriars) and surrounding modern buildings

Worcester's acerbic comment shows. The Coventry burial list, from a Franciscan document, has never been widely published so it serves to print it here for the first time for over 60 years and for the first time translated from the Latin. It is a very rare medieval record of monastic patronage and the claiming of burial rights, with few parallels in England. Formerly it has been described as a sixteenth-century document but it appears from the known dates of those mentioned in it, to be a sixteenth-century copy of an original, perhaps little later than *c.*1450-75. It contains evidence for intramural burial of 158 people. (*The* *bracketed italics are the author's.)*

Names of the Founders of the house of Friars Minor

Firstly

Ranulf Earl of Chester, Lord of Cheylesmore with the Lady Clementia, his consort. (*Ranulf d.1232, his body buried at Chester, his heart at Dieulacres Abbey near Leek and his entrails at Wallingford. His wife died in 1252 and was buried at Dieulacres Abbey*).

Secondly

Hugh de Albany, Earl of Arundel (*d.1243, immediate heir of Ranulf*)

Thirdly

Lord Roger de Montalt (*Mold, Wales, former stewards and heirs to the Earls of Chester*), who lies in the middle of the choir next to the high altar (*dead by c.1260*), with his consort, the Lady Cecilia, niece of the said Ranulf (Earl of Chester), who lies in the middle to his left

John de Montalt his son

Robert de Montalt, younger legitimate son of the above-mentioned John (*d.1275*)

Lord Roger de Montalt, elder son of the above-mentioned Lord Robert, with his consort the Lady Johanna, daughter of Lord Roger de Clifford

The Lady Isabella, consort of the younger Lord Robert de Montalt, daughter of Lord Roger de Clifford

Lord Thomas Hastang, Knight (a most vigorous man)and his wife the Lady Elizabeth lie by the north door (*floruit mid-fourteenth century*)

Names of other friends buried in the Choir below the step to the Presbytery

William Rivell (*floruit 1305*) and the Lady Alice Rivell his mother

Lady Johanna Chaunceys

Margaret de Braundeston (*Braunston, Warks*), Lady of Capworth

Emma, Lady of Wappenbury

Guy de la Greene

The heart of Thomas de Bray

The heart of Lord Richard de Mandeville (*of Berkeswell, in accordance with his will, dated 1298*)

Robert of Stone and Matilda , his wife

Lord John d' Odyngsels, Knight, once Lord of Long Itchington (*Three candidates from different generations – d.1337, 1381, 1403*).

Lord Nicholas Hastang, Rector of the church of East Leamington (*Leamington Hastings; Rector 1328*)

Lady Eleanor West
Lady Beatrice de Bishopden
Lady Margaret de Hartshill
Agnes, daughter of the Lord of Bradeston (*Braunston, Warks: floruit c. 1340*)

In the chapel of Lord Hastings, Earl of Pembroke are buried

Lord Henry Hastings (*d. 1268*) with Lady Joanna (*d. 1271*), his consort and daughter
  of lord William de Cantilupe,. She was also a sister of Thomas Cantiloupe,
  Bishop of Hereford
Lord John de Hastings (*d. 1313*), his son with the Lady Isabella (*d. 1305*), his consort
  and daughter of Lord William de Valence, Earl of Pembroke and Wexford.
Lady Joanna de Huntingfield daughter of the above John and Isabella.
Robert de Shottesbrooke, Knight, a most vigorous man and one time standard
  bearer to the same Lord Henry Hastings. He was afterwards his seneschal.
Lady Lorna de Latimer, daughter of the above-mentioned Henry.
Edmund de Segrave, son of Lord John de Segrave (*Lord John d. 1353*).

The names of others who lie beneath the said church

Thomas, son of Baron William Boteler of Werinton (*Lancs, the family had lands
  in Exhall*)
Joanna, daughter of William Bagot, Knight (*William, of Baginton, d. 1407*)
Lord Nicholas Pecche, Knight
Lord Robert de Verdun, the elder, Knight (*floruit c. 1290*), with Lady Margaret,
  his wife
Isabella Otteley
John de Clifton (*Warwickshire*) and Lucia, his wife
Alice de Draycote (*Warwickshire*)
Geoffrey de Whitley (*floruit 1308-32*)
Lord John de Solneye, Knight
Lady Marion de Birmingham
Lady Alicia de Wells
Henry de Vernoye, founder of two houses of Friars in Ireland
Joanna de Sackville, one time handmaiden to Lord Segrave
William de Aubeneye, once Lord of Hastull (*Asthill, Coventry; d. 1307-27*)
Robert de Sheppey and Matilda, his wife (*fl. 1290s*)
Radulfus Hunte
Henry Dodenhale (*Mayor of Coventry 1365*)
Adam Botoner, (*Mayor of Coventry 1374, '77 & '85; d. 1386*)

Agnes Michelle, Adam Botoner's mother

John Maxstoke and Alice, his wife (*Alice, of Hill Street, 1390s, predeceased by John*)

Alice, wife of Ralph Damet

William Horne

John Pomfret, Ball' and Agnes, his wife

Thomas Parker

Joanna Bowdy (*of Hill Street, 1390s*)

Philip Corley and Isabella, his wife

Adam Markyate (*Bedfordshire*)

Simon de Shepeye and Margaret, his wife

Robert Spencer and Isabella, his wife

John Spencer, son of Robert

John Multon

Nicholas Oxborough

John Marshall and Margaret, his wife

Robert Coke and Juliana, his wife, together with John, their son

Isold Belville

John de Toneworth (?Tamworth), who died at Abergavenny. (*Possibly John Tamworth, Cutler*)

Hugh de Melton

John de Toltham

Henry de Dancaster

Richard de Latymer

Eleanor de Stoneleigh

Isabella Leycester

Robert Rydwale (*Merchant of Coventry floruit c. 1300*)

Richard Lateuer

Roger Box

Agnes Sampson

Thomas the Warder

Agnes the Spicer

Lord John de Langford, Knight and Constable of Kenilworth Castle

Robert Dowbridge and Alice, his wife

Henry Verney and Alice, his wife

John Verdun, Knight

John Rotener

Roger Bray (*floruit 1334*) and Emma, his wife

Thomas Bray, son of Roger with his sons and daughters

William Wednesbury and Alice, his wife

Thomas de Clendon

Isabella Glym

John Exton (*Exton-by-Stamford, Northants, a manor held by the Zouche family of the Beauchamp Earls of Warwick: Katherine, Lady Beauchamp in the mid-fourteenth century was a benefactor of this house*)

Adam and Alice Rotener

John and Margery Manby

Geoffrey de Langley and Matilda (*de Brightwell*), his consort (*Lord of Pinley and Shortley; Geoffrey d.1274*)

Lady Margaret de Pinkney (*Moreton Pinkney, Northants; related to the Odyngsels of Long Itchington*)

William de Beuler

Walter de Langley son of the aforesaid Geoffrey (*d.1280*)

John de Langley (*of Pinley and Shortley, died c.1350-1400*)

Isabella de Hull (*Hull/Helenhull, now Stivichall*)

Richard Shipton with Mary, his consort (*Shipston-on-Stour, Warks*)

Sarah, wife of Robert de Stoke (*Lord of Stoke, Coventry*)

Henry de Ballard and Agnes

Richard de Weston and Alice (*?Weston-under-Wetherley, Warks*)

John de Claybrook (*Claybrook Magna/Parva, Warks*)

John de Mynoth

Alexander de Fillongley together with Richard Dubber and Beatrix

John Hunt

Agnes Marstock (*possibly Maxstoke, Warks*)

Eleanor Corby (*Northants*)

Henry Ygington, priest (*Long Itchington, Warks*)

John Wychard and Alice (*Alice d.1401*)

John Knight

Juliana, once Lady of Hasthull (*Asthill, nr Coventry*)

Robert Fasham, with Felicia his wife, who gave the spring at Deadmanswell (*the conduit-head on Beaumont Crescent (19) where the land was known as Fachamfeldes, the city was recommended to purchase the conduit head at the Dissolution; Robert Fasham probably died soon after 1324, having been active in business since 1280*)

Roger de Montalt, Junior (*died c.1275-1300*)

Simon Coleshill (*Warks, now West Midlands*)

Alice de Wiltshire

Juliana de Assefleye

Juliana de Willenhall (*Coventry*)

Simon de Tolham

Henry de Pailton (*Warks*) and Alice, his wife

Amicia, wife of Simon Child

William Lutemon (*floruit 1290s onwards, but died before 1335*)
Thomas Celer and Peter, his son
William Path (*?Alspath, Warks*)
John de Eton (*Nuneaton, Warks*)
Walter Tynell and Walter, his son
Richard de Rockingham (*Northants*)
Roger, the Chamberlain of Lord Thomas Blunt
Ralph Palmer, great benefactor with his wife
John Ward, first Mayor of Coventry (*Mayor 1345*)

While this list is very rare and certainly extensive, it does appear to run short of names somewhere around the third quarter of the fourteenth century. The latest few are early fifteenth century in date. As such it probably represents only those benefactors who achieved intramural burial in the first 150 years or so of the Friary's existence.

19 The well-house of Deadmanswell, given to the Franciscans at Greyfriars *c.*1300, Beaumont Crescent

CONTINUING BENEFACTION

It is from wills, principally, that an idea can be formed of the ongoing list of burials for the church, since it is known that none of the monastic houses in Coventry were short of benefactors in the decades leading up to the Dissolution. However, no list can hope to include the many scores of benefactors who wished for no more than interment in the Franciscans' cemetery to the north of the church. Like the Friars (who had their own separate cemetery), their burials went unsung, largely without the benefit of wills (because ordinary people had less goods to pass on and therefore less reason to make a will). In addition to the Benefactors' and the monastic cemeteries (a distinction common to all monastic houses), the Greyfriars may also have had need for a scholastic cemetery, such as has been excavated at the Norwich house. Here, like at Norwich, the house supported a *studium*, or monastic school of further education, its students drawn from the *custody*, or administrative area, of the Worcester Greyfriars. A Dissolution document records the presence of a school house and at least two distinct cemeteries.

From research into wills can be added therefore (in the church): Master Doctor Standyshe (died after 1506, when he was Franciscan Provincial): 1512 Henry Smyth, the acquisitive MP for Coventry from Fletchamstead, next to his parents (and friends) by the high altar; 1519 John Hardwen, Draper, in St Anne's Chapel in the church; Peter Warton, Yeoman, of Coventry, at the feet of Dr Standyshe (d.1525). The only moneyed benefactor who requested burial specifically in the churchyard is that of the eminent Coventry Draper, Henry Pisford (d.1525), who, along with his illustrious father, William Pisford, gave large amounts of money to the Greyfriars, with the specific intent of building and embellishing a Rood Chapel in the churchyard, already nearing fitting out in 1525 and completed by 1532.

Franciscan concern for the least fortunate in society manifested itself at Coventry in their practice of accepting execution victims. In 1330 the body of Roger Mortimer, Earl of March was buried there, following his hanging, drawing and quartering for the murder of Edward II. It may be that his proximity to Edward's widow, Isabella, at the Cheylesmore Manor was an affront and quickly became a matter of royal embarrassment since his own son quickly received permission to exhume the remains and rebury them at his own home at Wigmore (Salop). In 1487, one Thomas Harrington, an imposter posing as the son of the Duke of Clarence, was captured at the battle of Newark, brought to Coventry and beheaded, his body (and head?) being buried at the Greyfriars. Soon after, in 1495, Sir Henry Mumford and Sir Robert Mallory were beheaded for treason in Binley. Their heads were stuck on poles on Spon and Greyfriars gates, while their decapitated bodies were buried in the Greyfriars.

Most friars remain anonymous, although the names of a few survive. Naturally, none of the 11 named who signed the deed of surrender in October 1538 would have been buried in their own cemetery. Those whose names are known, and are buried there, constitute men of learning. Master Doctor James Standishe, Master from at least 1499 and elected Friar Provincial in 1506, has been mentioned above. He was known as an impressive preacher. Other than him the names are known of Christopher Hill, Warden of the Greyfriars in 1499; Master William Wall, Doctor of Divinity and Master of the Greyfriars in 1532; Friar Bredon, a somewhat mischievous and inflammatory preacher is mentioned between 1438 and 1446, as is his near-contemporary Friar John Norton, said to be a cultured man, learned in Philosophy and Theology. Such attributes as likely as not would have fitted him to the *studium* at Coventry.

RECONSTRUCTING GREYFRIARS

Reconstruction of the buildings of the Greyfriars is possible from a variety of sources including documents, antiquarian observations (which are afforded due scepticism where they are clearly fanciful) and past interpretations from architectural historians. Some valuable original documents complete the picture (*18*).

Observations by interested but largely untrained eyes have been regular but confusing. The site was disturbed when first Union Street (1820) and its successor New Union Street (1957) were laid out across the precinct. In the early 1930s the Methodist Central Hall disturbed burials to the north of the church, while in the early 1970s a basement car park probably removed the church presbytery and many burials, although no report of such was made. A small excavation in 2000 exposed a small piece of possible nave wall. Any view of the church is hampered by the remains of the 1828 building of Christchurch, a Neo-Gothic church by the eminent Birmingham partnership Rickman and Hutchinson in Bath Stone (they also designed the 1832 mock-tudor wing of Bond's Hospital in Coventry and the classical Drapers' Hall). It is unknown whether their work owed anything to what already lay there or even whether their new work removed any of the previous remains. It did, however, give the contemporary antiquarian William Reader the opportunity to measure and interpret the walls he found there. Fortunately he wrote these down and they were later published by his friend and contemporary Thomas Sharpe. They remain relevant although the interpretation of what he saw differs with hindsight. Through it all the fourteenth-century spire which marked the crossing of the church has stood, serving both the Friary and the Neo-Gothic church. It has now stood longer without a church than with one, since the later church was itself destroyed in the April 1941 Blitz on Coventry. It has undergone many repairs.

The church lay to east and west of the spire that stands alone today. The cloister lay on the south side of the church's aisled nave and was probably square. Its dimensions are roughly predictable but with caution. The measurements taken by William Reader in 1828 have been variously interpreted to produce putative church layouts. The one followed here is that of the historian of Franciscan architecture, A.R. Martin who suggested his plan of the church in 1937, from pre-Dissolution survey and Reader's work combined. Most of the rest of the layout is gleaned from the relatively formulaic monastic layout of Friaries plus two detailed documents, one which sets out the contents of the Hastings chapel and another from the Dissolution which mentions numerous buildings by name while detailing the measurements of parts of the church. In addition the will of Henry Pisford and another near-contemporary bequest add considerable detail.

The Hastings chapel, probably built in the early fourteenth century as principally known from a medieval document, was said to lie on the north side of the church. Commensurate with the status of the burials it contained, its windows were lavishly adorned in stained and painted glass with the coats of arms of the families who both founded it and whose members lay below it.

In 1499, John Smyth (of Fletchamstead) was recorded as having given over 100 marks (£66 5s) for building the 'over' part of the choir of the Greyfriars. This strongly suggests that the church was receiving some major overhaul at the end of the fifteenth century, or was even being rebuilt or heightened, a possibility strengthened by the will of Thomas Bradmeadow, draper, who left 40s for the repair of the church. In 1506 Thomas Bond, left £30 in his will 'for making the body of the church from the rode to the pilar as appereth by the old worke'. His will noted that he had already expended £60 on the work to that point. Certainly this is a wholly different structure from the one which was nearing completion in *c.*1232 when Ranulph Blondeville granted the Friars permission to roof it with shingles from the woods of Kenilworth. When surveyed in 1534 the later church, seemingly almost brand new to judge from the benefaction, appears to have been the only building in good repair:

> the hole churche ys newly covered all within thees 24 yeres (ie since 1510) and all the hole howse besydes is in moche ruyne, all covered thorowly with tile and nott worthe the stonding for any habitation. Adjoyning this fryery ys an old maner of the Kinges grace callyd Chyldesmore… The hall ys down butt many of the lodgyngs do stond…. Because the Kinges hignes hath as I here no convenyent lodging nye unto this cytie the tile of this olde fryery myght serve to repayer the sayd maner butt the tymbre of the howsyng is sterk nowgt. All the roff of the church ys very gudd tymbre.

The King's surveyors went on to state the following measurements, principally to calculate the potential income from the new lead roofs: quire 36 x 10 yards; rood chapel 3 x 4.5 yards; St Nicholas chapel 11.75 x 8 yards; north valence (a sort of transept or side-chapel) 11 x 7.5 yards; south valence 9.5 x 7.75 yards; nave 39.5 x 10 yards; north aisle 31 x 5 yards; south aisle 30.75 x 4.75 yards

The lead amounted to 1278 square yards of roofing sheet. Melted into half-ton sowes or plockes and shipped in consignments of a fother or cart-load each (19.5cwt, essentially 1 ton) standard grade church roofing lead amounted to 17 tons. By comparison, Charterhouse nearby would produce 55 tons, but presumably included all other buildings plus the guttering, window leads and other additions. The totals for the other of the city's monasteries are unknown. The going rate at the time was 2s 6d per fother or cart load, so a tidy sum was to be had from the lead, especially when compared with the stone for which *ten* loads commanded the exact same price and loading it paid only 4d a day. Essentially the smelting of the lead from the Greyfriars was a trial run in October 1538 for all the other monasteries in the city which were dissolved soon after. It was noted within a month of the house being surrendered to the Crown that the city's poor were already trying to loot the site, stripping the lead gutters. This kind of poverty-stricken desperation would provide Henry Over, Sheriff of Coventry, with good reason in January 1539 to set a guard on the Charterhouse, which he himself was angling to purchase after it too had been dissolved.

The lead half-fother sowes are occasionally found on excavations, such as at Rievaulx Abbey in 1920 where one of exactly the same weight was recovered, boat-shaped and measuring 113cm x 44cm x 18cm deep, and stamped with the crown. A much smaller version, perhaps a batch-end or leftover, was excavated on Much Park Street in Coventry in 1970.

Within the church, which, like all Greyfriars' churches was dedicated to St Francis of Assisi, were various altars: Our Lady of Pity lay on the north wall, presumably in the north aisle; also within the church were the altars of St Anne and St Nicholas, although it is possible that this latter was actually the dedication of the Hastings chapel

At the Dissolution the following buildings and areas are mentioned (*18*):

Le scolehouse; the lady Euyngherns chambre; a garden; les Garners; le warden's chambre; cellars; le Ffryers' orchard and another orchard; fish ponds; stable; hall; le cloister yarde; two gardens of cemeteries.

Not all these features are located, but those which are provide some idea of the layout of the precinct which was walled along Warwick Lane and Greyfriars Lane. The precinct was incomplete until 1289 when the original land grant was enlarged by Roger de Montalt out of former Benedictine Priory land, diverting Warwick Lane in the process, a diversion which should be demonstrable by archaeological means.

The Friars' Orchard mentioned later became known as Sheriff's Orchard. An inquisition of 1664 makes the link repeatedly clear and also details that the orchard lay entirely beyond the town wall, where The Quadrant now stands on the east side of Warwick Row. The orchard had its own postern gate in the wall but was not part of the Cheylesmore park, from which it was walled off from the start. A second gate was put in this wall to give access to pest-houses built in the park to isolate the sick in time of plague. It may have been this route which the Lord de Montalt is documented to have allowed for sick friars to have private access into the park, in order to relax and recuperate. His own Cheylesmore Manor lay cheek by jowl with the Greyfriars and the churchyard was in 1664 said to lie in front of the manor 'foreyard', separated by a dry stone wall. This would suggest the churchyard wrapped around the Greyfriars chancel towards where New Union Street now runs.

The Warden's chamber was simply the personal quarters of the Warden of the Friary, the most senior position in the Greyfriars' hierarchy, common to all their houses. He was the Franciscan equivalent of the Prior in other monastic orders. The separate mention may imply that he was housed in a separate building. Lady Euynghern is unknown. She may have been a long-term paying guest or corrodian, foisted upon the house by a wealthy benefactor or even the Crown. Alternatively the chamber which bore her name may simply have been so named following a generous benefaction by the lady herself. The Garners are probably storehouses, serving a function to which the cellars may also have been put.

Mention of the school house is confirmation of the presence of the studium, the school of theology which lay at Coventry, serving all the houses in the Worcester custody or administrative area, with custodial schools at London (for London custody), York (for York), Norwich (for Cambridge), Newcastle (for Newcastle), Stamford (for Oxford), Coventry (for Worcester), and Exeter (for Bristol). These served each custody although could attract students from anywhere in the province; some gained an international reputation for their teaching and were considered within the order as universities, such as Norwich which served the Cambridge custody, drawing the finest teachers from all over Europe (and probably students too). Coventry's studium may have enjoyed an equally rarefied atmosphere and was certainly one of the 21 '*studia particularia theologiae*', the prestigious schools of theology which were spread throughout Europe and were all listed in a document of Pope Benedict XII in 1336. At the Norwich house, excavations in 1998 showed that there was possibly a specific cemetery serving the school, which would have unfortunately been prey to all the plagues and diseases which affected all towns and monastic houses in the medieval period (and which were worse affected because of the gregarious nature of mendicant orders). The skeletons at the Norwich house probably derive from the school house there (dated 1291-1539) and showed a preponderance of young males but with some distinct clustering of graves around specific individuals. Three such were buried with their mouths packed out with ash, a rite not previously noted before in medieval burials, and one which may reflect humility or possibly genuine regret for ill-considered words in life. It is possible that they were teachers; part of such a cluster may be implied in the request of Peter Warton to be buried (in 1525) at the feet of Dr Standyshe in the Coventry. Greyfriars. The Benedictine Priory Cartulary of 1410 contains a document noting that the Friars' cemetery was located along Friars Minors Street (Greyfriars Lane). In all probability it today lies in the angle formed where the present Greyfriars Lane diverges from Warwick Lane, under a mixture of road and pavement, north of both Spire House and the Methodist Central Hall.

The speed with which the Greyfriars was rendered uninhabitable at the Dissolution was in relative contrast to the other houses, perhaps because it was the first. However the blight its ruins created in the landscape was considerable. In common with the other houses, its precinct remained almost entirely undeveloped when depicted by John Speed in 1610. Documents indicate that barns were built on the old churchyard in about 1640. Coins found during excavations in the ruins of both the Benedictine Priory and the Charterhouse indicate that Dissolution rubble was still being picked over through the seventeenth, and in some localised areas into the eighteenth century. This pattern is mirrored at the Greyfriars since when in 1636 a 25m section of the city wall collapsed on Gulson Road, the City Corporation ordered that it be rebuilt using stone from the Greyfriars churchyard.

Testing the documented archaeology of this site remains a priority, since it has not had substantial work directed at it. However, the issue continues to be clouded by the very nature of the site which remains by far the most fragmented of Coventry's monastic houses in terms of land ownership, doubly complicated by the existence of New Union Street right through the middle of the monastic cloister. Thus, in addition to development pressures, the site has been prey to the many service lines which have fed gas, water and electricity to local businesses. Nevertheless, remains of monastic buildings are usually substantial and contain (as documented here) numerous prestigious burials and cellars, where depth provides the greatest potential for preservation. There is much scope to continue sensible, rigorous enquiry and archaeological research in the field, however opportunistic development appears to render it.

6

Carmelites

'We stayed at the Whitefreers, which we know to be a right commodious place.' Elizabeth I

In 1342 the Carmelite order of Friars arrived at their newly founded house at the head of the London Road. Whitefriars, as it came to be known (after the Friars' white habits) was founded by the London-based merchant, Sir John Poultney who granted them a messuage and ten acres of land (4ha). This was followed in the next year by a grant of contiguous land by St Mary's Priory (probably the land itemised above). In 1344 a third grant was made to enlarge the house, followed by another in 1352, this time quantified as two messuages and a third of two others and a garden, in order to fashion the access road which became and still remains the Whitefriars Gate and lane from Much Park Street. There was yet a fourth land grant in 1413. Like the Franciscans, the Carmelites could only enlarge their holdings in this way, by the addition of contiguous plots. By the end of this process their precinct stretched from the River Sherbourne at Shut Lane to Much Park Street, and from New Gate to the rear of the gardens fronting Gosford Street (20).

Their precinct brought unexpected benefits but also responsibilities. In the 1360s the Carmelites were granted a window through the town wall and a postern gate of their own onto Gulson Road and with it a private bridge over the ditch. This, however, was on the proviso that they would wall it in within two days in the event of an alarm. This they presumably did in 1450 at the onset of Jack Cade's rebellion. Earlier in the 1420s the Carmelites were required to embank the length of wall along Gulson Road. Such measures were taken to absorb the shock of artillery projectiles, however crude they may seem to modern eyes. For any attack up the main road from London, the Whitefriars was in the firing line.

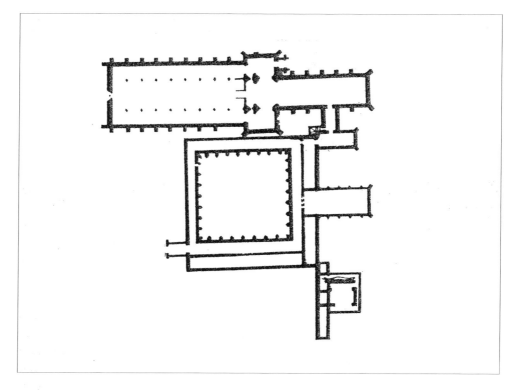

20 Plan of the Carmelite Friary (Whitefriars)

REMAINS

At the heart of the Carmelite mission was their immense church, with a long preaching nave. From the outset, Sir John Poultney employed one of the foremost craftsmen of his day, the master mason, William de Ramsey III, who set to work on the church. He had 20 years' experience behind him, including as advisor to the works at Lichfield Cathedral, St Stephen's Chapel, Westminster and Windsor Castle. His appointment would ordinarily have been a sound one, but in such precarious times nothing could be taken for granted. Within seven years both Poultney and Ramsey were dead, victims, like so many others, of the Black Death. Poultney was buried before the altar in the chancel of his new church, as yet far from completion. What is almost certainly his grave was excavated in 1977 and his tomb is today visible amid the conserved ruins of the Whitefriars church's east end. Poultneys would continue to patronise the house and succeeding generations were buried there in 1472 and 1507. Ramsey's legacy was less successful. Excavations on the church in the 1960s suggest that the change of mason led to a change in design and with it structural problems which entailed considerable strengthening of the central church spire at the beginning of the fifteenth century. This cannot have been helped by strong earthquakes recorded in 1382 and 1426. Subsequently the City Annals record that in 1446 'fell ye new worke at the White Friars'.

The standing part of the Whitefriars is the former east range of the Friars' cloister with their dormitory (*dorter*) above (*colour plate 8*). It dates to the later fourteenth century and bears the scars of other buildings which joined onto it. To the north lay the church, which was connected both via the cloister for daytime access, and by a night-stair from the dormitory which enabled the Friars to get to their night-time offices without stepping outside or into the unglazed cloister. The cloister itself is undershot, meaning that it is enclosed within the body of the building, rather than comprising a lean-to walkway within the central area or garth. It is made of a groined vault and takes up half of the ground floor (*cover and colour plate 9*). This would have been repeated on the remaining three sides of the square cloister. Leading off this passageway are two vaulted rooms, one of which has been traditionally called the warming room, since it contains a fireplace. Both rooms enjoy a second, direct access to a truncated room at the centre of the building which is the vestige of the Friars' chapter house, where they met in chapter to discuss the business of the house. Under the floor are the graves of the Wardens of the Friary and a number of other eminent Friars such as William of Coventry, an eminent theologian.

On the first floor the current massive space, 49m long (135ft), lay the dormitory (*colour plate 10*). Unlike the single floor space today, this was subdivided into individual cells or study bedrooms, which were partitioned off from each other to afford the Friars a level of privacy and enable them to retire to pray as well as sleep. Each was lit by a single window, a row of which survive at the northern end of the east wall. Otherwise, most of the medieval windows were replaced by larger, more fashionable ones after the Dissolution when this part of the house was bought by John Hales, Clerk to the Hanaper, as his own home. The massive timbered roof was for many years thought to be a sixteenth-century replacement from another building. However a recent archaeological survey, combined with tree-ring dating, has shown that the majority of the roof timbers is contemporary with the building.

Another range that would have been impressive would have been the south of the cloister. Here would have stood the refectory and kitchen, vital at this house since not only did it support the monastic community but it also gained a great reputation for entertainment and banqueting. Many feasts and guild dinners were held there, waited on by Friars themselves. This was especially so for those lesser guilds who could not afford their own guildhalls.

Renowned hosts

A document of 1477 serves to illustrate this since it lists the expenditure of such a feast at the Whitefriars, this for the Carpenters' Company:

Trencher Bread 2d
Minstrels 2d
To Friars 6s 8d
To Friars for singing 4d
Bread 3s 6d
Two and a half sisters of ale and half a sister of penny ale 3s
Two loins and four breasts of veal 1s 11d
Six loins of mutton 19d
Two breasts of mutton 3d
Twelve geese 4s 10.5d
Four sucking pigs 19d
Two marrow bones 1d
Milk 3d
Quarter of coals 4d
Frumenty 4d
Garlic and onions 3d
Vinegar 2d
Mustard 0.5d
Salt and verjuice 1d
Allsome 2d (*coarse bread for trenchers*)
To spit turners 5d
Dishwashers 2d
Faggots 2d
Vessels 4d
Spice 4d
To the cook 12d
Wayts 16d

Clearly seasonal entertainment in even the smaller monastery was a lavish affair. It must have been astounding at the Benedictine Priory in 1460-1 when Parliament was in residence for almost the whole year. Kitchens and banqueting halls are a regular archaeological mine of information, often because they also interact closely with other nearby buildings, such as bakehouses and brewhouses. This shopping list is telling since it indicates both the expenditure but also the lavish lifestyle being enjoyed. For instance, the production of cattle for slaughter as calves to produce veal either implies a fortuitous surplus of male calves (i.e.

non–milking) or possibly the breeding of such to maintain a dairy herd. Medieval cattle only lactated naturally for a maximum 150 days a year. The higher cost of their meat is in contrast to that of the mutton, only eaten when the sheep was older and could no longer produce a worthwhile fleece.

The entertainment in the form of minstrels is not unexpected, since music was always looked upon very kindly in the monastery; many instruments had good Biblical precedent as laid down in the Psalms. The official wayts or waits were a small band of musicians provided by the City Corporation and when not performing official functions would walk the streets at night, playing in the open air until the early hours, presumably to the annoyance of some, but the delight of others. Excavations at Whitefriars (1977), St Anne's Charterhouse (1981 and 1986), Derby Lane (1982) and on the town wall at Cox Street (1976) have all produced either lead (11, all from Whitefriars) and bone (eight in all) tuning pegs from stringed instruments, probably either harps or psalteries. To this may be added a bone flute mouthpiece from the Benedictine Priory's north range (2000). Documents make it clear that monasteries were well provided for with all manner of instruments, including organs. Coventry was in fact a centre of the performing arts and beside the much vaunted Mystery Plays enacted at the Greyfriars the city's musical excellence was widely known. In the mid–fifteenth century her actors, harpists and lute players are recorded as regular performers for the gentry at Maxstoke Priory, near Solihull, alongside private players in the pay of the likes of the Earls of Warwick and Huntingdon.

The occurrence of coal for heating is good evidence that it was readily available for special occasions at this date, possibly from Wyken where mines were certainly documented from 1523 and probably much earlier. As early as the fourteenth century the Black Prince's bailiffs who were attending to a land dispute at neighbouring Attoxhale (Woodway Grange in Henley Green) both had surnames indicating they were probably mining engineers. The area was later heavily mined for coal. The earliest reference so far for the coal industry in the area is of one Roger Creng, collier from Shilton, who in 1247 was outlawed for murder. He became a fugitive and his chattels (which probably included all his equipment), were claimed by none other than Richard de Erneys of Attoxhale, further proof that the potential of this area for coal-production was well known as early as the mid–thirteenth century.

The mere fourpence laid out on vessels for this feast may actually not be a purchase of large numbers of cups or dishes or whatever, but a tally of replacements for breakages, if indeed these constitute pottery at all; they may have been treen (turned wood) which survives very badly in the archaeological record. However they are cheap when compared with the 1459 price for a single brass ladle and a skimmer of 2s 3d, paid out for St Mary's Hall.

In common with all the other monastic houses in the city, building programmes were never quite finished. In 1506, the city draper Thomas Bond left in his will twenty marks (£13 6s 8d) 'to the White Freeres toward the finishing of there cloister'. In this same will he also donated to ongoing building projects at Charterhouse and Greyfriars.

The adjacent chancel of the church survived the Dissolution for some decades since John Hales chose to found a school there in 1545. His philanthropic ways were partly designed to curry favour with the King and he named his new school after him, King Henry VIII. He was a difficult person to deal with, exceptionally single-minded and the contemporary historian John Leland said of him at Whitefriars:

> The church is yet standinge, and a priest singeth there; but Hales with the clubbe foote hath gotten entret in this college, and none (but the devil) can get hym out.

Excavations in 1977 emptied the long deep troughs which had lain beneath the former choir stalls of the Whitefriars' chancel. Since the same stalls served the school, the originally grille-covered troughs, or 'resonance passages', which had served to amplify the sound of monastic plain-song back into the massive preaching-nave, had become choked with the rubbish and detritus of a generation of sixteenth-century schoolboys, comprising inkwells, styli, lace-tags, badges and marbles. Clearly classroom activities were not confined to structured learning. The oak stalls, some of which still survive, are engraved with the graffiti of names, initials and the tracks and runnels of a hundred games of marbles. Today, while the majority lie in the Old Grammar School, to where they were subsequently removed, one of the stalls remains on show in the Herbert Art Gallery and Museum, along with carved oak miserichords, the pull-down seat-perches which allowed medieval worshippers to rest against the stalls without ever getting too comfortable.

The city's efforts to get Hales out were considerable, since he and the authorities enjoyed a stormy relationship. Although the school still exists – and by the same name – its days at the Whitefriars were numbered and in a compromise with the city it moved out to the building of the former Benedictine St John's Hospital on the eponymous Hales Street. Here it stayed for 300 years; the building is still known as The Old Grammar School, with no apparent indicator of its previous longer-lived use. The great county and monastic historian, Sir William Dugdale was a pupil there in the seventeenth century, taught by the acclaimed classical translator, Dr Philemon Holland.

The destruction of the Whitefriars was seemingly a rather leisurely affair. The King's Commissioner Robert Burgoyne surveyed the house in 1545, a full six years after its Dissolution. The High Altar was only removed in 1547 and the bells were still apparently in the church in the 1550s, when the city sought to buy them from the Crown. Their efforts cannot have been altogether successful as one was removed in 1573, when the majority of the church was taken down. With the collapse of the steeple in the following year the city's dwindling count of seven stately medieval spires was reduced to four. Within a few years St Mary's central tower also fell and Coventry became the city of three spires. To many this was a cynical joke, now lost on generations of Coventrians. Even though the principal excavations on the house took place in the 1960s, the site of the precinct still yields indications of monastic tenure. In 2001 landscaping work on the new Coventry University Library uncovered burials in the monastic cemetery (east of the church), while in 2003 archaeologists from Warwickshire Museum uncovered foundations, probably of the precinct wall along the south side of Whitefriars Lane. Much work is still to be done on the house, particularly its precinct on all sides, areas ripe for redevelopment in the next generation or so.

7

Carthusians

'The Carthusian Order has never been reformed since it has never been deformed'
Carthusian saying

FALTERING BEGINNINGS

The last order to arrive in Coventry was the Carthusian. There was no inkling that any local lord harboured a particular penchant for their distinctively austere and eremitic form of monastic life in which the monks lived singly in individual cells and were totally cloistered from the world, their time given to prayer and contemplation in an altogether almost other-worldly demeanour.

Perhaps in imitation of their revered founder, St Bruno of Cologne's own beginnings, the first Prior originally brought only six Carthusian monks to Coventry, or more particularly, Shortley, in 1381, at the behest of their patron, Lord William Zouche the elder of Harringworth in Northamptonshire. The early years of the Priory were somewhat fraught with insufficient endowment and a debilitating local political situation with national ramifications. The new house or Charterhouse as such monasteries were and are known, was dedicated initially to St Anne and St Mary, although the latter was subsequently dropped, for reasons unknown, but possibly because of confusion with the dedication to St Mary of the existing all-powerful Cathedral Priory (*colour plate 11*).

Difficulty beset the new foundation from the start. Firstly, Zouche died in 1382 only a month after the Crown ratified his grant, whereupon his family reduced his testamentary bequest to the new house. Secondly, the younger Zouche, son and heir, proceeded to try to found his own Charterhouse near his chief manor of Totnes in Devon, in the converted buildings of a former Benedictine

Priory. This distraction was a complete failure and closed within three years. He then became embroiled (or was instrumental) in a court plot to depose or kill the King (Richard II, aged only 17). The plot was discovered and suddenly Zouche the younger's part was swept aside in an apparent act of effusive royal forgiveness. The King proclaimed himself with his child-bride Anne of Bohemia to be the founders of the new Coventry Charterhouse and in September 1385 laid the foundation stone of the church in person (*21*). Many of those suspected of being complicit in the former plot suddenly came forward and added their fawning support. Suddenly the new house had a fighting chance. Once more, however, Zouche and the plotters came to prominence as followers of a party of five disaffected and rebellious lords in 1388. Known as the Lords Appellant, their cause was futile and execution, exile or banishment from court became the punishment for their part. Zouche escaped with the last, least damaging of these but he never showed any further interest in the Coventry Charterhouse. Richard, however, did and continued to show exceptional favour throughout his controversial reign, a stance which carried much weight amongst those nobles who were still inclined to follow his lead. However his autocratic nature, inviting criticism and even violent opposition, meant that when he was deposed

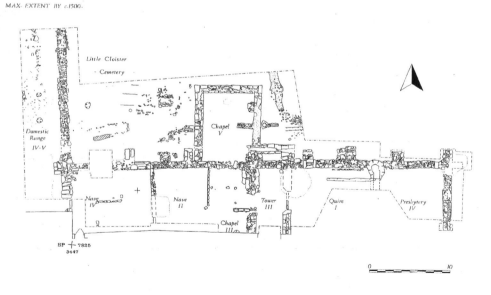

ST. ANNE'S CHARTERHOUSE.

CHURCH STRUCTURES AS EXCAVATED.

MAX. EXTENT BY c.1500.

21 Plan of St Anne's Carthusian Church (Charterhouse)

22 Charterhouse: the refectory, Prior's apartments and guest house (1417), looking west from the cloister. The second floor was inserted in the sixteenth century when a new roof was constructed

and killed in a coup in 1399, the stream of benefaction all but dried up with the accession of his former detractor, Henry IV. Costly purchases of outlying manors were needed to secure the Charterhouse's financial future. These were bought principally from the fabulously rich 'alien' priories in Normandy. However, far from ensuring the priory's future, the massive outlay nearly broke it.

Meanwhile, a bitter dispute had broken out between local lords over who could claim the rights and kudos of being the patron to the house. The 14 acres of land on which the new priory stood had been released to the elder Lord Zouche by Baldwin Freville II of Tamworth, whose father (also called Baldwin), a personal retainer of the Black Prince, had married into the Boteler family of Coventry and was Lord of Wyken. With the death of the Black Prince and Edward III, he had lost his influence. This was probably an attempt to regain it. However, his claim to the land was disputed and over 30 years the litigation continued, the matter being settled by crown intervention in February 1417 in favour of the Lord of Shortley, John Langley of Atherstone on Stour, whose forerunner, Geoffrey de Langley, had steered both Pinley and Shortley to economic success.

In thanks to God for the successful conclusion to the dispute, a wall-painting of the crucifixion was put up in the refectory of the Charterhouse (*colour plate 12*).

Ostensibly to mark the completion of the refectory, the painting is underwritten by an inscription

> This house has been finished, let there be the accustomed praise to Christ who shows favour to men…. Prior Soland had a hard task, Thomas Lambard was Procurator, putting aside the problems, afterwards…

The painting, probably completed in the 1420s, dates the completion of the structure perfectly (*22*). Soland was Prior in the period 1408-1417. To one side of the crucifixion stands the Roman centurion Longinus, saying 'Surely this man was the Son of God' (*Matthew 27: 54; Mark 15: 39*). However the centurion is portrayed as John de Langley, in early fifteenth-century armour since his similarly dressed retainer by his side carries a pennant bearing the Langley family badge (*23*). This is surely a matter of thanksgiving all round since 1417 was a year of triple celebration. The refectory was completed, Langley came into his manor in triumph (although he scarcely lived long enough to enjoy it) and simultaneously the Roman church emerged from a generation of schism.

23 Charterhouse: refectory wall-painting of the crucifixion. Sir John Langley of Atherstone upon Stour as the centurion Longinus. His speech ribbon reads in Latin 'Surely this man was the Son of God (see colour plate 12)

EXCAVATIONS

The church

Almost the entire church at the Charterhouse was archaeologically excavated between 1984 and 1987 (*21*). What emerged were the remains of an east–west aligned building which appears to have grown almost organically from a single cell chapel in the late fourteenth century to a multi-celled structure housing a tower, chantry chapels and a side chapel. Its last phase appears not to have been completed by the time it was dissolved in 1539.

In its earliest form of soon after 1385, the simple rectangular building measured 9m (29ft 6in) long x 8m (26ft 2in) wide. Its long axis was divided into bays of 3m (9ft 9in) width. A single beam slot marked the position of the sill beam on which lay a choir stall at which the monks would have sat. A stone sill supported the back of the stall. A shallow step up marked a simple division within this space which had been floored in local Stoke tiles. While the north and south walls were of buttressed stone, the east end was of timber framing and clearly designed to be temporary. Unfortunately subsequent reordering and then a high-explosive bomb in 1941 had removed most remains of the west wall.

The simple chapel was soon extended westwards to create a nave. This measured 18m (59ft) long x 8m (26ft 2in) wide. It was probably at this point that intramural burial of benefactors of the monastery began. A chamfered stone step lay within the nave and a screen would have divided nave from choir. The nave appears to have been built at around the same time as the adjacent refectory as the two respect each other in terms of sharing an alignment which is slightly eccentric to the cloister.

In a move perhaps not altogether well thought out, the monks then introduced a bell tower into the middle of the structure, measuring 12m (39ft 3in) north–south x 5.2m (17ft) east–west. This removed the former west wall of the original choir and any trace of the short-lived screen (although there would have been a replacement in the new scheme). This seems to have unbalanced the existing structure and when both the nave and choir were extended by 9m (29ft 6in) each at the same time *c.*1475, the whole church had to be re-buttressed, an act which would have necessitated at least some re-fenestration also.

The church continued to be tiled throughout using tiles made in nearby Stoke, although a plethora of benefactors' graves ensured that most semblance of original patterning was quickly lost. Elements of old designs continued to be reused, out of place. At the west end of the nave a last re-flooring of tiles set out a pattern of chequerboards in green and yellow, laid in bands and zones, eschewing the preference for stamped tiles of a preceding generation. No new stamped tiles appear to have been brought in to accompany new work after *c*.1450 and possibly earlier. This is in keeping with other, near-contemporary floors recorded in Warwickshire such as adjacent to the Beauchamp Chapel, Warwick and at Maxstoke Priory. A new restraint seems to have gripped floor designers at the same time, influencing kiln products.

Chantry chapel altars were set up in the new nave extension, close to the chantry founder's burial; thereafter family burials clustered around the progenitor. A small portable fifteenth-century polished blue Purbeck Marble altar table from just such a chantry altar was found during the excavations in 1986, ripped out and discarded at the Dissolution. Although cracked by its fall, when found it still polished up like new and is today displayed at the Herbert Art Gallery and Museum. Among the 48 burials excavated throughout the church between 1984 and 1987, seven are known by name from wills: John Langley, Lord of Pinley and Shortley (d.1457); Thomas Bickley of Coventry (d.1505); Margaret Wharton of Coventry (d.1507); Nicholas Fitzherbert (d.1508) and his parents; Thomas Hill, Draper, of Coventry (d.1518).

Eventually the available space in the church, always at a premium in a relatively small building serving a monastic order with strict rules over the use of space, simply ran out and the only solution was to build a side chapel onto the nave. This was done in the early sixteenth century, a fifth and final phase to the church's organic growth. The new chapel measured 8m (26ft) east–west x 9.5m (31ft) north–south. It was the only structure in the church complex not to be buttressed. It was divided in two by a short stubby foundation for a screen wall laid directly onto the natural clay and in each half stood the base of an altar. The floor was of thick mortar over rubble and sand which appeared so rough that it can scarcely have been intended as the final floor.

When the floor was removed, it became clear that there were no graves in this part of the church, indicating that whoever had the chapel built had not died before the monastery was dissolved in 1539. However, beneath the sub-floor lay a distinctive configuration of post-holes which indicated the original builders' scaffold used to construct the walls (*colour plate 13*). Counterpart post-holes lay outside the structure in a layout which enables the mode of construction to be carefully followed. Outside the chapel, massive stone splash-boards deflected the rainwater from the gutter-spouts onto clay makeup layers which, in addition to digging a drainage channel, were put down to reverse the run off of the ground slope, otherwise naturally inclined towards the new building. Confirmation of the late date of this chapel comes from the will of Henry Pisford (1525) who left £6 13s 4d 'towarde the reparacion and buldynge of the churche'.

Burials extended to the north of the nave, west of this late chapel, in an area which appears to have been flanked by a covered walkway or pentice. These burials may belong to a school for 12 poor clerks, aged seven to seventeen, which had been part of the life of the monastery for over a hundred years but which was nevertheless disbanded at the same time as the monastery was dissolved.

The monks' cells

Around the great cloister, in the usual Carthusian manner, stood the 12 cells in which lived each individual choir monk. Four of these on the east side of the cloister were partially excavated between 1980 and 1982 and part of a fifth, on the west side, in 1987. In addition the rear of the garden to one of those previously excavated was investigated in 1986.

The monks lived separate lives in simple three-room detached houses or 'cells' over two floors, each of which lay off the cloister and with its own walled garden. The name of each occupant at any one time remains unknown since each monk sought relative anonymity. This was such that over each entrance door from the cloister was set a letter of the alphabet, rather than the name of the occupant. One such door-head, believed to be a unique survival, stands reused within the late sixteenth-century second floor of the surviving Charterhouse building. It is of oak, carved into an arch with floral decorative motifs in the spandrels and bears in a central cartouche the letter 'i' (*24*). Thus it derives from the ninth cell of 12, A to L. Because of a document which lists the original benefactors of the

24 Oak Carthusian doorhead from cell I (*c.*1385), re-used in the sixteenth-century second floor of the Charterhouse

cells in 1382-5 and where each stood, it is known that the ninth cell was the westernmost of those on the south side of the cloister (where the former eighteenth-century cart hovel now stands as part of the Coventry Parks Club). This cell was paid for by Sir Nigel Loryng, at the behest of Robert Braybrook (King's Secretary and Chancellor 1382-3 and Bishop of London 1382-1404).

In all of the four cells excavated on the east side, the ground floor was divided up into two small rooms with a two-part lobby. Each of these cells stood in the north-west corner of its plot, so must have been lit from the east and/or south sides. Generally they had no windows into the great cloister and certainly none overlooking the neighbouring yard to the north. Such a layout ensured privacy (essential to the rules of the order) warmth (in that the coldest, north side was sheltered by the next cell to the north) and the early morning sun (necessary for rising at dawn). Light was maximised within the high walls by the inside being limewashed.

Each cell measured 6.3m (20ft 7in) x 5.7m (18ft 7in). It is not known how the cells were configured on the upper storey but they may (unusually for English Carthusians) have housed each monk's bedroom and oratory, including a fireplace since none was present in any of the excavated ground floor rooms. While the monks were daily accustomed to long periods of prayer and contemplation, they were also encouraged to spend their time engaged in manual tasks such as the illumination of religious manuscripts, carpentry and gardening, the last two being based upon the Biblical examples of Christ's trade and Adam as gardener of Eden. To the side and rear of their cell lay at least a pentice or often a glazed gallery in which the monk could work in a well-lit but covered environment. In two of the excavated yards adjacent to the cells there is some evidence that the monks were engaged in activities more akin to industry, since there were water channels and drains in elaborate configurations which suggest more than just the incidental collection of rainwater for drinking or washing. In one was dug a well with a well-house placed over it. In the garden of one cell were excavated footpaths and the edges of raised beds, picked out in unused roof tiles set end to end. This is very much in common with the gardens at Mount Grace Priory in Yorkshire, overall the best preserved of the English Charterhouses. The gardens on this east side of the cloister appear to have measured 14.3m (48ft) deep x 10.9m (36ft) wide.

STANDING REMAINS

The crucifixion wall-painting of the south wall of the first-floor refectory has already been described above. The monks would have viewed this on the few but

25 Charterhouse: the church high altar reused as a lintel for a post-Dissolution fireplace

regular occasions on which they met together to eat in silence with their minds on God and their eyes, if they strayed from their food, on the panorama of St Anne, St Mary and the Crucifixion. The second floor of the surviving building is a late sixteenth-century insertion, although the finely-carved timbered ceiling beams set on wall-posts on carved stone corbels are original. Reset into an inserted second-floor room as a fireplace lintel, lies the original sandstone high altar table of the church, a somewhat ignominious end. It still bears the five requisite incised crosses, representing the wounds of Christ: two in His hands, two in His feet and one in His side (25).

Also in this building were the ground-floor Prior's lodgings (26). While his quarters were no less austere than those of his monks, his suite was located at a point where he could deal most effectively with the needs of his monks in the great cloister on the east and those of his lay brethren, based around a smaller cloister, to the west. The tasks of the Prior (and often those of other officials, such as Procurator) were often considered onerous since they meant repeated dealings with the outside world. Since Carthusians were always in the first place professed as monks, this exposure was considered an unwelcome fall from their religious vocation. Thus it is not uncommon to find Priors or other officials requesting 'mercy' of the general chapter, release from their onerous duties and with it reversion to their professed rank of Brother. The last prior, John Bochard,

26 The Prior's lodgings, refectory and guest apartments (completed 1417)

seems to have had three separate terms of office during the immensely difficult time between 1530 and 1539. He died in 1543, as a secular priest at the church of St Bartholomew the Great, Smithfield, London, where he was buried; he was probably the only Coventry Prior not to be buried in his own Charterhouse. His will indicates that he still owned the chalice given him by Henry VIII's Commissioners, part of a gift which helped buy his compliance in dissolving the house.

Between 1381 and 1539, the Priors at Coventry were drawn from most echelons of society. One Prior, Sir Thomas Tarleton (1521-30) was clearly of knightly class. This was also true of some choir monks, such as John Rodmondby who in 1486 was described as 'of noble birth'. Others have come down to us simply known by their Christian name. At least one Prior climbed the ranks, John Norton, who was Procurator before becoming Prior *c.*1486. Others still might be transferred to the Priorate direct from other houses, perhaps when no Coventry monk was suitable for this unlooked-for promotion. Thus in the 1470s Robert Odiham was promoted from being Procurator of the London house to the Priorate of Coventry

Most ordinary monks were locally recruited and thus brought local support for the order. Many of the surnames of known monks are known from other, official and mercantile documents in Coventry, and after the Dissolution some of the last choir monks lived out their declining years in Coventry on their government pensions, in common with their pensioned Benedictine brothers from the Priory.

FINDS

In common with all the monasteries, large areas were habitually kept clean, so often there is a lack of finds. However, enough areas have been excavated to begin to understand the likely uses to which different parts of the cloister and precinct might have been put, aided by a wider understanding of the strict segregation common to this day in Carthusian houses.

Pottery was ubiquitous but very distinct differences can be seen between the cells and the outer precinct north of the church. In the latter were found many examples of imported tablewares such as Raeren types, as seen throughout the city. However, in the cells these were almost absent. In contrast from the cells there was a preponderance of local redwares, not seen in the outer cloister. The absence of finewares from the cells, especially imported material, is in stark contrast to the material culture of Mount Grace Priory, Yorkshire, where one cell in particular was lavished with such material.

The cells in general produced largely tableware forms in small quantities such as cups and flagons while the outer precinct areas excavated produced significantly larger proportions of these plus forms such as cisterns, cucurbits and jugs, largely for food storage and preparation. This is in keeping with Carthusian tradition of food being prepared by lay brethren or servants and taken on a tray to each choir monk to be eaten in his own cell. This seems to be confirmed by a general lack of preparation-type vessels in any of the excavated cells. Similarly the lack of ostentation in the forms recovered, may reflect Carthusian preference as construed in the Coventry community. The base of a single chafing dish (for warming food at the table), found adjacent to one of the cells on the southern side of the cloister may suggest that the monk at that far-flung end of the great cloister was rather too used to receiving his meals too cold for his taste.

Related to the monks' employment and devotions were a variety of writing implements in bone and copper alloy, sharpened styli for marking out parchments before writing. There were also tuning pegs for musical instruments. There was always a strong case for musical accompaniment in many religious offices, although the Carthusians have traditionally been accredited as being less musically inclined than their cousins such as the Benedictines or most orders of Friars. Books were represented by numerous small clasp fragments, cover mountings and decorated reinforcements. At least three thimbles in late medieval layers indicate the self-sufficiency in mending garments and soft furnishings if not in making them, while a brass dairy skimmer/strainer suggests that the monks may have made their own cheese, a regular monastic by-product, even today.

Despite extensive excavations much of the Charterhouse remains unexplored and it is arguably the best-preserved of Coventry's monasteries, simply because it has never been redeveloped. Its rarity and its preservation are such that it today constitutes a Scheduled Ancient Monument and the standing building is listed Grade I. It is still partly surrounded by the listed precinct wall, which was built to keep out the distractions of the secular world, such as rowdy games of bowls which caused them great disturbance and anxiety in 1518. Despite not being finished as late as 1506 (when Thomas Bond, former Mayor of Coventry, bequeathed £20 to complete it), the seclusion it brought has helped to keep the integrity of the precinct through 400 years.

8

Institution and infrastructure

'From Henry Wentbridge: rent for a tenement in New Street which he has recently built. The … whole street was built in Earl Ranulf's orchard which he gave to Richard Gardener who gave it to the Prior and Convent.' St Mary's Priory 1411

While the presence of the monasteries and friaries in and around the City was ubiquitous, not all churches exuded overt monasticism. The rest took in the Bishop's own influence, or that of ordinary parish priests or clerics in hospitals and non-parochial chapels. Their priests were put in place by sponsors, the holders of the so-called 'advowson' or right to the presentation of a vicar. Often the sponsor was indeed the Prior and Convent of the Benedictine Priory whose place in the city was unique. However, sometimes it was the Bishop of Coventry and Lichfield, at others it was a secular patron where the mainstream monastic influence was weaker.

Alongside the Bishop and the (theoretically) subservient Prior, lay the growing power of the mercantile classes of the boom-town economy of medieval Coventry. Their confidence manifested itself, like in so many other major towns, such as London, York and Bristol, in a coalescence of like-minded individuals to form trading guilds along religious lines. Their sense of belonging and ownership of a successful town, people and infrastructure, led to a powerful but rigid local government. Under a seemingly all-powerful exterior seethed personal feuds, enmity and shady dealing, complicated by old allegiances which bound many to their traditional seigneurial overlords. Growing fortunes were at stake and the currency for the most part was land.

The church land was as near sacrosanct as anything could be, and while it could rarely be touched with impunity, the church could be brought round by the gift of more land, more rents or more properties. Individuals also knew that secular wheeling and dealing was encouraged since the richer the parishioner, the bigger the tithe to the mother church. Gifts to the church also bought redemption from time in purgatory when the excesses of earthly living were believed to come to an end.

The city approaching the end of the fourteenth century was a hive of industry, with ecclesiastical and civic building works just about everywhere. The Cathedral and Priory were being updated, while nearby the Bishop's own palace had reached its apogee. St Michael's Church tower, the work of the renowned master-mason Robert Skyllington, was just being prepared to receive its new spire. The Charterhouse was a relatively new building site, as still was Whitefriars after two generations of construction. Greyfriars' spire was new and the city walls were still in their infancy. There was money being spent everywhere on massive building projects. Since 1350, some sense of self-belief had clearly overtaken the city, helped by a redistribution of wealth brought about by a generation of plague and pestilence. In 1393, a massive gift of property by scores of individuals set up the new Holy Trinity Guild with a financial base second to none. The stage was set for Coventry's rapid rise on the twin foundations of church and government. However, there was a price to be paid for growth, both at the time for the city's society, as well as today for the archaeologist.

THE BISHOP'S PALACE

The church's place at the centre of power was nothing new. The Bishop had already had his See in Coventry since about 1102, worshipping from St Mary's Cathedral and with plans for a new palace next door. Although nothing is visible above ground today, the site of the Bishops' palace remains at the heart of the ecclesiastical centre of the city, lying just outside the east wall of Sir Basil Spence's New Cathedral of 1962 and spreading across Priory Street into the heart of Coventry University. A surprising amount of detail has come to light concerning this once prestigious residence.

Its earliest reference is related to its construction, and survives in the incomparable *Magnum Registrum Album*, 'The Great Register' of the Bishops of Coventry and Lichfield which charts events in the life of the double See before the Coventry element was made redundant in 1539 (finally to be reconstituted in its own right in 1918). In 1224-5, the register records:

> Brother Geoffrey, the Prior and Convent of Coventry grant to Alexander de Stavenby,
> Bishop of Coventry and his successors, to enhance the dignity of the Bishopric, the plot

outside their cemetery on which the houses of Reginald, their late mason stood, with the houses thereon, extending lengthwise along the cemetery wall from the gate of the aforesaid houses to the garden of the Earl of Chester and Lincoln, and in breadth from the cemetery wall to Robert Briton's land; for a residence to be built there; reserving to themselves both sides of the cemetery wall, free from any attachments of building, with free access for rebuilding or repairing the same.

After only 60 years, the growing influence of the Bishop forced a rethink of existing arrangements, and in 1283 the same register records when Roger de Meuland, Bishop of Coventry and Lichfield on the one hand, and Brother Thomas Pavi and the Convent of Coventry agreed that:

...seeing that the Bishop's house is dilapidated and the site too confined the Prior and Convent undertake to grant to the Bishop an adjoining site or one close by of equal size and 200 marks (£133; 1 mark = 13s 4d) for the repair of the existing house and the construction of additional buildings in which the Bishop at his visitation may accommodate his retinue with himself and entertain them.

The Bishop may not have been too regular a visitor at some periods because in 1364 it appears to have been rented out by Bishop Robert de Stretton, although at a very high cost (three and a half times the average rent of a contemporary principal residence, or *capital messuage*). This betrays the sumptuous apartments and the kudos of such an abode:

The Bishop leases his palace in the city of Coventry with its gardens and appurtenances to Nicholas de Crowland, Chaplain and Henry de Kele, citizen of Coventry, for four years at a rent of 46s 8d per annum. Reserving the use thereof to himself and his household when at Coventry, and to his clerks (priests) at such times as the annual synods are held there. If the rent is in arrears he may re-enter and take possession of the contents. The tenant to do repairs.

Powers of distraint by the landlord (forfeiture of the tenant's own goods) may seem a high price to pay for rent arrears, but the upkeep of such a palace could clearly become a major problem. After all the original complex had become dilapidated after only 60 years.

At its height the palace would have had to contain, as a minimum, a great hall for both reception and dining, kitchens, sleeping apartments for the Bishop, others for guests and the Bishop's entourage, storage rooms, gardens and stables. These would have been arranged very commodiously, as befitting the station of the Bishop. The original complex even had access to a prison in the adjacent cathedral priory. The earliest tenant is recorded in 1221; Robert de Rode, a chaplain, who killed his servant, Gervaise. His eventual fate is unknown although monastic statutes provided for a killer in holy orders to be imprisoned and fed on bread and water for the rest of his life. The later description of the palace makes it clear that it also acquired a banqueting house, probably in the fifteenth century (when such structures began to become fashionable) and fish ponds.

Perhaps the best description of the palace is found in a survey of 1646, long after the complex had ceased to perform its original function. A copy is held in Coventry Archives.

A survey of the Bishop's palace there as it now standeth, with all gardens, orchards, lands and appurtenances thereunto belonging, taken 22nd day of January 1646 … we think that Richard, heretofore Bishop of Coventry and Lichfield was seized in the right of his Bishopric and in the site of the messuage or dwelling house with appurtenances called the palace in the City of Coventry and of all houses, edifices, gardens and orchards thereunto belonging. Which house was then ruined and in decay, that the said Richard, in consideration that one John Rumridge constructed and built divers buildings belonging to the same by his indenture bearing the date the 10th day of July in the 37th year of the reign of King Henry VIII (1546), did demise and let to the said John Rumridge all that site (etc) for 99 years for the yearly rent of 3s 4d (seemingly a pale shadow of its former self) … with liberty to have and enjoy the said palace for his entertainment during … his residence …. The palace contains two large bays of building and two small bays of building and at the end of the term was out of repair (1645). But one room there has been repaired since by the company of clothiers. ..there are also sixteen private gardens … two others … eleven others (many sizes and tenants given).. orchards and gardens lie near the palace, worth yearly 7s'

The surveyor, possibly coming upon the palace for official purposes for the first time in many years, was forced to rely thereafter upon the statements of two elderly men, and the memories of their youth, in order to ascertain the detailed layout of the grounds of the palace, which had apparently become subdivided and much altered. The survey continues:

Robert Everitt, Gardner, aged 80 years, says he knows the house … and has known it 60 years … with an orchard at the east end of the palace … which had in ancient times trees standing in it, which are now decayed … and he has planted some more trees in it. And says he knows the nether orchard and that there was a Banqueting House in it for long since … and one or two fish pools (possibly water-filled quarries). Thomas Potter, aged 79, says that he knows the palace.. and the plot of ground lying to the north in the occupation of Mr Miller, lying open to the great orchard at the upper end heretofore, divided from the orchard and garden now in the possession of Mr Burton, and another wall in the middle of the great orchard which Mr Warren pulled down ... he remembers the great orchard and in it a Banqueting House and two fish pools, one of which is filled up ... he remembers also a causeway or alley (the eponymous Miller's Alley) which led to Bustall Dye House (The Bastille House just north of the nineteenth-century Cope Street and possibly once the Priory/Bishop's Prison) and says that Mr Warren...pulled it down about 50 years since (i.e. c.1590 – although it is shown on John Speed's map of 1610; the gardener's memory may not have been so reliable on the timescale involved).

The Bastille House lay where the 1960s' swimming baths now stand, close to the town wall, while the fish ponds probably lay at roughly the same elevation since their water supply would need to be regulated from the Sherbourne. The orchard and banqueting house lay east of what is now Priory Street and north of the former New Street, where the surviving graveyard now stands, overspill in the eighteenth century from St Michael's. The University buildings of the 1960s have wrapped around this, leaving open the possibility of the banqueting house's preservation beneath and amongst the graves. The last standing remains of the palace appear on the 1851 Board of Health Map of Coventry but the four wings around a central courtyard, shown on Speed's map in 1610 have gone. The site of some of the buildings lies under the verge adjacent to the New Cathedral, by the side of Priory Street. Much was lost, unrecorded, when the New Cathedral was built.

ST MICHAEL'S CHURCH

The two dominant parish churches of medieval Coventry, St Michael's and Holy Trinity, dominate the hilltop just adjacent to the palace site. That they were in fact once dwarfed by the Cathedral of St Mary today seems inconceivable. The juxtaposition of the three churches in a forest of spires and pinnacles on top of the hill presented a sight which would have lingered long in the memory, when few other buildings reached higher than their eaves. However, it is easy to forget that each church grew organically and many generations would have known each as little more than a building site and the only forest would have been not of pinnacles but scaffolding.

Before its consecration as (all too briefly) a cathedral in 1918, St Michael's was reckoned to be the biggest parish church in England (*colour plate 14*). It was certainly one of the four biggest (with Yarmouth, Boston and Hull). The loss of its interior to the Blitz in 1940 was and is still mourned, not least since it contained the finest surviving medieval stone and wood carving in the city (*27*), together with the largest collection of medieval stained and painted glass. John Leland

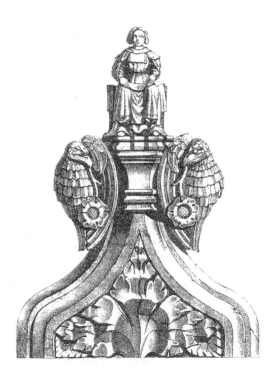

27 Fifteenth-century carved oak pew ends, formerly in St Michael's Church, destroyed 14/15 November 1940. From a nineteenth-century print

described it in *c*.1543 as 'an excedynge goodly and ample peace of worke'. Today the shell remains an impressive testament to both the skill of its builders and the unutterable waste of war. It is inextricably linked to the public psyche as the Old Cathedral, given this name to mark it out from Sir Basil Spence's magnificent New Cathedral, but ironically betraying the fact that the original cathedral, St Mary's, had long since disappeared from sight and from public memory.

The earliest part of St Michael's which survives is the south door on Bayley Lane. This is Early English in style and bears great similarities to the contemporary west-door remains found in the excavation of the Benedictine Cathedral of St Mary. This may not be a surprise since they may have enjoyed the same school of masons in the early thirteenth century. The remainder of the shell is truly Perpendicular late medieval in character, dominated by the two-phase early fifteenth-century spire paid for by the Botoner family of Coventry. It remains one of the tallest spires in England (after Salisbury and Norwich Cathedrals) and its existence is remarkable since it survived both the Blitz of 1940 and an episode of underpinning in the 1880s when it was found to be subsiding. Early photographs of the 1860s show that by then it had become a sorry sight, eroded by weather and the very new threat of pollution. Well-documented restoration as a result has unfortunately left little of its medieval detail (*28*).

28 St Michael's Coventry, the Cathedral, 1918-40. The magnificent late fourteenth-century tower, probably by Robert Skyllington. The spire was a later addition. Viewed from the Castle Bakehouse site

The earliest church on the site, however, was probably twelfth century in date, and Romanesque in character. It probably looked something like St Mary Magdalene, Wyken, and then grew quickly by degrees until the existing plan was far too small for the needs of the growing parish. It is likely that this early chapel was the castle chapel built by and for the Earl of Chester. As such it belongs to the period *c*.1100–1140. How soon it was enlarged is not yet known, nor where under the current footprint the early church lay, other than to speculate that its Early English south door seems improbably large if it was ever added to a Wyken-sized chapel. Some intermediate twelfth- to thirteenth-century building seems plausible, before the dramatic growth to the structure whose ruins are seen today. It was not until the advowson of the church came into the hands of the Benedictine Priory in the mid-thirteenth century (along with those of all its dependent chapels, as a gift of the de Montalt Earls) that St Michael's can be seen as part of the monastic establishment, to which its prior independence must have been challenging.

St Michael's at its greatest extent in the sixteenth century was full of chantry chapels and altars (*29*). All parts of the church would have been subdivided. Contemporary surveys and other documents attest to 11 altars with different dedications and 13 Chantry chapels, the earliest of which was founded in 1323. A few it gained briefly at the Dissolution, such as Copston's Chantry, moved from St Mary's when that was closed down. The 1522 muster rolls for the city show

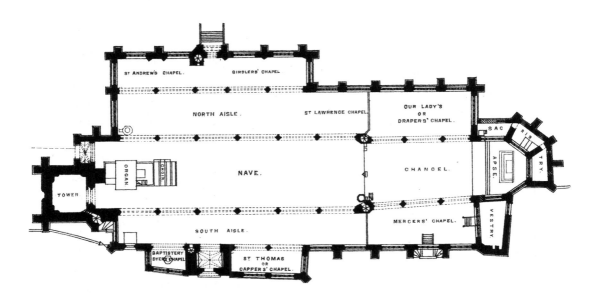

29 St Michael's Church. Nineteenth-century plan

that St Michael's was served by 19 parish priests and seven chantry priests.

In 1990 the (then revolutionary) technique of ground-probing radar was deployed to investigate the extent of buried vaults and undercrofts beneath the church. This was in connection with ideas to use the space. While the work did indicate that such vaults remain intact beneath the north and south aisles, the church is also riddled with seventeenth- to nineteenth-century intramural burials, many of them in brick-lined shafts, some in lead coffins, which totally blocked the radar signal from deeper penetration. They will have denuded the earlier remains, a considerable loss. Recovery of the vestiges of the plan of the earlier church or churches will probably have to wait for traditional archaeological interventions. Somewhere in the massive cemetery which St Michael's shared with both the Benedictine Cathedral Priory and Holy Trinity church, lay another chapel, possibly a mortuary chapel, known as the Chapel-on-the-Hill from a few documents. It may lie within the existing graveyard, now largely cleared of headstones, and might in future benefit from geophysical prospection. In 2012–13 further research has taken place on St Michael's undercrofts.

HOLY TRINITY CHURCH

Just as St Michael's had begun as the Earl of Chester's own parish church from the twelfth century, so Holy Trinity began as that of the Prior of St Mary's. John Leland, in his inimitable curt style, described Holy Trinity at its greatest extent *c.*1543, as 'a right fayre piece of worke' (*colour plate 15*). Just so; even after its incongruous nineteenth-century re-facing in Bath Stone. Just like St Michael's, Holy Trinity was minutely subdivided into separate altars and chapels/chantries, eight of the former and 14 of the latter. The 1522 muster rolls record ten parish priests and three chantry priests. The piscina (holy water drain) belonging to the Tanners' chapel still survives, its pattern probably repeated all over the church (*30* and *31*). Two similar piscinae were excavated in the neighbouring St Mary's Cathedral in 1966 (Copston's Chantry by the south door) and 2000 (west end of the north aisle, in an unnamed chantry chapel). The individual altars would have stood very close by.

From the fifteenth century, a recently restored Doom painting above the central tower crossing dominated the public part of Holy Trinity – the nave. Such depictions were largely didactic, backing up the teaching from the pulpit, and were joined by scenes carved in stone and wood and blown in stained or painted glass. In a society in which only a minority had any formal learning and could afford books, the illiterate majority received moral teaching directly from their church and looked to that same church for encouragement and guidance.

Left: 30 Tanners' Chapel Piscina, Holy Trinity
Church, just one of many chantry chapels

Below: 31 Holy Trinity Church. Nineteenth-
century plan

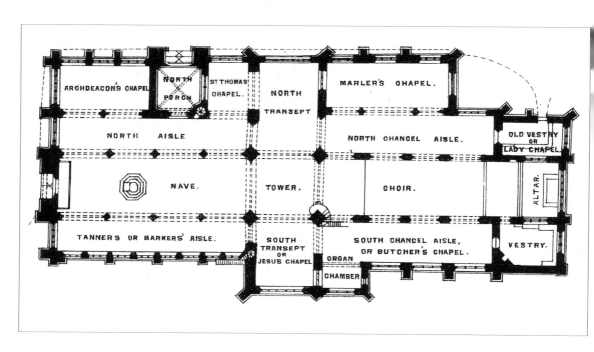

The artistic motifs employed in almost all aspects of church buildings rarely went without deeper meaning.

Just as the St Michael's seen today supplanted an earlier church, somewhere beneath Holy Trinity lie the remains of the church of the Holy Cross, a possibly eleventh-century foundation. Nothing is known of this building other than the sparsest of documentary references, but its foundation may have been contemporary with Godiva's monastery. It seemingly occupied the prime hilltop site, helping to dictate the position of the Romanesque cathedral. This might suggest that it predates Godiva's better-known foundation. Naturally its earliest form is unknown. If of eleventh-century date or even earlier (and this is a big 'if'), the likes of Earl's Barton Church (Northamptonshire) or Deerhurst (Gloucestershire) are potential comparisons in form from the relatively small number of Saxon chapels known.

At the time of writing (2003-4) there are plans to reorder the interior of Holy Trinity, work which may involve considerable sub-floor interventions. Earlier work in 1990 showed that, in common with St Michael's, the interior is riddled with post-medieval burials, many of them in destructive brick-lined shafts and vaults so the sub-surface remains of any early church are likely to have been denuded. The loss of the early churches was the price to pay for Holy Trinity's success.

One particular burial environment makes Holy Trinity a church of more than local or regional significance. That is the Marler Chapel complex of 1526. This slightly unprepossessing chapel lies on the north side of the chancel of Holy Trinity. As with so many similar chapels it was privately funded as a chantry in which prayers were to be said for the soul of the benefactor and his or her family. On his death Richard Marler was by far the wealthiest man in Coventry, owning over 50 houses. However, this chapel is in no way magnificent nor ostentatious. In fact commentators agree that he actually left it insufficiently endowed. Beneath the chapel, however, lies the archaeological gem of a vaulted undercroft, a charnel house, stacked full with human bone. The construction of the chapel disturbed so many bodies that the undercroft was built to accommodate the mountain of exhumed bones and pay them a form of reverence. The charnel house remains unopened since it was finally closed to disturbed bones, full to bursting, in 1698, the rarest of archaeological burial environments.

ST JOHN THE BAPTIST'S CHURCH

At the western end of the city, almost squeezed to the outer margins, lies one church which is an anomaly within the medieval urban fabric. Unlike the other great churches of the city, the collegiate church of St John the Baptist is entirely a creation of the fourteenth century, although today it mainly reflects later restoration. Its site has always been problematic since it lies partly over a former thirteenth-century water mill whose mill pool continued to saturate the local substrate. By the mid-fourteenth century, the choice of sites for new major churches was almost nil. It is little wonder that St John's ended up on a nightmarish site, little-suited to the mass of its structure. It represents real economic growth, but at a price. During 2000-1 large parts of the west end of the church were extensively underpinned to halt a problem of subsidence which had been previously addressed in the nineteenth century. This provided the opportunity for extensive archaeological recording both below the floors and within the standing fabric (*colour plate 16*).

Only the briefest glimpse was seen of the problematic topography of the site. At a depth of 1.5m below the nave floor a test pit through what seemed like natural geology (Keuper Marl) hit upon the *in situ*, blackened roots of a tree, totally saturated. Clearly the clay was not natural at all but a massive dump of such material, deposited to raise the pre-existing ground level where a single document previously recorded an adjacent water mill. Unfortunately this is part of the problem St John's has encountered since it not only slides upon the real, underlying natural clay and the natural groundwater levels, but is also largely impermeable to fresh rainwater. Thus the church sits upon two superimposed ground levels; one natural, one unnatural, but both of clay and both separated by trapped water. Here Coventry recorded its highest floods in 1900, which inundated the church.

St John's was founded and quickly completed by William Walssheman (Welshman) in the second quarter of the fourteenth century, in honour of (and on land donated by) the Dowager Queen Isabella, widow of Edward II and mother of Edward III. She was beloved of Coventry and regularly resided in her dotage at Cheylesmore Manor. Walssheman had much to be thankful for since he had risen to the rank of Keeper of the Royal Wardrobe. In this position he seems to have accrued massive wealth, much of which reflected well on Coventry as a whole. It was during the life of Isabella and the 50 year reign of her son that the Royal Wardrobe's cloth purchases switched from continental cloth to English, a substantial proportion being Coventry cloth bought at the annual Coventry cloth fair. Walssheman may have had a lot to do with this. He owned the Drapery between Earl Street and Bayley Lane outright and even after his own death and his family's eventual passage into obscurity, a Welsh drapery continued to exist within it.

The church of St John the Baptist comprises a cruciform body with a central tower topped with distinctive bartizans. Both the chancel and the nave are fully

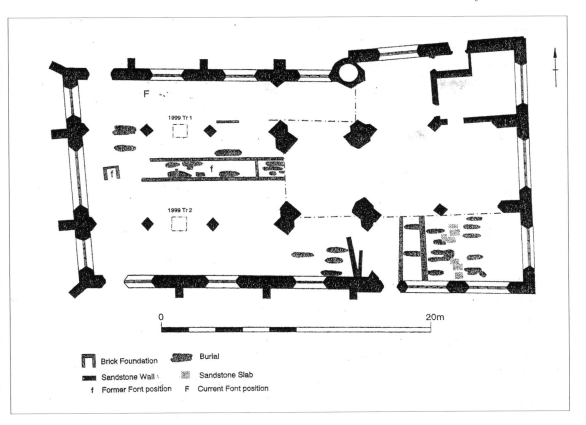

32 St John the Baptist Church, plan from excavations, 2000–2001. *Northamptonshire Archaeology*

aisled, the arcades carried on improbably slender piers, unlike the earlier, more sturdy counterparts of St Michael's and Holy Trinity (*32*). The whole body is lit by a lofty clerestory, but the detail of which archaeological recording has shown to be the work of G.G. Scott in the nineteenth century. Although he has long been thought to have copied the original work he found there, so little of any earlier clerestory work survives that this cannot be confirmed. Even Scott's own clerestory has now had to be restored, so bad has been the movement of the stonework in the long-standing subsidence problem. Nineteenth-century commentators make it clear that Scott completely redressed the entire church in its current red sandstone, replacing a greenish-grey local variant which existed before. Looking back in the late 1870s, W.G. Fretton described it as its former 'venerable grey suit'. Only the north nave aisle and the nave north clerestory appear to contain areas of original medieval work, and in confirmation of Fretton's observation, they are of the greenish grey stone (*colour plate 16*). The details of much of its original appearance are hard to gauge, since a penchant for drawing and painting the church in the eighteenth, nineteenth and twentieth centuries indicates that such things as the window tracery and the parapets changed from decade to decade or artist to artist. Some show the parapets as continuous, others as crenellated. They also change with bewildering regularity. The few windows which were once thought to be unchanged, and which used to contain medieval stained or painted glass, were blown out during the Second World War. In almost every way St John's is a nineteenth-century approximation of what architectural restorers thought a medieval church should look like. One thing the restorers could not do was redress the subsidence caused by the topographical problems. This had been exacerbated by the lofty clerestory and arcades, one of the piers of which was leaning alarmingly. It was totally rebuilt and underpinned by Scott, but then had to be underpinned again in 2000 since the problem had resurfaced. It was not helped by Scott's rebuilt arches of the south arcade being improperly centred, their springers being eccentric to the sweep of the arches and all this causing clerestory shafts to bend, and tracery to crumble like cake under the shifting weight of the roof and walls.

As if the medieval problems and the restorer's remedies were not enough, the church has also suffered major but relatively undocumented post-medieval alterations, due to the fact that it languished for many decades in the seventeenth century without priest or congregation. It was used briefly as a prison for captured royalist rank and file during the Civil War (the officers were held at the Earl Marshall's house in Much Park Street). Following the creation of its own parish in 1734, major repairs began. The nave roof was renewed in 1764 and has been subsequently much patched, having been, amongst other things, fire-damaged. Its coffering and wall-posts seem to be too numerous, being eccentric to the medieval bay-divisions, and resulting in a disturbing incongruity of the nave roof proportions as a whole, when compared to the earlier walls.

The nearby attachment of Bond's Hospital left the church with a chantry link; indeed it was served by seven such priests in 1522. For much of its early history it had also enjoyed the service of an anchorite or hermit who lived in a purpose-built hovel north of the chancel. In the mid-sixteenth century the Reformation put its very future in jeopardy. Its survival was never assured and its history during the seventeenth and eighteenth centuries was often beset by difficulty. Its biggest threat has always been the unsuitable topography. Now stabilised once more it remains a singular piece of church architecture, albeit predominantly an approximation of the medieval.

EARLY CHAPELRIES

Whereas St John's is definitely a church without a precursor, the difficulty of tracing the early development by accretion of St Michael's and Holy Trinity can only be alleviated by studying the sites of the small early chapels of the city which never developed further, usually because funds were not available. At the beginning these great churches began as simple, small foundations. As will be seen their models lie in the suburbs of Coventry.

At the very southern edge of Stoke Green lies the site of Pinley Chapel. Little is known of this small church building other than that it was founded by Geoffrey de Langley, Lord of Pinley, in the thirteenth century. However, the chapel is the site of the earliest known example of archaeological recording in Coventry, dating from *c.*1815. The 1817 version of Sir William Dugdale's Antiquities of Warwickshire records that the chapel remains were found

> on premises belonging to Mr Percy, and that gentleman is about to make further excavations, with a view to ascertain with all precision that is attainable, their character, extent &c

It was, however, left to a later antiquarian, Thomas Sharpe, to report Mr Percy's results in his 1835 book on Warwickshire:

> some remains of buildings, evidently of still greater age, were discovered about twenty years ago, within the same lordship, amongst which the walls of a private chapel, with piscina and locker, were very perfect .... The south wall was tolerably perfect, having a couple of round-headed lights at its eastern end, and just below them a mutilated stoup or piscina, with traces of a priest's door .... On the south of what appeared to have been this chancel site stood a substantial stone building of two stories, the chimney pieces apparently of Tudor date .... The garth or chapel yard was an enclosure of considerable size and was separated from the surrounding property by a ditch, traces of which were plainly discernible. Evident indications of foundations to the south and west showed plainly that the building was once of large size. Hewn and moulded stones were turned up at different periods ....

A further, drawn record appears to have been made since in 1869 it was reported to the *Coventry Times* by their regular correspondent known as '*Viator*' 'I saw the remains just before their demolition, and took several sketches thereof. In the cottage was a fine carved oak chimney piece ... to the best of my recollection Elizabethan'. The whereabouts of any sketches is no longer known, or whether they even survived '*Viator*'. Sharpe's description remains the only one, and it is an exceptional description for its day. The excavator, Mr Percy (who subsequently moved to Leamington Spa) seems to have recorded the chancel

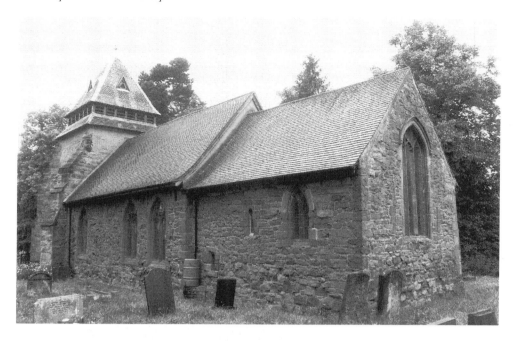

33 St Mary Magdalene, Wyken. An archetypal twelfth-century two-cell plan, the tower added later. The church is a model for other Norman chapels in Coventry

of a small single- or two-cell medieval chapel, perhaps not unlike the surviving church of St Mary Magdalene in Wyken (*33*). The adjacent late medieval house is more enigmatic since there is no ready identification. By the time Rev Blythe wrote his History of Stoke, in 1897, the remains were below ground and he barely mentioned the site, other than to acknowledge Thomas Sharpe's earlier record. The sites of both chapel and house, south-east of Stoke Green, remain of great archaeological significance in Coventry. Both would repay more up to date rigorous archaeological scrutiny and excavation.

Further out to the east lies Willenhall. Here St James' Chapel, unlike Pinley, was once a parish church. It was owned by the Benedictine Priory and was the first church any visitor from London would glimpse on their approach to the city, other than the spires of Coventry's skyline within the walls. The parish it served is known today as Willenhall. However, until the fifteenth century the principal grouping of parishioners would have been found in the hamlet of Newton which stood north of the London Road and east of the River Sherbourne. Dominated by the great Tithe Barn of the Benedictine Priory, the hamlet lay along the sides of a hollow-way which linked the end of St James' Lane with the bridge over the river. Newton was probably a casualty of the natural disasters which struck repeatedly throughout the fourteenth century, and

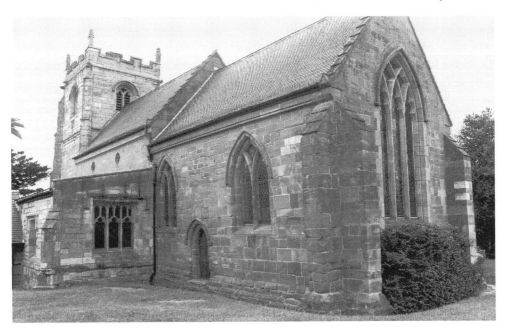

34 St Mary's, Walsgrave: how St Mary Magdalen, Wyken, might have developed had finance been forthcoming

in 1410 was almost depopulated. Willenhall is known to have been particularly badly affected by the Black Death. Seemingly only the Tithe Barn and St James' Chapel survived. The barn finally disappeared in the middle of the nineteenth century (but was mapped in 1838) apparently used for its original purpose (but with secular owners) right up until the end, while the chapel was probably subject to a long, slow decline, bereft of its parishioners. The manor house nearby, across St James' Lane (then Weeping Lane) survived into the nineteenth century but the parish after the Dissolution owed its allegiance to Holy Trinity Church; the local focus had long since gone.

St James' chapel lay on the rising ground west of the lane which now bears its name. Nineteenth-century maps make it clear that it stood within its own graveyard, which may not have been disturbed, despite the presence of a post-war estate over the top of it. It may be that the remains are deeply buried, or that 1950s and 1960s estate building work destroyed remains which went unreported in less enlightened times. The church itself is likely to have been of Romanesque or Early English design, perhaps (like Pinley) similar to Wyken. The later medieval loss of Newton means that it may not have been much altered since the finances were never there after the middle of the fourteenth century. When the existing estates on top of its site are due for demolition, then its location is one whose investigation would shed light on the church, the people of medieval Willenhall and the disasters and faltering economy of the fourteenth and fifteenth centuries. The sites of the chapel and the Tithe Barn are in physical terms distant outliers to the city but their importance is closely linked with the influence and economy of the dominant Cathedral Priory.

ST MARY MAGDALEN, WYKEN

As has been mentioned above, only one church in Coventry remains today which is truly early medieval in character. While it is probably a lookalike in plan for both the destroyed Pinley and Willenhall, it should also be seen as a model for the Norman, Romanesque St Michael's and Holy Trinity. St Mary Magdalene,

Right: 35 St Mary Magdalene, Wyken. Chancel, east wall showing two of the original three tiny Norman windows, blocked up

Opposite page: 36 St Mary Magdalene, Wyken. Nave north wall, painting of St Christopher carrying Christ. The first view on entering the church by its original south door (see colour plate 25)

Wyken is the key to Coventry's Romanesque parish churches (*33*). Never extended and altered in the way that its original contemporaries in the wealthier medieval parishes at Allesley (All Saints), Stoke (St Michael's), Walsgrave (St Mary's) (*34*), the bomb-damaged Foleshill (St Lawrence's), and the entirely rebuilt Stivichall (St James'), it retains much of the simplest of Norman layouts. Its slightly obscure location, on a purely local road, far from a main artery out of the city, conspired with the very sparsely populated parish, to ensure that the twelfth-century features of this church were relatively undamaged by medieval progress.

St Mary Magdalene's two-cell plan of chancel and un-aisled nave is lit by a mixture of small, twelfth-century windows and a few later ones which were widened to admit more light. Some early blocked windows are still visible in the fabric of the chancel (*35*). The simple Romanesque west door which stands at the base of the later medieval west tower, originally opened on the south side of the nave but was moved when the tower was built in the fifteenth century. Opposite the original door position from the fourteenth century lay the magnificent wall-painting of St Christopher carrying the Christ-child across the river (*36*). The subject of this saint was often placed opposite the main door since it was the first image a traveller or pilgrim saw when entering the church, St Christopher being the patron saint of travellers. Thus the visitor was reminded to give thanks for his or her safe arrival.

HOSPITALS

Inevitably for a city, alongside great opulence and mercantile success lay grinding poverty and destitution, made all the more appalling by the absence of any welfare state or health service. Only the church could try to fill this gap, and did. The city possessed numerous ecclesiastical hospitals, none of which has yet been the subject of excavation. Far from being places for sick in the modern sense of hospitals, they were actually almshouses and care homes, while providing shelter for pilgrims and travellers. They comprised St John's Hospital (founded 1165 for 20 local poor), St Margaret's for Lepers at Spon (1181), SS James and Christopher at Spon, Guild Merchants' Hospital (1340 for 13 poor pilgrims), Walsh's Hospital (1370), Bond's Hospital (1506, for 10 poor men of the Holy Trinity Guild), and Ford's Hospital (1526 for six poor men and their wives, later reduced to five) (*colour plate 17*). Many minor hospitals followed the Augustinian Rule so were essentially monastic. SS James and Christopher owed its allegiance to Basingwerk Abbey, a Welsh Cistercian house and latterly as a free chapel of Studley Priory. Thus there was plenty of monastic representation for the poor, the sick and those simply travelling to or through Coventry as pilgrims. Today the buildings survive of the church which lay at the heart of St Johns, the core of Bonds and almost the whole of Ford's, despite a direct hit from a German bomb in 1941. While none have ever yet been the subject of archaeological investigation, they are today listed buildings. It is believed that only the Leper Hospital of St Margaret's (also known as St Leonard's, in the eponymous Chapelfields) would have had its own cemetery attached, since all the others would have existed within the sufferance of the Benedictine house, which controlled parochial burials. Only St Margaret's lay at a distance due to the stigma attached to the sufferers of leprosy and the powerlessness of medieval society to combat the disease's virulence. It survived as a barn into the nineteenth century but its remains now lie under nineteenth-century houses and gardens. SS James and Christopher in Spon Street is a well-photographed ruin; nothing is known of it nor of the Guild Merchant's and Walsh's hospitals, since none has yet been the subject of archaeological scrutiny.

St John the Baptist's hospital, latterly known as The Old Grammar School, was directly responsible to its mother house, St Mary's Benedictine Priory. Its remit to look after 20 poor was probably often overstretched. The complement is known to have comprised both Benedictine monks and nuns, who would have needed separate cloisters and apartments attached. In their gift lay the valuable Grange and Manor Farm of Harnall, known as Prior's Harnall. It stood off Harnall Lane and its land stretched from Cook Street Gate to Swan Lane, taking in most of what is now Hillfields. Originally the Hospital's conventual buildings stretched south across what is now Hales Street into The Burges and north along

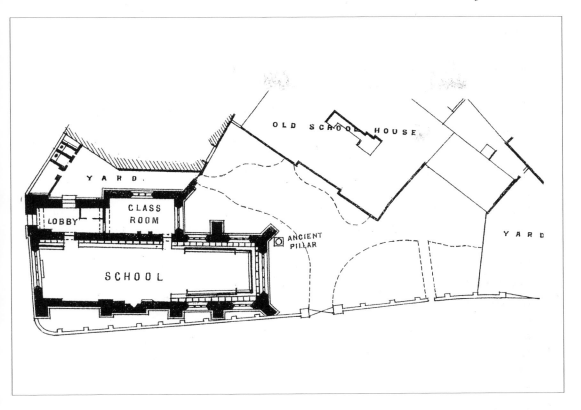

37 Benedictine Hospital of St John the Baptist. Nineteenth-century plan

Silver Street, once part of Cook Street (*37*). Its monastic links ensured that it did not survive the Dissolution as a hospital but it became the second home of John Hales' King Henry VIII school after he left Whitefriars in the 1550s. There the school remained until the 1880s when it moved to its current site on Warwick Road. Today the church survives, dwarfed by the modern skyline.

Today only Bonds Hospital and Ford's Hospital survive as hospitals or, as now construed, Alms Houses. Their secular founders ensured their continuance by not associating them too closely with the monastic orders and they remain startling timber-framed survivals in a modern cityscape of harsher materials.

Monastic attempts to look after the people who were the church's sustenance were everywhere. At first sight the secular city's attempts to provide for the poor and the destitute seem to be lost beneath the weight of business matters and the creation of an atmosphere to breed success. As will be seen, however, there are hints at a civic conscience amidst the prestigious building programmes.

GUILDHALLS

At the head of the guild provisions was St Mary's Hall (*38*). Although a meeting hall, St Mary's was always a religious institution to boot since the trading guild which met there, the Holy Trinity Guild, did so within a religious framework of piety and devotion. It was formed out of the amalgamation of three other, older guilds and was fabulously endowed with lands and property in the city from 1393. The artistry and iconography of the magnificent building which stands today is entirely of religious origin and the setting, hard by the parish church of St Michael, is a purposeful juxtaposition of church and state; anyone of superior social standing sought to become a member, whether Coventrian or a trading partner from beyond the city. Membership included merchants and churchmen from all over the country and even royalty.

St Mary's Hall was by no means unique as a purpose-built meeting hall. The Shearmen and Tailors' guild met in St George's Chapel, built out over Gosford Bridge, while the Whittawers had their Pageant House constructed off Hill Street, in the heart of their industrial leather-working zone. Other groups, such as the Carpenters, preferred the hospitality of and entertainment at Whitefriars. St Nicholas' Hall, Jesus Hall and doubtless others, ensured there was no shortage of imposing suites where commercial clients could be wined and dined and

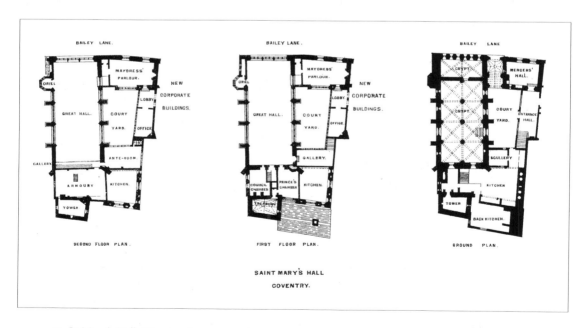

38 St Mary's Hall. Nineteenth-century plan

thanks given for business done, as well as the moveable property and wealth of each guild stored, including the paper records of their land and property deals.

The location of the hall on Bayley Lane is one which recalls the earlier prominence of Coventry castle. This is confirmed by deeds relating to a medieval property on Earl Street (where the Council House of 1916 now stands) which was recorded as backing onto the castle ditch; and of course the 'Bayley' significance of the name Bayley Lane. The owner of the property in the late thirteenth century was the Att Mur family (whose name means 'at the wall'). This would put the southern line of the castle defences at the rear of St Mary's Hall, close to where Caesar's Tower (also known as the Treasury) now stands. Anecdotal evidence attests that this was originally part of the castle (*13*). Since it took a direct hit from a German bomb in World War Two, and is today mostly a reconstruction, it seems unlikely that anything short of excavation beneath it will confirm an appropriate twelfth-century date or not.

Next door to the west lay the buildings which became known as The Castle Bakehouse (now Castle Yard). With the new Drapery lying a short distance on the other side (the first one in the thirteenth century had lain outside the Cathedral forecourt towards West Orchard), St Mary's Hall was built on a site which enjoyed, and continued to assume, an historical significance for power and prestige and which lay at the heart of the city's growing commercial enterprise.

No concerted excavation has ever taken place in St Mary's Hall, since its stunning structure, including the expansive undercroft *is* the archaeology. The depth of the huge vaulted undercroft makes it unlikely (but not impossible) that anything older survives beneath. The later timber additions across the courtyard are more likely to conceal earlier remains beneath. At the time of writing (2004), there are plans to refurbish the great medieval kitchen adjacent to the hall to give public access. This will probably involve some archaeological excavation, both in removing modern accretions and services, and in preparing a new floor. Herein lies the first opportunity to look at the archaeology of St Mary's Hall. It will benefit from some superb historical records which detail every aspect of repair and refurbishment which took place from the fifteenth century, from the purchase of utensils for the voluminous kitchen (*39*), to mending the tile floors and replacing the lead in the windows.

The movement of secular property, much of it to guilds or under their auspices, was a regular occurrence, and was part of the social fabric of medieval Coventry. Gifts of land, a house here, the value of a rent there, could cement social alliances for life. But for those whose sole contact with the land owner was simply to pay the rent at a pre-arranged festival, a life of commerce was a dream most often not realised. Such people, though not strictly poor in a city of growing opportunity, were nevertheless at the mercy of events.

39 St Mary's Hall: the medieval kitchen *c.*1800. Contemporary print published in 1870, from an engraving of an original drawing in the Aylesford Collection. *Birmingham City Archives*

WELFARE

It was perhaps to combat a stream of social disasters that at least two streets were laid out from 1388. One lay in each half of the city. One was monastic, the other secular. The visitations of the Black Death in 1349 and again in 1364, with the enigmatic Great Plague of Coventry in 1386 meant that the city was robbed of large numbers of both its prominent citizenry and of landless poor, probably in equal measure. The records of the Benedictine Priory suggest that in the villages which are today's suburbs, the death rate in 1349 alone ran at over 50 per cent. The Priory itself, with its monks in close confines and prey to infection, suffered horribly and word had to be sent to France for new recruits, so depleted were their ranks, including novices. Although there is evidence that rents were replenished relatively quickly, there was a severe manpower shortage on the land. Many, unable to work their holdings at a profit, moved to the city in a wave of population movements seen right across the country. As if to make matters worse in Coventry, the new town wall and ditch were causing hardship for many as their course scythed across houses and gardens all around the town.

It is in exactly this period that the Benedictine Priory built St Mary's Street (later New Street), aligned between Mill Lane (Cox Street) and St Michael's Church. It is today the site of the core of Coventry University. Simultaneously came the efforts of a group of prominent citizens, including the industrious Botoners, who began developing Dead Lane (later St John's Street) four and five houses at a time, connecting the southern ends of Much and Little Park Streets. So quickly were these whole streets put up (1388-1411) that it is tempting to see them as a joint civic and ecclesiastical attempt to address the social ill of homelessness caused by difficult planning issues and a sudden press for space amongst existing housing. From photographs of long-lived examples which survived until the 1950s it is clear that many were far from high-quality and documents show that most had little more than a yard attached, carved out of existing plots. Part of the north side of St Mary's Street even backed directly onto a stone quarry; the rest probably spoilt the view for the Bishop's banqueting house in the Palace grounds! However, they represent the only new large-scale intramural domestic developments until the construction of New Buildings (the street between Butcher Row and Priory Mill) to house refugees in the 1640s.

ADMINISTRATION

Medieval Coventry was in every way a religious city. The dominance of the Benedictine Priory was overwhelming and the very obvious division into only two parishes, each with its own parish church, stands in stark contrast to other, less rich walled towns in which urban parish churches proliferated. To many historians this has been largely the result of the Earl/Prior division, with origins in secular administration. However, it has as much to do with the date of Coventry's growth. Those towns in which the numbers of urban parishes proliferate expanded predominantly in the period 1000-1200. London heads the list with over 100 parishes, then Norwich with about 60, York, 40, Lincoln 35, Canterbury 22. Even Northampton had seven with a further four having semi-parochial rights. However all of them were large, walled towns by 1200. By contrast the diminutive Coventry was then only just emerging from a village-like existence, clustered around the Benedictine Cathedral and strung out along the main east—west road of Earl Street, High Street and Smithford Street. Coventry's dramatic rise was only just beginning in 1200.

Therefore a Coventry on the verge of greatness inherited an Anglo-Norman parochial system which had fossilised to serve Coventry the village, not Coventry the boom-town. When growth might have allowed new parishes to be created, there was simply no need since the whole area was Priory controlled one way or another, and the Priory would, quite sensibly, get no benefit from diluting the value of the tithe to support more church buildings and more parishes. From the thirteenth century it would be bad enough having to compete with Friars for burial fees, without denuding their own income unnecessarily! It is telling that in some towns in which parishes proliferated early on, the widespread urban economic downturn of the fifteenth century quickly began to drain some very ancient urban parishes of resources as numbers of people tithing dropped dramatically and churches, long at the centre of tiny parishes, began to be lost, the weak being subsumed in stronger neighbours. Norwich, for example, lost some 30 parishes. With its restricted two-parish set-up, Coventry had actually inherited a very strong parochial foundation against such economic attrition. It even stood it in good stead when the Priory was dissolved since the undiluted tithing base was intact for the post-Reformation church. The old collegiate church of St John the Baptist was the exception. Languishing through the sixteenth and seventeenth centuries, it did not gain parochial rights until the eighteenth century, and it was not until the nineteenth that new parishes could safely be created, to meet the challenge of a massive growth in population.

This particular issue is unlikely to be much helped by further archaeological fieldwork in Coventry, other than to shed light on the physical nature of the administrative boundaries and discern comparative levels and rates of development on either side, encouraged or held back by degrees of lordly influence. Discovery of the Palace, the early nature of the city's great churches, those two early parish churches, is likely to be hampered by the sheer size and destructive mass of their successors; rather those sites of Pinley and Willenhall, Chapelfields and Wyken are just as well placed to illuminate the architecture of the Norman town and the burial environments of ordinary folk before monastic dominance spread over all aspects of the city's life from the thirteenth century. The sites of the two street developments, St Mary's/New Street and Dead Lane/St John's Street are sadly denuded by post-war development. Parts alone may survive to illuminate their history further and their unusual place in the city's development as possible safety nets to manage the ills brought about by plague, population movements and insensitive construction programmes.

9

Death and burial

'I trowe I shal nat lyven tyl tomorowe. For which I wolde alweys, on aventure, to the devysen of my sepulture the forme.' Geoffrey Chaucer: *Canterbury Tales*; *Troilus and Criseyde*

The medieval church existed for the cure of souls. There was no single way of approaching this, and as long as no new group strayed into the area of heresy (as defined by the papacy at any one time), a plethora of choices greeted the worshipper who kept a weather eye on their eventual passage into the next world. While a modern citizen may choose in a post-modern world, a course which embraces one of any number of faiths, the medieval citizen was spoilt for choice in a different way. In Coventry, he or she would be expected to become Christian, and could, if they wished, espouse Benedictine ways (St Mary's), Cistercian (Combe and Stoneleigh), Franciscan (Greyfriars), Carmelite (Whitefriars) or Carthusian (Charterhouse). Each had their own particular way of doing things, since each order had sprung up partly as a reaction to what it saw as the dissolute ways of those who had gone before. Many prominent Coventry citizens chose to be buried in the churches of these monastic orders. Their particular brands of religious piety were felt to be of singular benefit in a bid to speed their course to heaven through the trials of purgatory.

CEMETERIES

Over the years some 80 medieval skeletons have been excavated in controlled conditions on the sites of the city's monasteries, together with disarticulated remains of a similar number. It is almost certain that this represents only a small proportion of those actually still in the ground, and they are known to have been drawn mainly from a restricted group, monastic benefactors. It is necessary to be selective over which cemeteries are chosen for detailed research purposes since the shorter the space of time represented by a group of burials, the better the results, simply because it forms a distinct population group. Those cemeteries which began in use in the twelfth century and are still in use (most of the parish churches), contain human remains which are ultimately very jumbled, often five or six bodies deep and always so intercut that less than 25 per cent are incomplete skeletons. Most are bereft of legs, arms, heads or even wholly represented by one of these elements alone. The other bones, disturbed by subsequent burials, are most often simply thrown back into the fill of subsequent graves, sometimes afforded a degree of reverence, more often not. This is the situation not only in all long-lived cemeteries, but also in intensively used ones where space is limited relative to population size. This can be seen in the 1999-2000 excavations of the post-medieval cemetery which was an overspill graveyard for Holy Trinity on Priory Row. Used in the relatively short period 1776-1851, it contained over 2,500 skeletons (*colour plate 18*), of which perhaps only two out of ten were complete.

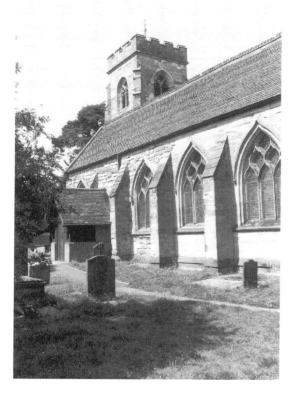

40 St Michael's Church, Stoke

1 *Right:* The castle bakehouse ovens behind 22 Bayley Lane, 1990

2 *Below:* St Mary's Cathedral Priory: north-east undercrofts, 2001. *Barry Lewis*

3 Above: St Mary's Cathedral: the view east along the excavated nave, 2000. Note the human scale of this gigantic building of which bay two can be seen here in the centre; six bays were excavated

4 Left: St Mary's Cathedral: the floors and stair of the main west end entrance, 2000

5 St Mary's Cathedral Priory: fourteenth-century painted and gilded stonework from the Chapterhouse, depicting a scene from the Bible (Revelation 4), 2001. *Barry Lewis*

6 Coombe Abbey: the stone north range (sub-dorter) amidst later brick foundations, 1993

7 *Left:* The fourteenth century spire of the Greyfriars c.2000

8 *Below:* Whitefriars: the east range from the cloister, 1990

9 Whitefriars: the undershot cloister looking south, 1987

10 Whitefriars: the first-floor dormitory looking north, 1991

11 St Anne's Charterhouse: excavations with the refectory block behind, 1986

12 St Anne's Charterhouse: the refectory wall painting of 1417, 1990

13 *Left:* St Anne's Charterhouse: sixteenth-century chapel construction levels, 1986

14 *Below:* St Michael's Church: the conserved ruins of 1940 looking east *c.*1995

15 *Right:* Holy Trinity Church: undergoing spire conservation, 1992–2000

16 *Below:* St John the Baptist church (*c.*1350) from the north-west 2001. *Bob Fielding*

17 Fords Hospital (1526): courtyard c.1990

18 Holy Trinity overspill cemetery(1776-1851), c.2500 bodies lay on the Dissolution rubble of St Mary's Cathedral, 1999. Its very creation indicates the overflowing nature of the existing provision of graves

19 A complete early fourteenth-century jug of local Cannon Park-type from Derby Lane, 1982

20 St Mary's Cathedral Priory: the refectory floor collapsed into the vaulted cellar beneath, 2000

21 Cheylesmore Manor: the gatehouse, now the city's Register Office, 1990

22 Cheylesmore Manor fourteenth-century east range, 1992. Note the stair bases to the first-floor apartments

23 *Above:* Cheylesmore Manor: buried carcasses
– conspicuous consumption or oversupply? 1992

24 *Right:* Priory Mill, 2001: the fifteenth-century
mill race within the many mill buldings. *Barry
Lewis*

25 *Above:* The fourteenth-century windmill depicted in the church of St Mary Magdalene, Wyken, 2003

26 *Below:* A mortar-mixer's barrel next to the town wall at Cheylesmore Manor; still malleable lime putty removed, 1992

27 *Left:* The town wall at The Cheylesmore, looking east towards Friars Road, 1991

28 *Below:* The town wall and the defensive tower of *c.*1390 at The Cheylesmore, Friars Road behind, 1991.

29 The town wall at The Cheylesmore showing a mason's butt-joint break for winter, c.1390, 1991

30 Construction of the Chapel of Industry, Coventry Cathedral c.1960. *W.F.Soden*

Research suggests that the average parish churchyard begun in the early medieval period contains upwards of 10,000 graves. This idea can be said to apply to Allesley (All Saints), Binley (St Bartholomew), Coventry (Holy Trinity, St John and St Michael), Foleshill (St Lawrence), Stivichall (St James), Stoke (St Michael) (*40*), Walsgrave (St Mary) and Wyken (St Mary Magdalen). In fact, owing to the growth of Coventry in the post-medieval and modern periods and the spread of its suburbs into these former rural parishes, the estimate of 10,000 burials in some of the above churchyards is probably very conservative.

Thus when dealing with human remains of past populations, it is incumbent upon the archaeologist to be fully aware of the limitations of the evidence before work begins. Those groups with the shortest date range form the best research material since such cemeteries are most complete and provide a snapshot of a population. Thus in Coventry the best are the monasteries and those other churches which were (occasionally) begun and were certainly lost at a known point in the relatively distant past.

In Coventry, therefore, the sites with the greatest potential are St Mary's Cathedral and Priory (intramural burials), St Anne's Charterhouse, the Franciscan and Carmelite Friaries (Greyfriars and Whitefriars); all of the locations of their cemeteries are known. In addition there are those small chapels long since destroyed, as at Fletchamstead Templar manor, Gosford Green (St Margaret), Pinley (dedication not known), Spon (St James and St Christopher), Willenhall (St James) and medieval hospitals at Chapelfields (St Margaret) and Hales Street (St John). One outstanding exemplar would be the former parish church of St Nicholas, north of the Coventry canal basin which went out of use in the sixteenth century but may have been in use as early as the tenth. There may be other non-parochial chapels, their existence strongly suspected from documents but otherwise unproven, such as at Caludon, Coundon and Keresley.

CHARNEL

A singularly rare and startling burial assemblage in Coventry lies below the Marler Chapel, a subdivision within Holy Trinity Church. This space was a vaulted undercroft used as a charnel house, into which were placed the thousands of large bones which were disturbed by grave digging; this normally meant those bones most visible to the grave digger. In reality this usually amounted to the skulls and the long bones, such as the thigh and upper arm; sometimes the lower limb bones were also kept. Created in the 1520s, possibly to house the hundreds of burials disturbed in its own chapel's digging, the Marler charnel house was used until 1698 when it was totally full and could no longer be used sensibly, whereupon it was blocked up. It remains today, a tremendous resource for the future for the study of Coventry's medieval and early post-medieval population. It is also one of only a handful of intact charnel houses in Britain. Another is said to have exist close to St Michael's, the so-called 'chapel-on-the-hill' but its exact whereabouts and whether its contents are intact are unknown. It probably lies north of St Michael's and may have acted as a mortuary chapel for the three city-centre churches which shared the same enormous graveyard. Many great churches maintained charnel houses for centuries but firstly the Reformation drastically reduced the numbers of sites observing the practice and subsequently the sense of the macabre they engendered has, particularly in Protestant northern Europe, put modern generations off the practice. A preference for cremation, together with the closure of many churchyards in ecclesiastical law, have combined to ease the pressure on England's more ancient cemeteries. There has never been any Biblical basis for reverence to human remains (since the Christian message is aimed solely at the living) and the whole approach adopted by the medieval church was a mixture of the application of whatever culture already existed locally, combined with the creation of wholly new rituals which had no basis in scripture except with the preparation of the body for burial in which attempts were made to mimic the washing and anointing of Christ's own body in a first-century Jewish rite. The copying of the rites of Christ's death had many forms. A temporary sepulchre was commonly built against the north side of most churches each year for the Easter period and priests or anchorites would often live in them to mimic Christ in the tomb between Good Friday and Easter Sunday.

The few English charnel houses which remain today (such as Holy Trinity or that at Rothwell, Northants) are little seen by the general public and their former effects as a *memento mori* are largely lost. When viewed, their aspect is startling.

CLAIMING THE DEAD

Of the medieval cemeteries or groups of probable medieval burials known to lie in Coventry, the following inhumations have been excavated: Whitefriars (20), St Mary's Cathedral and Priory (17 – but 30 otherwise located), Charterhouse (48) and St John the Baptist (30). A further 79 individuals have been represented by disarticulated bone. Since these totals span the period 870-1539, they clearly represent only the tiniest proportion of those actually buried. Medieval burial archaeology, even within known monastic or other churchyards, represents one of the least understood aspects of the city's medieval past. Besides those in churchyards as we know them, it is recorded in the City Annals that when the city fell victim to the Black Death in 1349 the churchyards were so full of fresh burials that fields outside the town had to be purchased in which to continue burials. Likewise during the reign of John (1199-1216) the King quarrelled with Rome leading to his excommunication and to 'the interdict', during which no one, even Bishops, was allowed to be buried in consecrated ground. It will be an almighty shock to the public and an archaeological find of immense importance, when any such burial field is found, whether from 1208-14 or 1349. The best candidate is probably towards Hillfields since here lay the nearest Benedictine Priory lands, and the Priory controlled all non-monastic burial in the city. An entry in the Priory Cartulary (1410) hints at St John's Hospital controlling Harnall burials since it firmly restates that the Prior is the founder and due to 'his long suffering should be compensated and an agreement made for burial rites lest they [the hospital] should claim by prescription and continuous possession'. It seems that they may have assumed responsibilities for burials for and in Harnall in the years preceding.

St Mary's also controlled burials at its dependent churches in Warwickshire, a responsibility it chose to demonstrate and enforce from time to time. In the thirteenth century it was enacted that the dead of Shilton parish should be buried at the mother house (St Michael's) in Coventry (since the curate was in the pay of the Prior), requiring a funeral procession which needed to travel 6 miles through Henley Green, Wyken and Stoke! St Mary's also felt the need in 1410 to reiterate that the Prior was the Rector at Stivichall and his chaplain there was to bury the dead at Coventry; another sinuous funeral route, trailing miles through the fields of Astill and Earlsdon.

In addition to the set-piece excavations, a few isolated medieval burials have been found over the years which drew contemporary comment, including a handful from the Greyfriars, disturbed in the 1930s when the Methodist Central Hall was built at the lower end of Warwick Lane, behind Hertford Street, and some in the late nineteenth century at St Lawrence's Church, Foleshill. Apart from these most everyday disturbances in churchyards in use draw no comment since their disturbance takes place in wholly ordinary circumstances in the pursuance of the continuing life of the church. In Coventry archaeological excavations on Priory Row in 1999-2001 accounted for over 2,500 eighteenth- and nineteenth-century skeletons from Holy Trinity (spectacular groups in themselves) (*colour plate 18*) but by comparison the current total of archaeologically excavated medieval bodies from Coventry is relatively small (*c.*190). However, these few are disproportionately interesting since they reflect certain, known parts of medieval society and exhibit remarkable traits in pathology and the graves themselves are records of contemporary views of the dead person's social standing and their family's view of the pre-Reformation afterlife.

BURIAL CHOICES

In medieval life a person was expected to grant a tenth of their produce or their wealth to their mother church, the practice of tithing. As a preparation for death, however, the dying person was expected to have a contrite heart; a symbol of their repentance was the purchase of papal indulgences and eventually, as enshrined in their last will and testament, the payment of a priest or monk to pray for their soul (and often other members of their families), in order to shorten the time they would spend in purgatory, being punished for their sins before progressing on to heaven. The more practical bequests were often those made *'cum corpore meo sepeliendo'* (with my body for burial).

Thus, in 1479, Alice Braytoft, wife of a former mayor of Coventry, bequeathed to St Anne's Charterhouse 3s 4d for an obituary mass to be said (one of many hundreds known scattered across all the churches), while in 1520 Sir Edward Belknappe of Weston under Wetherley left his body for burial there if he happened to die in Warwickshire. The most archaeologically interesting at the Charterhouse is the will in 1508 of Nicholas Fitzherbert who left 13s 4d (one mark) with his body for burial next to his parents, with a further £3 6s 8d for a gravestone to be laid over all three of them. This may have been a stone tomb, part of which was discovered in the excavation of the church in 1986 (*41*).

41 Fifteenth-century sandstone tomb chest excavated at Charterhouse, 1986. Possibly from the Fitzherbert tomb; *c.*2m long. *Harriet Anne Jacklin*

There are many more instances of such bequests, some great, some more modest. The medieval list of 158 named benefactors buried in the Franciscan church (Greyfriars) is a unique record in English monastic annals and will one day be invaluable when the nave of this former Friary is excavated (as it probably will be, ahead of redevelopment). Some graves were probably destroyed by the construction of Christchurch in the 1820s (itself lost in the Blitz of April 1941) or in the construction of the contemporary Union Street or its post-Second World War successor, New Union Street. Nevertheless a majority will have survived, since medieval graves in churches tend to have been more deeply buried than their extramural counterparts in the cemeteries in order to allow for the continued use of the floor above.

Money which would buy a plot in a monastery church was simply not available to most ordinary people. Thus it was the wider monastic cemetery or more often the local parish church, such as Holy Trinity and St Michael's (or the surrounding village churches in today's suburbs) which provided the simple funeral necessary for most. With such a hierarchical society, paupers, naturally, got the most basic service. The parish churches of St Michael's and Holy Trinity shared a common graveyard with their mother-church, St Mary's cathedral, who claimed all the burial fees. However, it was by no means always a simple matter to get the dead buried. When the King's Commissioner, Dr John London, wrote to the Chancellor Sir Thomas Cromwell during his dissolution of the Greyfriars in October 1538, he was vitriolic about the nearby Benedictines. He alleged that they followed a heinous practice of allowing the bodies of plague victims to be piled up in the south porch of the Cathedral, up to 20 at a time. They apparently agreed to bury them – and even then seemingly unhurried – only when the requisite burial fee was paid by the family, comprising 1s at the least for a poor person (a year's rent of a cottage). If not just propaganda therefore, the cemetery may be expected to contain quite a number of multiple burials.

Even when not hard-pressed by plagues, the choice of burial method, beyond the actual location, might also be decided by cost. While almost everyone could be provided for cheaply with a winding sheet, simply wrapping the body with a knot at both ends, there were other options available. A small, but significant proportion of excavated burials took place with the body wrapped in a linen shroud, with the ends tucked in and secured with a single copper alloy pin. The pin remains the only indication in the ground of this mode of burial and is often found close to one of the shoulders or upper arm. Circumstantial evidence for a shroud alone is found in the absence of suggestions of anything else since material such as the traditional cloth rarely survives in the ground.

For a little more outlay a coffin could be used, and contemporary illustrations suggest this might even be combined with a shroud. During the thirteenth century there was a preference for massive, monolithic stone coffins. One found in 1987 in St Mary's Cathedral chancel under 10 Priory Row was of non-local limestone and must have been expensive to bring in since it could literally weigh a ton. Similar ones were found at nearby Coombe Abbey. Hollowed out of a single block, with a similar lid, the lozenge-shaped stone box was carved to wrap around the head and shoulders of the body, cradling the head which also rested on a slight shelf. A central hole at the midpoint allowed the body fluids to escape during decomposition. Clearly such a massive coffin-type could not have been part of a funeral procession but was made ready to receive the body at the grave-side committal. It was perhaps more symbolic of a rock-cut tomb, such as Christ had occupied. Less contrived was just such a rock-cut grave, cut to the exact shape of such a stone coffin, found in the nave of the same St Mary's Cathedral in 2000. This deep grave just in front of the monastic screen bore the chisel-marks around

42 Rock-cut thirteenth-century tomb burial in front of the monastic screen in the nave of St Mary's Cathedral. He may have been a pilgrim who died far from home

the head where the mummiform shape had been created in the natural sandstone bedrock (*42*). Unusually, the dead man was buried in his woollen clothes, a patch of which survived beneath the copper alloy buckle of a waist belt. He also still wore the vestiges of calf-length leather boots, a common attribute of pilgrim burials, such as one found in perfect condition at Sandwell Priory in the 1980s where the incumbent also carried, and was buried with, a 6ft long staff.

A variation existed throughout the medieval period in the provision of stone-built tombs, which in certain cases might support tomb chests or monumental effigies. The grave was simply dug wider than necessary and lined with stone which was mortared into position. Such tombs have been excavated at the Whitefriars chancel (where they can still be seen), in the chapter house and south aisle of St Mary's Cathedral (*43*) (where the tomb interior was also plastered and limewashed) and below the rood loft at St Anne's Charterhouse (probably the origin of the tomb chest and the grave which may have belonged to the Fitzherberts).

43 Prestigious tomb burial in the Copstone Chantry, St Mary's Cathedral

44 The Purbeck marble tomb of Benedictine Sub-Prior John Aylmer. A priest from 1279 and a monk in 1295, he became sub-prior sometime after 1301 and died *c*.1310-30

Most recently, and perhaps most spectacular, was the grave of a sub-prior of St Mary's Priory, whose tomb lay at the east end of the Priory chapter house (*44*). It was discovered a metre below the ground adjacent to the former John F. Kennedy House in 2003 during foundation work nearing the end of the Phoenix initiative. There the stone-built tomb was capped with an enormous slab of polished blue Purbeck (Dorset) marble fashioned in the marble workshops of London. Within it were cut a central crucifix and calvary and a border bearing a legend in medieval French:

> As you pass this place pray for the Sub-prior who lies here. His name was Dom John Aylmer; you shall have 100 days indulgence.

John Aylmer, priest, appeared as a witness of a document relating to Harnall (Hillfields) in the 1280s when he is also known from another contemporary document. He had certainly become a monk by 1295 and probably became sub-prior after 1301; the exact date of his death remains unknown, it was probably *c*.1310-30. The tomb was re-covered and now lies, undisturbed following recording, just south of Youell House, west of Hill Top.

Doubtless other such tombs and coffins exist in Coventry, particularly at the Greyfriars, since there the list of benefactor burials includes many of considerable social standing. There is architectural evidence for monumental effigies at both St Mary's Cathedral in which a sculpted lion was found in 2000 (a traditional footrest to a reclining figure), and at St Anne's Charterhouse where the stone mailed foot of just such a figure was excavated in 1987.

The graves of the wealthy were often very carefully sited. It was normal practice for wealthy individuals or families to found chantry chapels within the body of a church in which the obituary masses which were the proviso of the bequest would be said. Usually having a specific dedication, the progenitor-cum-founder's grave or tomb and those of his subsequent family would be grouped before the altar.

It is rare to be able to put a designation to an excavated chantry or other chapel, and thus begin to identify those who were buried within. While there appear to be two such nave chantries and two in a side chapel excavated at Charterhouse, none are identifiable as belonging to a particular family. At St Mary's Cathedral there were 10 chantries, their names known. Of these, two were recognised in the excavations of 1999-2000 but only one of them is identifiable to name, that of Copstone's Chantry, the location of which was described by the county historian Sir William Dugdale, writing in the seventeenth century. He stated that Copstone's Chantry was *Capella sancti Clementis iuxta porticum ecclesiae Cathedralis Coventriae* (the chapel of St Clement next to the porch of Coventry Cathedral). This chapel was found immediately west of the south porch in excavation. It is possible that Dugdale actually saw and remembered this structure still standing since the roof of the south aisle here remained standing into the seventeenth century, much longer than the rest of the nave and aisles, and was home to a pack of feral dogs. Wide, deep holes had been dug through the tiled floor and the benefactors' bodies dug up. Rubbish accompanied those few bones which were tossed back in.

The chantry was founded in 1291 by William de Copstone, presumably for himself, his family and descendants. Within the centre of the bay disturbed from the central grave was a copper-alloy-handled knife and patches of fine chain mail, an expensive delicate type which was used to protect the face. There is thus the possibility that someone here was buried in at least some armour. To this may be added a startling injury observed on a skull disturbed from the central grave (45). The owner of the disarticulated skull had received not one but two blows (one from the front and one behind) from an axe or sword which had split the side of the head, separating a considerable portion of bone and cracking the skull towards front and back. Amazingly, with no apparent infection, the victim survived both the blows and any rudimentary medical attention and considerable

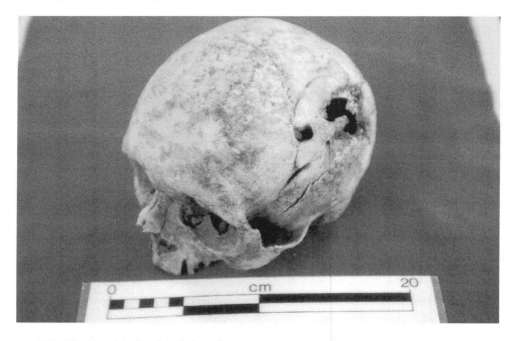

45 Old soldier? Disarticulated skull from the Copstone Chantry (founded 1299), St Mary's Cathedral. The individual survived two massive bone-splitting blows to the scalp, but was probably permanently disabled

healing was observed, such that he may have lived many years after the injury. He may however, have been beset by a form of epilepsy as a result. It is tempting to view these disturbed finds as evidence for the corrodian Roger de Cestria, King's Serjeant at Arms, who was sent to the Priory in 1301 by Edward I, having been maimed in battle and who was not fit for further service.

Since the Copstone Chantry and its functions are known to have been transferred to St Michael's church at the Dissolution, it may be that the very intensive and focused disturbance of the graves in this chantry within St Mary's represents the deliberate transference of the founder's remains to the new chantry site, just ahead of St Mary's closure and demolition. In this the apparent desecration may not actually have been one by tomb robbers but instead was a deliberate act to provide continuity across the divide of the Dissolution, with continued reverence of the medieval dead in an atmosphere of reformation. While no conclusive evidence has yet been found that this is the case, there are documented examples of this practice elsewhere across the country.

For ordinary people, there was simply not the choice of buying a stone coffin or having a tomb built, both of which are rare enough to be considered luxuries afforded only to the wealthy. The simple winding sheet, however, was surpassed by a basic wooden coffin, for which the only evidence to survive is the rusted lumps of iron oxide which once formed nails. The pressured movements of the soils and clays and the outward heave with which many bodies bloat and explode after burial often distort the remains of the wooden coffin, at the mercy of the city's acidic clays, apart from burials in waterlogged conditions. At Charterhouse in 1986 a rare coffin was reconstructed on paper from a perfect three-dimensional nail plot, which indicated a lozenge-shaped box tapering from head to foot. There was no widening at the shoulder and top and bottom leaves were simply nailed onto the side- and end-assemblies.

Occasionally the presence of a few nails may indicate the strengthening of a coffin which may have otherwise been pegged with dowels or perhaps even simply dovetailed. In the burial of Carthusian monks it was and remains normal practice to use only a plank on which to lower the body and there is no reason why the presence of a single nail alone should not imply that such a plank might have been used, and that it was actually any old reused building timber, nails and all. Usually the only way to be sure of the presence of a coffin is either the occurrence of numerous (perhaps a dozen or more) nails and the recovery of the coffin shape within the cut of the grave. Some excavators have tried to use the posture of the body, particularly the feet, as a guide to the presence of a coffin but in Coventry, more often than not, the destructively heavy clay which distorts the coffin and contents, makes this a wholly unreliable method of conjecture.

ANOMALOUS BURIALS

Three further burials at the Charterhouse are worthy of comment. One, at the east end of the church, was clearly a person of some importance, since the grave lay in front of the High Altar. This may have been William la Zouche, the nominal founder. This is made more likely by the fact that this was not a primary burial, but a reburial. Although a full-length grave was dug, the bones lay jumbled within a small box- or casket-shaped cut at the east end of the grave. In addition, the majority of the hand and foot bones were missing, a sure sign that the body has been moved from elsewhere. William Lord Zouche of Harringworth (Northamptonshire) had died in 1382, before his foundation at the Charterhouse could gain a financial foothold. The King, Richard II, in what was at the time probably a highly politicised act, stepped in and carried through the foundation, professing himself and his Queen, Anne of Bohemia, to be the founders. They laid the foundation stone of the church in 1385. The part of the church in which the particular body was found was not built, however, until probably *c.*1475. Thus the body which was re-interred was entirely de-fleshed, and the hundreds of tiny hand and foot bones were simply not retrieved in the original act of exhumation. It is not known where the earlier burial site lies. While there are other potential candidates for this reburial, Zouche remains the most likely.

Reburial of a body was sometimes a necessity since the person died far from his intended sepulchre. Such seems to have happened to John de Toneworth/Tamworth who is buried in the Greyfriars church but who was recorded as having died in Abergavenny. Since the journey was probably a week long, he may have been buried initially in Wales and only moved when nature had defleshed his bones. It is possible that he was subjected to the practice of *mos teutonicus* (the German custom), wherein the flesh was boiled off the bones and the two buried separately, the fatty products where the practice occurred, the bones sent home or to the intended place of burial of the deceased. It was a grisly business and the Papacy tried to outlaw it, not altogether successfully. That bodies were butchered on their owners' wishes seems clear; witness the two deceased Franciscan benefactors, de Bray and de Mandeville, whose hearts were cut out and buried in the church of the Greyfriars at the end of the thirteenth century.

Below the church tower of the Charterhouse lay another apparently re-interred body, probably dating from after 1450. This, however, had more sinister undertones. Here all of the body was present but had been dismembered. Thus, the torso, head, legs and arms lay separate but stacked on top of each other. It is entirely plausible that this individual had been quartered in the well-known grisly capital punishment of hanging, drawing and quartering. It was probably not a simple site-to-site re-interment since all the body was present. More such burials are likely to have been carried out at the Franciscan house, Greyfriars, since the Coventry house of that order was well-known for receiving execution victims. A few are documented, including notorious rebels and miscreants.

In the nave of the Charterhouse church lay two instances of reverence to the bones of an earlier burial. In one, the existing bones had been boxed up in a casket which was replaced next to the new coffin. In the other, more graphically, the disturbed skull of one and the arm bones of another were replaced, skull-and-crossbones fashion, on the legs of the new burial. This grave dates between *c*.1475 and 1539 and may be one of the earliest examples of this common *memento mori* motif seen later on innumerable seventeenth-century gravestones and immortalised in the common psyche as the Jolly Roger flag design of naval legend.

While so many terminal diseases and illnesses affect only the soft tissue of a body, leaving archaeologists little or no clue as to the cause of death, occasionally some do emerge which have not only had an effect on the bone but which may also have contributed to the death of the individual or at least seriously affected their abilities to lead a fully physical life. Amongst the medieval skeletons at Coventry one in particular highlights the dangers of a lack of hygiene in past societies. At the Charterhouse one man had been buried with his right leg slightly raised, the knee bent. Within the lower end of the femur was a gaping hole, probably the site of a tuberculosis infection. This was probably the result of infected milk in the centuries before pasteurisation. While it may not have been the cause of his death, his lifestyle would have been seriously affected from the outset by severe and chronic pain. He would have been unable to walk far without crutches.

In the same assemblage was evidence of rickets, osteoarthritis, work-related stress, degenerative spinal problems and a range of fractures, together with appalling tooth decay. The stature of the mature individuals was no different to today, there being an adult range amongst the 48 articulated Charterhouse burials of 1.63m (5ft 2in) to 1.91m 6ft 3in. Likewise the life-expectancy of individuals was good, and any who survived the deadly childhood diseases, today taken for granted as mild, could expect to live to respectable old age. The traditional idea of life being nasty, brutish and short is steadily being shown to be a misconception for the majority with better skeletal ageing techniques and, plague and war aside, it is possible that it was a normal expectation for better-nourished adults to attain three-score-years-and-ten. Without a degree of longevity, it becomes increasingly difficult for any society to pass on skills and training and heredity becomes a nightmare of orphaned children needing executors and wards to administer estates during their minority. While these circumstances did arise, and can be glimpsed in the State Papers (*Inquisitions Post Mortem*), they were not the normal state of affairs.

Despite there being relatively few burials to work from so far, there is a wealth of evidence amongst the excavated examples, for pathologies, diet and burial rites observed, backed up by good documentation. A great deal more waits to be addressed, principally at the notable sites of the Priory church, Greyfriars church and around the churches of St Michael's and Holy Trinity. All of the others may yet make unanticipated contributions, including the parish churches and the small medieval chapelries such as at Pinley or the leper house of St Margaret, Chapelfields. The burial fields of the Black Death and the unconsecrated plots used for the interdict of King John complete a whole variety of sites whose potential is yet to be fully realised.

10

Trade and industry

'The towne rose by makynge of clothe and cappes, that now decayinge the glory of the city decayethe.' John Leland c.1543

THE WOOL TRADE

Without doubt the single largest trade on which medieval Coventry grew and prospered was that of wool and consequently woven woollen cloth. In particular the city became internationally known for its blue cloth, Coventry Blue, coloured with a dye which had a reputation for being fast, combined with a wool quality which was rarely bettered. In the fourteenth century only fleeces from Yorkshire could command higher prices than those from Warwickshire. Before 1350 most Warwickshire wool, and by inference all wool sold at Coventry, was bought up by Italian merchants for manufacture into cloth in Italy. The producers were predominantly the monasteries; at Coombe Abbey excavations uncovered a monastic drain which was still partly clogged with a material analysed as limescale, soap-based carbonates and lanolin, all from constant washing of fleeces. At some point the skills of broadcloth manufacture were acquired in Coventry and less local wool was exported as was the case nationwide, although it is clear from records that considerable quantities of unwoven wool still left the city for Bristol and Southampton and the sea routes to Italy. By the end of the fourteenth century Coventry's cloth had gained its reputation for excellence. However the economic conditions for Coventry were not looking good; top quality wool in the fifteenth century was no longer Warwickshire produce, but that of the Cotswolds. The quality of Coventry's cloth and its dye had to make up for what the raw material lacked. For some time it did just that and much more. At the start of the fifteenth century cloth was the largest single export of English merchants to any destination in Europe. Ships carrying wine from Bordeaux to Bristol and Southampton took back cloth and corn; homeward voyages carrying Spanish iron from Bayonne in south-west France returned with cloth; ships carrying codfish from Norway and later Iceland returned laden with cloth. To Italy went English cloth. All Europe wanted English cloth. Until about 1310 the English Royal Wardrobe bought mainly foreign cloths; by the late 1320s its cloth purchases were English, bought mainly at the great fairs of London and Coventry. Yet the fifteenth century was a turbulent period and all established trade routes, however long they had been in existence, and however well run they were, remained at the mercy of international politics.

There was an in-built fragility to the renowned export of Coventry Blue, in that it was dependent upon two vital imports for its dyeing process, woad from Tuscany, Piedmont and Toulouse together with alum from Asia Minor. This dependency is amply demonstrated in the records of Southampton, where Coventry imported vast quantities of Genoese woad and its mordant, alum. During the 1440s Coventry imported 200-300 balets of woad each year; in the 1460s this had risen to 600-700 (a balet = half a bale, weighing *c*.113kg/*c*.250lb each). The brokage books for Southampton record that in 1443-4 there were 59 separate road cargoes which headed for Coventry, marked by the large quantities which were sent with regular carriers in rumbling, slow-moving convoys of three, four or more carts, each drawn by a team of up to eight oxen or draught horses. The Genoese supplied most of the woad, a near-monopoly made even stronger when in the 1450s war with France made the French source, Toulouse, unreliable, along with Gascon wine. Ironically, even then most of the Toulouse woad was probably carried on Genoese vessels since English ships found increasing difficulty using the hostile ports of Bordeaux and La Rochelle. The Genoese also enjoyed a complete monopoly on the trade in alum until 1455, since they controlled the then sole known source, the alum mines of Foglia, in Asia Minor. When Genoa lost these mines to the Turks in 1455, the supply all but dwindled away. Existing Italian stocks kept going through the remainder of that decade but at a much reduced level; some competing Florentine galleys even managed to deal successfully with the Turks and they recovered some of the trade. The Genoese monopoly was broken but so was the trade. So desperate were the English dyers that Florentine merchants paid in alum for their English exports, a wholly unsatisfactory long-term solution since it robbed the economy of cash. By the last quarter of the fifteenth century the writing was on the wall for the Coventry industry. The city's cornerstone would fast be undermined. There was little foresight as to the collapse of the market and woad, which had been a common small-scale crop here in England remained almost unknown in our fields until the seventeenth century. The last continental woad ship is reputed to have docked in England in 1638.

In addition to woad and alum Coventry also imported through Southampton madder by the balet (red dye, for which alum, in 108lb loads, was also the mordant), canvas by the ell or 'C' (one ell = 114cm/45in, C = 120 ells), oil by the pipe (572 litres/126 gallons) or tun (1145 litres/252 gallons) and wine by the pipe or tun.

The nature of the final leg of this vital Genoese trade through Southampton may be best served by resorting to the brokage book. On 4 October 1443, William Hekle paid duty for carriage to Coventry on two cart loads containing five C of canvas (600 ells or 685m/750 yards) belonging to the agent Angelo de Negri (10d customs duty), seven balets of woad (0.8 tons) belonging to John Goolde (customs free), seven balets of woad belonging to William Per (customs free) and four C canvas (548m/600 yards) belonging to the agent Gregorio Catana (8d customs duty).

It is tempting to imagine that the two English importers were exempt from duty because Coventry was lobbying for such freedom, a campaign which met with success in 1456 (a wholly ironic date since the alum supply was then about to plummet). William Hekle belonged to a family of carters from Bursledon, just east of Southampton; a John Hekle also crops up in the records with consignments. It seems clear, however, that William was not merely a haulier but the overseer of the business. The periods between his appearances in the records as entering Southampton with Coventry goods for the port and his immediate return inland to Coventry are sometimes so short (as little as two days) that he simply cannot have travelled all the way with the consignment. Thus on 2 November 1443 he entered the port with wool and left with a load for Coventry. He did the same on 4 November; he cannot have done more than merely accompany each consignment at the ends of their respective outward and return legs. The journey from the coast to Coventry and back again was far more than a day. He was probably coming from home to oversee dispatch and arrival of his clients' shipments.

There was no let-up in the trade through the winter, testament to the fact that the roads were in good repair. Each cart appears to have carried more than a ton of goods. Later, on 28 August 1444, William Hekle, bound for Coventry, paid duty for three cart loads with 30 balets of woad (3.3 tons) belonging to William Warwick, and in two carts towards Coventry with 10 balets of woad (1.1 tons), two balets of alum (227kg/500lb), one balet of madder (113kg/250lb) and one pipe (572 litres/126 gall) of oil belonging to John Goolde (4s customs, 4d brokage, 5d portage).

The magnitude of Coventry's mercantile dependency on this trade can be gauged by the fact that in the year 1443-4 alone, 59 such cargoes left that one port for the city, comprising chiefly 631 balets of woad, weighing 71 tons, surpassed only in 1460-1 with 695 balets, a staggering 78 tons. Some of the City's principal officers were instrumental in the trade and their names crop up in national documents, such as Thomas Rastell of Greyfriars Lane, Warden of the Corporation in 1443-4 (and eventually MP for Warwick in 1472-5), or William Warwick, City Chamberlain in 1447.

Unsurprisingly, throughout the 1440s and the 1460s as a whole, in a ranking of English towns based on woad consumption from orders through the port at Southampton, Coventry always stood between second and fourth, with 1809 and 2319 balets in each decade (204 and 262 tons); only London and Salisbury imported more on a regular basis, with Winchester the occasional strong finisher.

Naturally, this was not the only foreign import which Coventry was able to purchase with the revenues from its lucrative woollen cloth industry, but it was the most important. Nor was all the trade through Southampton. Contacts through the east coast ports of Lynn and Boston were commonplace, as they were through Bristol. The clothiers and dyers, whose opulent homes were often concentrated, although not exclusively, around Earl Street and Jordan Well (formerly part of Gosford Street), were often men with widespread contacts in society circles and whose material culture probably matched the size and complexity of their homes, some of which were drawn in detail by Nathaniel Troughton in the nineteenth century.

Not all high-level cloth dealing brought guaranteed wealth, however. In 1463 William Dove, Woolman of Coventry, was pardoned for not appearing at Bristol to answer for his debts of £17 (a considerable sum) owing to one (perhaps rightly-named) Thomas Shiplode of that city. Later, in 1503, Henry Kebull, Mercer, received a pardon for smuggling. A pardon however, acknowledges guilt; it is not an acquittal. Up to that point Kebull had been apparently a pillar of society; a merchant of the staple at Calais, he was also a member of Coventry Corporation 1472-94 and was Sheriff of Coventry four times between 1480 and 1489. Clearly there was illegal money to be made alongside legitimate wealth. Women too could engage in high-level trade and many women were members in their own right of the prestigious Holy Trinity Guild, which met at St Mary's Hall. The lot of both male and female merchants could at times, however, also be precarious. In 1398 armed Hansa merchants captured off Boston a ship laden with cloth and goods of three Coventry merchants worth in excess of £350, at that time a not-so-small fortune. They also beat up the merchants' associates on board. Later, Holy Trinity Guild member Margery Russell in the early fifteenth century obtained royal letters to seize goods of Spanish merchants to recoup a massive £800 of which she in turn had been robbed by men of Santander.

The organic nature of cloth is such that exceptional ground conditions are needed for its preservation. Rarely do such conditions exist. However, in the Broadgate excavations of 1974-5 a few fibres of flax were found attached to shoe leather. When examined under a microscope they showed as blue-dyed, a colour interpreted as being woad-related.

In the 1960s excavations at St Mary's Cathedral, patches of fabric were recovered from a grave under the nave. Preserved in the modified, anaerobic environment of the grave were patches of clothing under a leather belt and copper alloy buckle of the person buried. While the dye in the cloth appeared to be brown, the cloth itself was woollen and of the finest Merino quality. Recent excavations in Hill Street (2005) found pieces of coarse cloth from medieval pits, while work at Far Gosford Street (2006) has found dyeing evidence in woad and madder seeds.

EUROPEAN TRADE ROUTES

In excavations at the Whitefriars and at St Mary's Cathedral, high-quality imported European pottery has been recovered. From the former came Italian Maiolica, while from the latter was recovered small amounts of Saintonge ware; both may indirectly be related to the woad supply as both come from the regions from which the woad came or through which it had to travel to the French Atlantic ports and both these monastic houses were known to be regular meeting places for influential trading guilds and merchants.

Another possibility is that they were brought back as a result of the pilgrimage routes which passed to Rome, through northern Italy, or to Spain's Santiago de Compostella, which passed through the Saintonge, an area at the northern edge of Aquitaine, equating to the modern Poitou-Charentes region of France.

The city's monasteries and friaries, in particular, maintained close personal contact with the continent, simply because their mother houses lay there. For the Benedictines and Franciscans, this was Italy (Monte Cassino and Assisi, respectively); for the Cistercians and Carthusians it was France (Citeaux, near Dijon and Grenoble, respectively). At regular intervals a deputation was required from each monastery to report to its mother house for matters of administration. As a result of the church's Great Schism, during which a Pope in Rome opposed another in Avignon, England backed the traditional Roman papacy. Consequently for Englishmen, travel to Rome across a generally hostile France could be extremely hazardous. The result was that chapters were often either not held or were rearranged. For the period of the Great Schism in the church (1378-1417), Coventry's delegation from St Anne's Charterhouse had to travel to

Seitz in Austria for that order's quadrennial general chapter meeting, a journey which could take six months. When Aquitaine was lost to England in the middle of the fifteenth century, the overland routes once more became problematic and the ports were denied to many English ships.

The monasteries too benefited from the direct trade through the ports. The Cistercians of Coombe Abbey fought hard to maintain a private quay against local mercantile protectionism on the River Wensum at Norwich. Their wool would have been exported there and small amounts of Grimston-type pottery in Coventry attest the two-way trade through East Anglian ports; although this was always more widespread and stronger through (King's) Lynn. In relation to the other side of the country, in 1464 Edward IV granted the Charterhouse a yearly tun of wine at the port of Bristol, during a brief period of respite with France. It was joined some years later by a second tun from London. Finally in 1494 Henry VII granted a third tun, again from Bristol. So between 1494 and its dissolution in January 1539, the thirty or so occupants of St Anne's Charterhouse could perhaps count upon an annual documented supply of 3435 litres/756 gallons of (probably) what is now called Claret, from the Bordeaux region of France, part of Aquitaine. While this may seem an excessive amount to modern tastes, it is rather a reflection that the water quality could not always be relied upon for healthy drinking. Whether their wine supply was always reliable is debatable, given the vagaries of England's political relationship with France in the fifteenth century.

One possible example of a fine wine was excavated at the castle bakehouse site on Bayley Lane. Naturally enough the wine itself had gone but there was recovered the fragments of a smashed bottle of fourteenth or fifteenth century date, wrapped in a rush basket. Both glass and basket were in exceptionally poor condition and could not be reconstructed. Similarly from a benefactor's grave at the Charterhouse came the remains of a glass goblet in finest Venetian glass made with a distinctive broken-threading method. It indicates appreciation of the finest goods money could buy, and in this case a type of vessel well beyond what English glaziers could produce at that time. The first recorded imports of Venetian glass are through Southampton in 1481. It was a startling piece to be buried both in a Christian grave and in the austerity of a Carthusian church; it was also an indication of the level of wealth which might be dispensed with in a funereal context. How much greater might have been the wealth which the family retained for the living?

More indicative of popular consumption in the later medieval period are the numerous drinking vessels which began to be imported, slowly at first, but subsequently in the later fifteenth century in a flood from Germany and the Low Countries. They appear on many sites, regardless of status, since they are

46 Rare seventeenth-century mammiform costrel in French Martincamp stoneware from 121–4 Spon Street, 1990. *Photographed by kind permission of Coventry and District Archaeological Society*

of no great beauty or refinement. Their type can be graphically seen in Peter Breughel's well-known painting 'The Peasant Wedding' (1568), which now hangs in Vienna, in which a basketful of such vessels lies in the corner of the alehouse where a wedding breakfast is being served. Such mugs (for they are such) and other simple vessels are known to archaeologists generally by their place of origin: Paffrath (thirteenth century ladles), Raeren, Siegburg, Frechen (all near the Dutch/German border) and Martincamp (northern France), produced well into the seventeenth century (*46*).

With the exception of the Martincamp vessel (which are usually very fragmentary), Coventry sites are by no means unusual in producing such imports, and as much as anything they indicate a people's change in dining habits since they seem not to have replaced anything similar. They may reflect an increase in the consumption of beer as brewed at that time in the Low Countries. They do, however, reflect a thriving overland trade from the ports to northern Europe, where lay another of the City's clientele for its cloth, the fabulously wealthy ports of the Hanseatic League, which lined the Baltic from Denmark to Lithuania and could be reached directly by sea or overland via Amsterdam and Rotterdam. Since a large proportion of Coventry's woollen cloth exports left England through Lynn and the east coast, the Dutch/German connection must have been a reasonable proposition.

The same ships which brought the new types of pottery in also brought large quantities of glass from the Rhine, still a considerably sought-after commodity, since the new English glass-houses of Sussex and the West Midlands were incapable of producing anything like the quality of the imports, whether Venetian (as above) or Rhenish. Unfortunately all of the port books are relatively late in date; few early equivalents survive (Southampton's Brokage Books being a notable exception). However, from Boston in Lincolnshire between 1601 and 1640 comes a long and detailed record of imports and exports to the Low Countries and the Baltic. Ships plying this long distance trade are principally from Boston, (Kings) Lynn, Hull, Amsterdam, Rotterdam, Emden, Elbing, Danzig (Gdansk), and Norway.

Documented arrivals and the clear evidence of the archaeological record shows that, although Coventry lies almost as far from any English port as it is possible to be, both the secular and religious material culture reflects a degree of regular, close contact with northern and southern Europe. The links have already turned up in pottery, glass and the rarest of fibres; there are likely to be others yet.

While Coventry imported the best that Europe and the ports had to offer, such as wine, woad, alum and madder, iron from Spain, fish from Iceland and Norway, its cloth was its principal ambassador, to the Hanseatic League, to France and to Portugal, to Italy to Iceland and to the Crown. On the back of this grew up other industries, perhaps not so pivotal, but equally important to the face of Coventry and to the fashion and artistic variety of England and western Europe. Alongside the cloth went dress accessories and metalworking trades, masonry, carpentry, alabaster-working and wall-painting. Many have produced related archaeological finds.

ROADS AND TRADE

Necessarily the city's trade depended in no small part upon the road system. It is a myth of previous poor teaching of medieval history that travel was difficult and that no one went far. Roads were often not actually a physical entity but a right of way, ultimately sanctioned by the monarch. In the medieval period the old Roman road system was still in relatively good repair; on the Gough map of Britain (*c.*1280-1360) 40 per cent of the roads depicted are former Roman roads, such as survive today at Wheeldale Moor and Blackstone Edge in Lancashire. It is telling that on the Gough map the road networks converge principally on a very few centres, including Coventry. The four major travelling groups who needed the roads were the monarch, the church, the civil service and traders. Ironically, the last group was the largest, for whom there is the least documentation.

A measure of the constant use to which roads were put can be gauged by study of the reign of King John (1199-1216). His court left more than copious records and his whereabouts are known for virtually every day of his reign. He and his retinue, which comprised both the royal household and the whole government, included 20 carts and wagons. They were constantly on the move and in some periods moved up to 13 times a month. While there was a preference for travel in late summer, there was certainly no appreciable let-up for winter (as has already been seen for the woad supplies from Southampton). John's movements are far from exceptional, indeed his itinerant lifestyle was typical of all nobility at that time, but with the added responsibility of government being dispensed from wherever the royal person happened to be. In the 1320s the whole field army over-wintered at Coventry on its way to Scotland. In 1397 Richard II, the Duke of Brittany and 10,000 troops were quartered around Gosford Green, probably camped on every field from Cheylesmore to Stoke! Later, the entire government worked from Coventry for the year 1460-1. Clearly the infrastructure was as solid as any and within the city, documents reveal that the main roads had been paved or metalled since around 1285.

The church needed the roads since England became a major source of European pilgrimage and established its own internal pilgrim network. The lure of both Jerusalem and Rome remained high throughout the medieval period although the journeys there were long, arduous and frequently very dangerous. Almost as important was the journey to Santiago de Compostella in Spain to pay homage to the remains of St James. The sanctified relics of saints were collected in many places to ensure that crowds flocked to an increasing number of pilgrimage centres. In England, Canterbury became the most important: the place of martyrdom of the Archbishop Thomas Beckett. In Coventry, all the monastic houses purported to house sacred relics. At St Mary's Priory the saintly possessions were said to include a piece of the true cross and the jawbone of the ass which had been wielded as a weapon by Samson. Most pilgrimage centres issued official badges to their visitors as proof of their visit and thus a means to claim papal indulgences (time off their stay in purgatory). The most famous was that of Santiago de Compostella, a scallop shell, the emblem of St James. An example of just such a badge, in copper alloy, was excavated at Ernesford Grange in 1971.

Although the civil service and numerous trading groups needed the roads, it is only due to such things as port books that we possess any records of their movements at all. It is only through archaeology that the likes of pottery, tile, stone and other goods can be traced to their points of origin. The cost of carriage of any commodity was the single biggest expense in a purchase and so it was probably rare that any cart went anywhere unladen. This not only applied to the likes of William Hekle's port-bound loads but to goods everywhere. Thus a cart from Nuneaton with pottery for Coventry market would return to Nuneaton laden with Coventry goods.

LOCAL TRADE

Indeed the immediate hinterland could and did provide more trading opportunities than anywhere else, since the countryside provided most of what the city needed, from food to raw materials. Surplus could be sold at the weekly specialist fairs in the streets or the Great Fair, held annually, which lasted a whole week. From Warwickshire came wool, grain, livestock, fuel and building materials. The Forest of Arden provided cattle (en route from Wales), charcoal, faggots, wax and honey, while from the Felden areas came grain and wool. So great was Coventry's demand for fuel that during the fifteenth century some Coventry merchants were going out for their fuel requirements, since the existing supplies were insufficient. Coal was arriving in small quantities, possibly from Nuneaton, although by no later than 1524 this was supplemented by supplies from (probably amongst others) Sir Henry Willoughby's coal pit in Wyken. As early as 1388 coal was being used to heat the homes of the wealthy, such as at Cheylesmore Manor as related in State Papers, when Richard II came to stay. This must have been a distinct preference, since Cheylesmore park was hardly lacking in good firewood. A Shilton collier is known in the middle of the thirteenth century, when the trade would have been exceptionally dangerous. Charcoal is ever-present on all of Coventry's archaeological sites and this universal fuel was used to both heat homes and drive industry. Coal was generally needed only where temperatures needed to be raised a little more than wood allowed.

Simply because they needed the most carriage, the most expensive materials were building materials, chiefly stone and timber. Allied to this were the subsidiary building supplies such as tiles. While the last of these came mainly from Stoke, the others had a variety of sources.

Stone and stonemasons

Stone quarries were a valuable commodity and could be traded between landowners. Thus the considerable quarries which lay within the Priory Manor of Prior's Harnall, were actually owned by the Abbot and convent of Coombe Abbey from before 1224. It was from here that the stone was cut which built Coombe Abbey in the second half of the twelfth century, under the supervision of John the mason. With subsequent extensions in the thirteenth century, the quarries were so massive that by the nineteenth century, although long since disused, they and their landscaped spoil heaps were still a major landmark as part of the estate of Primrose Hill House, and were described by the diarist Joseph Gutteridge (1816-99) in the *Coventry Herald*:

> The highest part of Hill Fields is called Primrose Hill …. This hill is beautifully wooded with stately elms of two species, the common and wych elm, maples of two or three species and pines of several kinds. One part of this hill had been quarried very extensively and to a great depth for the valuable sandstone it contained. The stone was used in the construction of the city walls and gates about six hundred years ago. In the deep holes made by the excavations, forest trees now grow, towering by straight stems to a height of thirty or forty feet, their heads making one umbrageous mass of foliage almost impenetrable to the sun's rays. The sides of the excavations are terraced in all directions under the shade of the trees and at the more open parts. It well deserved the name it bore, for in my early recollection it was a mass of primroses and daffodils, while the lower and damper parts were yellow with the flowers of the lesser pile wort.

Other quarries are known to have lain in the royal park at Cheylesmore, at Allesley, Pinley and Whitley. The first of these eventually provided an impromptu emplacement for Charles I's artillery when he bombarded New Gate in 1642; they were later in 1847 landscaped into a sylvan idyll by William Paxton for the London Road cemetery (*47*). Archaeological and documentary evidence also points to early quarries lying within the city at locations in Hill Street, Well Street and Bayley Lane. Excavations in 2004 along Whitefriars Street uncovered huge sandstone quarry pits to the rear of the Phoenix pub, filled in with domestic and industrial waste in the thirteenth to fourteenth centuries (*48*).

Masons were always present in the medieval city since it enjoyed such copious supplies of freestone. With a constant flow of monastic and mendicant clients, and a growing secular middle-class, masons were in great demand. The earliest known mason in the City is probably William the Englishman who worked on Canterbury Cathedral in the period 1179-84. He may have carried out the initial work on the Cathedral and Benedictine Priory in the 1190s. Later on, the work on the Cathedral was completed by Reginald the mason, who operated a lodge close to Priory Street and died shortly before 1224. In the 1340s the master mason who began the Carmelite Church was William de Ramsey III, a man of high renown. By 1373 the construction of St Michael's Church tower had attracted master mason Robert Skyllington from his previous work for John of Gaunt at Kenilworth Castle and the choir of St Mary's Church, Warwick. After that he would proceed to Leicester and Tutbury Castle, seemingly at home with

47 The Cheylesmore quarries, landscaped into Joseph Paxton's 1847 London Road cemetery

many of the Midlands' stone-types. His less-renowned contemporaries, however, seem an altogether rougher crowd, who in 1380 were involved in a professional quarrel (or common brawl). Two affidavits in the Sessions of the Peace show that one man was killed and another injured:

> The constables state that Thomas de Whateley, mason, William de Needham, mason, Clement Mason and William de Darley, mason, on the Sunday before the feast of St Augustine in the third year of the reign of Richard II (1379-80) at Coventry by force of arms attacked one Wendelburgh, mason and beat, wounded him and worked him over so that he was in fear for his life.

> The constables state on oath that Thomas de Whateley, mason (on the same date and at Coventry) murdered John of Lyveden, mason.

The names indicate that most of these men were not local. Darley (Derbyshire) and Lyveden (Northamptonshire) are both stone-producing areas with their own industries and it may be that their expertise was needed in a post-Black Death Coventry alongside a denuded workforce. In 1380 they may have been working anywhere in the city, from the walls to St Mary's Priory (which had long-standing links with Darley Abbey), or on Whitefriars or St Michael's Church tower. Charterhouse was not begun for a further two years. One such mason probably bound to church building was John Eyres, who crops up twice in two years in the Coroner's Rolls. In 1379 he was a witness under oath when a Stoke tiler was found face down in a pond. Only one year later he himself was found murdered (it seems to be a mason was inherently risky!). He was said to have had ecclesiastical rights which probably means he was bound to the church.

Otherwise it was to largely anonymous men of local extraction to whom the city turned. They lived both in the city and its suburbs, their superior and relatively imperishable handiwork, showing complete confidence in the qualities of the local Triassic sandstone, is regularly discovered in excavation, reflecting changes in architectural fashion from the Romanesque, through experimental Early English and the flamboyance and grace of Gothic to the lightness of the Perpendicular. They were equally at home with figurative sculpture as with structural building work. In a post-hole excavated at Charterhouse in 1986 was an early sixteenth-century mason's chisel, 285mm long and finely wrought to be of use as an implement to produce a delicate finish on the stone. What the city did not produce in local stone could be had elsewhere. Probably from London workshops came Dorset's finest export, Purbeck Marble, used here to make a finely-wrought screen in St Mary's Cathedral, the massive Benedictine chapter house tomb-slab of Sub-Prior John Aylmer (fl. 1280-post 1302) with its formulaic Norman-French inscription and a simple, portable altar table in the fifteenth-century Charterhouse nave. All bear the hallmarks of this fossiliferous stone: a characteristic blue-green colour and a smooth sheen which polishes magnificently and still shines when excavated after hundreds of years of burial.

During their life the Cheylesmore Park quarries generated considerable documents and contributed to non-royal building programmes. Thus in 1358 there appears in the Black Prince's Register:

> Licence to the Friars Minor (i.e. Franciscans at Greyfriars) to take as much stone as necessary from his quarry in Cheylesmore for the enlargement of their house and to take earth in any suitable place on the Prince's soil which shall be assigned to them by the Prince's steward there for making their partitions and walls and plastering their houses.

In 1362 the grant of stone was extended to the Carmelites at Whitefriars who may already have exhausted nearer pits behind Gosford Street (*48*). Whether the king would have been as generous with Sir Nicholas Revel's proposed 1363 foundation of an additional house, of Austin Friars, remains unanswerable as it was never carried through despite a genuine royal enquiry as to its viability. The earlier 1358 grant was ratified in 1385 in the Patent Rolls by the young King

48 A huge rubbish-filled fourteenth-century stone quarry pit, one of several over 2m deep at 68-70 Whitefriars Street, 2004. *Northamptonshire Archaeology*

Richard II who gave additional permission:

> with free egress and ingress for their workmen and the carriage of the stone … also the right of digging earth for the walls and plaster, with leave to have a postern gate into the park.

How long the need for masons lasted in the city is difficult to tell. By the mid-sixteenth century, however, the Dissolution of the monasteries had robbed the masons of some of their principal clients. In 1541 two masons from far afield, Thomas Philips of Bristol and John Pettit of Wellingborough, were engaged to construct a new 56ft high Coventry Cross to be built in Broadgate. It may indicate that all of Coventry's stone quarries were either exhausted or filled in since the freestone was to come from quarries in Attleborough and Rowington, with the harder stone of the stepped plinth to be robbed from the dissolved Benedictine Priory.

Timber and carpenters

Timber also was in evidence in large quantities in Cheylesmore park for both the manor and other needs. In 1360 it was used to repair the manor. Four years later timber was cut to repair Park Mill. Richard II in 1385 appointed James Boteler:

> Bailiff of the manor and park of Cheylesmore, with orders to cut down and sell 3000 faggots in the park and to apply the proceeds towards repair of park pales and of the manor house.

Later, in 1421, Henry V issued licence for:

> Robert Castell, steward of the manor of Chailesmore (sic), to receive twelve oaks within the park of Chailesmore for the repair of the manor and also to cut down underwood for sale to the value of 40 marks (£27 6s 8d) ....

Naturally, it was not just the royal lands which contained valuable woodland which was of use, but all major holdings included some proportions of wood in order to reach an optimum value both for the use of their raw materials and for their sale. Thus in 1191 St Mary's Priory was granted 113ha (280 acres) of wood and waste in Exhall and Keresley with freedom, if they wished, to convert the whole into arable land. That amount of wood might build an entire town and doubtless, at that date, lacking conventual buildings only recently destroyed by the maverick Bishop of Coventry, Hugh Nonant, the possibilities for rebuilding with ready timber were much appreciated by the Benedictine community and facilitated a speedy reconstruction programme.

The other monastic orders also owned woodland. At the Dissolution of the Monasteries in 1539, contemporary inventories show that St Anne's Charterhouse owned a grove outside New Gate called Boles Grove and another at Exhall (Robyns Grove). Likewise Coombe Abbey in 1291 was assessed by Pope Nicholas IV as having an entire Grange-farm of 121ha (300 acres) specialising in managed woodland (its location is unclear, but the Cistercian rule dictated that it should lie within a day's journey of the Abbey).

As suggested above, the orders of Friars had to rely on the grants of others for their raw materials and these were not commodities in which they could trade. This was enshrined in the monastic rule of these mendicant (begging) orders of monks, whose way of life did not permit them to own land beyond their own precinct. True, they could enlarge their precinct by the gift of land, as did the Coventry Franciscans by the grant of former Priory land on Greyfriars Lane by Roger de Montalt in 1289 and the Carmelites' repeated enlargement of their precinct (it was a common practice; the Austin Friars of Northampton did so six times in the thirteenth century, the Norwich Franciscans three times). However, each new plot had to be contiguous with the existing main precinct. Thus opportunities for self-sufficiency in raw materials were almost non-existent. In a rare gift of materials from a distance, Edward I in 1291 granted the Coventry Franciscans six oaks from the royal forest of Kinefare (Kinver, Staffordshire), charging the felling to Roger Lestrange, Justice of the royal forest south of the River Trent. This personal royal gift indicates the excellent quality of roads which must have existed to link the city with such a comparatively remote place. It in no way implies a local unavailability of suitable timber, it merely reflects the situation in which at that date the Crown had no local stake in managed woodland (such as Cheylesmore Manor, then still a baronial holding) so Kinver may simply have been the nearest possible royal source for such timber. Carriage to Coventry, whether in its raw state as trunks or pre-fabricated into trusses or frames, would have been an expensive additional cost, not lost upon the recipient Friars. The oak would probably have come via Stourbridge, Halesowen, Birmingham, Meriden and Allesley, a distance of some 56km (35 miles).

While most of the medieval stone mason's skill was introduced gradually from the continent from the eleventh century, there already existed a superior tradition of carpentry and timber-working for all scales of structure. With timber supplies generally close at hand, this gave rise to workmanship which is all too perishable in the English climate. The medieval timbered town which sadly burned so brightly in the bombing of November 1940 and April 1941 was a jewel of medieval English carpentry. Regardless of whether decisions to clear Butcher Row in the 1930s and New Street in the 1950s are condemned with hindsight by apparently more enlightened generations, they were far less contentious at the time and within the wider spirit of the mid-twentieth century when towns and cities were being renewed.

The survivors of those clearances and the ravages of centuries of wind and rain are relatively few in number but no less remarkable for that. While the only records of the church fittings of St Michael's are a few excellent drawings and photographs (27), both ecclesiastical and secular examples do survive elsewhere. Occasional buildings such as those which still grace Bayley Lane (7 and 8), the Burges, Spon Street and Gosford Street are statutorily listed for their architectural and historical merit.

The surviving medieval churches and monastic buildings at Whitefriars, Charterhouse and St John's Hospital still contain fine examples of the medieval carpenter's craft and the carver's art. For example at the Charterhouse is found arguably the only wooden medieval Carthusian door-head in the country, made c.1381-5, deriving from Cell 'I', on the west side of the cloister (24). Close to it is a complete suite of early fifteenth-century ceiling beams carved with vines and flowers. They rest upon wall-posts perched on sculpted angelic stone corbels (49).

49 Angelic corbel (1417)
supporting a wall-post
of the roof to the Prior's
apartments, Charterhouse

Metals and foundrymen

Principally from Jordan Well (1955), Broadgate (1974-5) Cox Street (1976),
Derby Lane (1984), Much Park Street (1971, 1986), Bayley Lane (1988, 1990) and
Whitefriars Street (1995, 2003, 2004) comes copious evidence of the metalworkers
who produced in bronze, pewter, latten and related alloys the hundreds of fittings
and accessories, which both helped adorn not just the clothing of local people,
but also their shoes, belts, armour, horse tack and homes. While no furnaces
have yet been excavated, these sites have produced both crucibles for bronze-
smelting and globules of melted metals, including (at Derby Lane) a pit filled
with scraps of copper alloy objects awaiting melting down for re-casting. On
some of these sites, such as Much Park Street and Bayley Lane, the broken, heat-

50 Some of the discarded fourteenth-century stone moulds excavated at John Foundur's tenement, Bayley Lane, 1988. *Photographed by kind permission of the Herbert Art Gallery and Museum*

cracked, worn or merely old, unfashionable stone moulds in local Lias mudstone were discarded by the dozen in the domestic and industrial rubbish pits which characterise the back yards of parts of these streets. Most date to the thirteenth to fifteenth centuries and are testament to the accent placed on personal dress and fashion in the medieval period. At Bayley Lane in 1988 the excavated plot (the former Delph, quarry site) was documented in 1411 as the property of one John Foundour (foundryman) from the late fourteenth century. Here a number of unfinished or blank moulds was recovered, suggesting another dependent, but undocumented industry, that of mould-maker (*50*).

Larger items were also produced in copper alloys. A small workshop existed in the city producing intricate brasses for tombs; however this is one of the industries which died out most startlingly at the Dissolution in 1539 and has left very little material evidence. Dissolution levels indicate a frenzy to remove every piece of brass from monastic tombs, even the individual letters and full stops of inscriptions (as in John Aylmer's Benedictine chapter house tomb), all to be melted down and re-cast (*44*).

Art and artists

Surviving wall-paintings at Charterhouse, Holy Trinity and St Mary Magdalene, Wyken, together with those rarest of excavated painted stonework indicate how beautifully decorated many of the principal buildings in the city were. The painted and gilded pieces of stonework excavated from St Mary's Benedictine Priory chapter house caused a storm in the world of art historians, so fine are they. They are felt to surpass even those of Westminster Abbey in the quality of their execution (*colour plate 4*). Further pieces, less intricate but just as bright and bold, were excavated from Whitefriars in the 1960s. Distinctive pieces of figurative brightly painted plaster have even been recovered from domestic contexts (Bayley Lane, 1988), depicting the bold head of a devilkin and insects (now in the Herbert Art Gallery and Museum). There was clearly a school of more than just competent artists who, if not actually established in Coventry, could find some fabulously wealthy commissions here. Art historians are convinced that their level of expertise and method of execution betrays a studied continental influence. While painters were not feted in the same way they are today, their skills do mark them out as extraordinary craftsmen. Their principal clients disappeared with the Dissolution, but both polychrome and austere monochrome post-Dissolution paintings do survive at Charterhouse. Unsurprisingly they are said to continue to show continental and, in particular, Italian influence.

Another specialist trade was represented in medieval Coventry in the person of a small number of alabaster carvers. Although the light raw material came from Nottinghamshire, documents attest a number of these craftsmen in the fourteenth to fifteenth centuries. From the Charterhouse come two excavated alabaster statuettes, probably altar pieces, depicting St Denis and St Lawrence. The two carry the indications of the methods of their martyrdom (St Denis holds his severed head wearing a mitre – in addition to that still on his shoulders – and Lawrence the grid-iron on which he was roasted). They were apparently buried for safe-keeping at the Dissolution and dug up by the eighteenth-century gardener John Whittingham. They are today in the possession of St Osburg's Church.

The glass workshops which produced the great medieval glazier John Thornton lay in Coventry. They may have lain close to Thornton's own house, which stood on the west side of The Burges. Before he went on to conceive the Great Rose Window in York Minster in the early fifteenth century, Thornton's work probably graced windows in a variety of Coventry churches. His genius, and that of the Coventry schools of glazing, was mainly lost in the frenzy of iconoclasm and destruction which accompanied the Dissolution of the monasteries in Coventry, windows deliberately smashed in; in excavation thousands of pieces of glass have been found to litter the half-robbed monastic floors beneath where windows stood, pushed in from the outside and stripped of lead where they lay. The merest hints survive of the former glazing schemes, such as a Tree of Jesse (Christ's earthly family tree) excavated at Whitefriars in the 1960s. Most would have had didactic religious themes but were also graced with delicate observations of the natural world and the intricate architectural forms of contemporary buildings.

Recycling waste

Little was wasted in medieval society and in Coventry, as in many other towns, small, cottage-industries reused animal bone, horn and deer antler for pins, styli, handles, buttons, tuning pegs, ice-skates and a whole host of small objects which today are made from a wide variety of materials. Pinners' bones (for holding lengths of wire while cutting and sharpening pins) and sixteenth-century buttoners' bones (usually cow ribs from which buttons were drilled out with a hollow drill) are common on many sites.

Just as bones were reused, so the skins of slaughtered livestock were valuable since leather in particular was the only hard-wearing, waterproofed material available for shoes, work garments, horse tack and belts of all kinds. The early medieval town may have had leather-tanning carried out at its heart but the acutely smelly nature of the industry (involving defleshing skins and boiling or scraping off copious animal fats) meant that the City Leet eventually banished the tanners and their likes out to the margins of settlement. The principal group of tanners, barkers, dubbers (waterproofers) and whittawers was, by the fourteenth century, to be found on Hill Street and Well Street, all the way out to Hill (Naull's) Mill, working on plots irrigated by the waters of the Radford Brook, but when the City wall was constructed between these streets in the 1390s, their noisome industry was excluded. Their waste was amply described by the diarist Joseph Gutteridge (1816-99):

> The north bank of the Cherry Orchard (north of Upper Well Street) in its upper part was supported by thousands of ox horns and skulls packed together so tightly as to keep the high ground of the orchard from falling into the lane (Abbots Lane, between Hill Cross and Spon Street, now beneath Ringway Hill Cross).

During a watching brief on the construction of 1960s buildings on the east side of Bond Street, a similar deposit of cattle horn cores was seen at depth. The head and horns were the last elements to be detatched from the carcass, usually by the tanner. This site is adjacent to the Belgrade Theatre, at the heart of the city's later medieval and post-medieval tanning industry.

Thus for 500 years there was constant interaction with the locality, for inspiration and for raw materials. The daily existence of the city depended on what its hinterland could produce and import, in terms of personnel, raw materials and in food. In time the city became a centre of artistic endeavour and excellence. It had all the trappings and variety of a successful mercantile society with links around the region, the nation and Europe.

11

The ceramics trades

'Demise to Thomas and Agnes Clement Stoke Manor except suit of court, wood, underwood and tile quarries, allowing them to use trees. Grant of 30 acres and three crofts for tiling for 40s a year, allowing them the shredding of trees there.'
Coventry Borough Archive 1416

POTTER

The archaeology of Coventry's medieval ceramics is dominated by two local groups and their study: the producer and his wares on the one hand, and the consumers on the other. In some ways the consumer leads the potter since if the potter produces unfashionable material he goes out of business. The relationship is one key to the use and supply of Coventry's pottery in the medieval period. It is an industry of fashion and function. There was also great competition and the small-scale early medieval potteries of Coventry would, in the thirteenth century, be swamped by the volume of the output of their fashionable Nuneaton competitors in the space of one generation.

There has been considerable work done on the pottery industries of medieval Coventry, borne out of many excavations. However, ongoing work is showing that very much still needs to be done to understand the patterns of supply and demand of this important and ubiquitous archaeological commodity.

Most pottery industries were based in rural areas where they could capitalise upon the ready availability of suitable clay, water supplies and copious quantities of wood. Kilns were a fire hazard of the first order since a newly-fired kiln, when drawing well, could have flames and showers of sparks leaping 5m (16ft) into the air. This was spectacularly proven by an archaeological experimental night-

51 Experimental medieval pottery kiln fired at Baginton, 1985. Although cooling, the sooted rim hints at the billowing flames of the overnight firing at over 1000°C. Note the ring of sensors

firing of a replica medieval kiln at Baginton, near Coventry in 1985 (*51*). Kiln temperatures could reach 1000°C. As a result there were probably few pottery kilns within the city itself, although occasional documents do refer to potters within Coventry. Other towns risked this potentially hazardous coexistence too, such as Birmingham (Deritend), Warwick (Market Street) and Shrewsbury (Hallgate).

Potters and kilns

Potters seem to be named far less in documents than tilers, an observation which may be due to the fact that local potters generally flourished in a period which has produced comparatively few surviving documents (the twelfth to thirteenth centuries) when set against tilers of the fourteenth to sixteenth centuries. Such early references also reflect an age when many craftsmen bore no surname other than that of their trade, such as John le (the) Potter, Peter the Smyth or Brian the Woolmonger. Increasingly from the early fourteenth century names changed and proper surnames as are understood today arose and John the Potter's son might be known by his father's name but choose another trade. Only then is that trade communicated if the writer of a document feels it necessary to include it. Thus by the late fourteenth century, many people who might be well known from documents seem to ply an unknown trade simply because it was felt unnecessary to record it. It has also been argued that potters were largely poor and that many female or dependent relatives traded on behalf of the head of the household, both recipes for non-appearance in many documents.

Documents however do mention some potters and imply their trade all around the city at various times. In the 1240s a Robert le Potere is mentioned at Wyken, working out of land owned by the Langley family of Pinley but no kilns have been located. Witness also Roger le Proude, Potter, in Gosford Street in 1328. Between 1340 and 1450 the registers of the prestigious Holy Trinity Guild indicate that membership was bestowed upon two potters, John Somely and Thomas Boner, together with their respective wives, although the location of their potteries is unknown. At the eponymous Potters Harnall on the western edge of Hillfields lay an early industry about which little is currently known except that by the time the area was dealt with in documents during the fourteenth century, the industry had vanished. Potters Green on the borders of Foleshill and Walsgrave has medieval beginnings since the name appears on medieval documents; but again no firm indication of pottery production has yet been reported there although the area may have been the home to Margery le Potter, described as of nearby Henley Green, who paid rent to the Benedictine Priory in 1410-1. This is a rare occurrence of a documented female potter, although long suspected from the size of finger marks and handprints on many medieval pots. A second Potters Green is attested in Stoke documents in the 1270s and 1280s, possibly adjacent to the Binley Road. On the north side of the city documentary evidence has recently come to light of a pottery industry in Radford, as yet undated. At the University of Warwick's Westwood campus there are probable pottery kilns near Tocil Wood. Further afield there was a Potters' Pit Field in Baginton at the end of the medieval period but, like Radford and Westwood no detailed evidence of the industry there has yet come to light. The search for kilns goes on.

The products

However, in 1976 a dump of waster pottery (kiln-shattered or heat-warped waste sherds) was found during the construction of a supermarket at Lychgate Road in Cannon Park, Canley. The pottery recovered was dated on stylistic grounds, plus the presence of a few sherds of another, well-dated type, to the second half of the thirteenth century. The distinctive red-firing clay jugs splashed sparingly with a reddish-green glaze have become known as Cannon Park Ware from the name of the estate. They seem to have been part of a local redware tradition which crops up in vessels found at St Anne's Charterhouse from the late fourteenth century. Since its 1976 identification it has been recognised in small but not insignificant quantities on numerous other Coventry sites along with others in Warwickshire (*colour plate 19*). Its kilns have yet to be located but they probably lie within half a kilometre of the Canley waster site. Identification of pottery kilns in documents remains difficult since the word kiln is used for a variety of different purposes, including pottery, tile, brick, lime-burning and malting. The word is also interchangeable with 'oven' or 'furnace' allowing for metalworking or agricultural purposes and any pottery connection is left unspoken. Excavated evidence, however unplanned its discovery, remains the best initial guide to the industry.

By far the biggest early local product found on local excavations is what has become known as Coventry Ware. This occurs in two basic fabrics which are also associated in the city with specific forms. Coventry A Ware, otherwise known as Coventry Sandy Ware, is red-firing and rarely glazed. Although present in jug forms from the thirteenth century, it is predominantly a fabric used for storage/cooking pots, often with out-turned, flattened rims simply decorated with thumb-impressions, to give the effect of a 'pie crust'. Its earliest appearance seems to be in the mid-twelfth century, possibly slightly earlier and is usually wheel-turned.

Meanwhile the A Ware's companion, uninspiringly termed Coventry D Ware, is more distinctive in both fabric and form. It was usually comparatively crudely made, using coils or slabs of clay (rather than wheel-turning), to produce large heavy vessels dominated by the tripod-pitcher form. A massive cistern type of vessel with a bung-hole drain is also known from Ernesford Grange. This is the only example known in this (usually much later) form. The ware has been relatively closely dated to the period *c*.1150-1240 after which its disappearance from the archaeological record is startlingly rapid. Thus it is a type fossil for later twelfth century deposits in the city. Formerly, little was known about it other than from the largest group excavated at Broadgate in 1974-5 and it continued to be used mainly for dating purposes. More recently however (1998), extensive excavations at the deserted medieval settlement of Coton Park, adjacent to the M1, near Rugby, recovered a rural assemblage which was dominated by this ware, in a range of forms not seen in any of the Coventry material. Where the forms excavated in Coventry seem mainly to have been distinctive tripod-pitchers, those at Coton seem to have been more a mixture of bowls and cooking pots;

a case perhaps of the different functions expected of their pottery by urban and rural communities. A Coventry link, however, may be provided by the fact that Coton, which was deserted soon after *c.*1400, was dominated by Coton Grange, a Grange farm of Coombe Abbey. It was Coombe which had considerable holdings in Harnall, including a quarry and it is tempting to surmise that the Coventry D Ware and possibly the Coventry A Ware are the products of the early, little-understood Hillfields industry of Potters Harnall. Only the discovery of kilns or associated material there will settle the issue. Recent work (2003) by Birmingham University showed that the medieval ground surface, comprising the black waterlogged shoreline and reed-beds of the once much larger Swanswell, still survives along the west side of Stoney Stanton Road at about 1.5m below the modern ground surface. This is at the heart of Potters Harnall. There is every chance of the survival of kilns in the area

Before *c.*1150 there appears to have been little local material on offer. Excavations which have ventured into discrete, sealed contexts of this early date, such as the castle ditch at the corner of Hay Lane and Bayley Lane found a predominance (but in small quantities) of St Neots-type shelly wares of a type seen in copious amounts in Warwick (a Saxon *burh*), Coton Park and further afield in Northamptonshire in the period *c.*1000-1200. In contexts known to post-date the mid-twelfth century this has disappeared completely. In the castle ditch excavation, the shelly wares were accompanied by Coventry D ware and a rare Stamford Ware costrel (pottery bottle) in a developed fabric archaeomagnetically dated at a kiln site in Stamford to the period 1125-1150.

Stamford Ware from the Lincolnshire town of that name continues to be the earliest well-dated pottery on offer in Coventry. Never present except in tantalisingly small quantities, it is distinguished by its (at that time) revolutionary yellow and pale green glaze which was beyond the capabilities of almost all other early medieval English potteries in the eleventh to twelfth centuries. The sherds found in Coventry, however, have generally been non-diagnostic body sherds in very small quantities and though the type is often said to be late-Saxon when it appears closer to Stamford, its appearance in Coventry has never yet been proven unequivocally to pre-date the Norman Conquest. However, it was certainly in the city in the first half of the twelfth century at Broadgate (1975), Bayley Lane (1988) and Hay Lane (1990).

The demise of the early Coventry Wares in the mid-thirteenth century was, it seems, in no small part due to the rapid and widespread success of the Nuneaton potteries, based at Chilvers Coton (52). This success coincided with (and was owed to) a sudden increase in the range of forms being potted and in the quality and technology being brought to bear. This was not an isolated phenomenon and new tall (baluster) jug forms of the later thirteenth century are everywhere to be

52 Late thirteenth-century pit group of pottery from the Castle Bakehouse, Bayley Lane, 1990, all made in Nuneaton

seen combined with a growing confidence in glazing methods and decoration. Clearly there was a social dining revolution going on which was reflected in the material everyone wanted at table. The new pottery, however, is not restricted to houses of status but suddenly appears throughout the archaeological record about 1250. The lead glazes, predominantly green when fired, have been said by some to betray an aspiration to status in that they reflect a wish to copy the patina of bronze or copper alloys. This seems too simple an explanation since, in fact, both such pottery and metal vessels appear in the same horizons in domestic situations which pertain to all levels of society.

Cheap commodities

Pottery in the medieval period was everywhere. It usually forms the largest bulk find on any medieval excavation, and this is certainly true in Coventry (*53*). All classes of household used pottery and its appearance anywhere should cause no surprise. As a measure of status, however, it is simply the wrong material because it was freely available and relatively cheap. Work in recent years on the composition of the 'royal wardrobe' has shown that a better artefactual measure of status is to consider the range of materials which were available at table. For a royal household, this was composed of a wide range: gold, silver, pewter, latten, bronze, glass, horn, pottery, leather and wood. Naturally only certain of these materials are commonly found in the archaeological record and documentary evidence is needed to attest the presence of others. The most desirable and the greatest statement of wealth, the metals, whether precious or not, are in the medieval period usually specimen or communal pieces, such as table-centres which are not only durable but when they do break, wear out, or go out of fashion can be re-smelted into something else, such as was attested by a smelting pit full of assorted bronze vessel scraps on the former Derby Lane (1984). Leather and wood, the cheapest, only survive in waterlogged ground conditions, as does horn. Thus the archaeologist is usually left with only glass and pottery and occasional pieces of metal on which to base understanding of the daily dining habits of the medieval consumer. Fortunately it is clear that the ubiquitous nature of pottery and its enduring appeal, through many changes of fashion, themselves a barometer of wider social change, makes this medium one which is relevant to all medieval sites.

53 Thirteenth- to fourteenth-century pottery found in various excavations. The tallest jug (top right) stands *c.*40cm high. *Photographed by kind permission of the Herbert Art Gallery and Museum*

In the later medieval period most pots cost very little, and each firing of a kiln accounted for the finishing of hundreds of vessels which may have taken many days to throw. The average price for a pot was between a farthing and a ha'penny (but could go as high as four pence). Often the records of pottery purchases are scarce since it was so common a commodity. Occasionally such receipts do occur.

In 1431 Maxstoke Castle in Warwickshire purchased four gallons of wine and an incidental two pots at a penny each. In 1407 the executors of the Bishop of Salisbury spent £130 on expenses for his funeral for 1,500 guests. This included 271 clay pots for the buttery, costing 13s 3d (a ha'penny each). Around the Midlands the price was not dissimilar. Naturally the potter's outlay was on raw materials, records of payments for clay are widespread (as the potter rarely owned the land on which he worked) and fuel also was an expense, usually wood although increasingly coal in small quantities. Coal would eventually enable advances in both clay and glaze technology since it facilitated higher firing temperatures than either wood or charcoal. Clay payments varied tremendously, presumably since the demand varied from place to place. Where there were numerous clay sources locally the price was probably lower. At Worcester in the twelfth century a potter was paying sixpence for clay and was also providing two pots per week to his clay supplier. The basic clay price of sixpence was the same for a potter in Burslem in the fourteenth century. The Benedictines at St Mary's Priory in Coventry, never unaware of the value of their holdings could, in 1410-1, charge 3s 4d annual rent on their land at Potters' Marston (Leics) simply (and explicitly) as a reflection of the clay source which was exploited there.

Some inflation may be visible in the price of pottery, however. In the thirteenth century, Staffordshire records show pottery being bought at 1s 3d for 100 vessels. In the fourteenth century the same number at Cleobury Mortimer in Shropshire cost 2s 6d.

Pottery, being relatively fragile by its very nature, was not as highly prized as other materials and, of course, it was not suitable for all culinary purposes. Thus in 1459 the mayor and aldermen at Coventry paid one Robert Burnell 2s 3d for a brass ladle and skimmer for the kitchen at St Mary's Hall, considerably more than a pottery type would be (and they were available). A few years later in 1466 they paid John Tynker two pence for mending 'the great dish' in the hall, presumably a charger so big as to be unwieldy and fragile in ceramic. The employment of a 'tinker' is very likely to indicate a metal dish, but this is not certain since pottery was occasionally mended using metal clamps and wire. Such clamps, or pot-menders, made of folded bronze sheets, have been found at Whitefriars (1977), Charterhouse (1986) and most recently behind Far Gosford Street (2003).

Fashions

During so long a period as the middle ages (in terms of Coventry's archaeology roughly from the Norman Conquest to the civil war) fashion changed continuously. Pottery was no exception and the principal earlier types in use and made locally have already been described. However, it is the changing forms of the vessels themselves which can indicate just as much about fashion and the art of dining which, as ever, could be a situation to impress just as much as to nourish. Changes in foodstuffs and methods of preparation form the basis of changes, for the most part as the more formal feasting of the nobility extended down the social scale to the guilds and the guest-feasts laid on by the monasteries for their patrons and benefactors. Influential groups regularly hired the monastic guest houses and in some cases the refectories for entertainment.

During the fourteenth century and increasingly during the fifteenth the previous standard range of storage/cooking pot and baluster jug, was greatly enlarged to include pipkins (as modern saucepans), a wider range sizes and shapes of jugs, cisterns (for storage), skillets (small frying pans for making sauces) and chafing dishes (a stand/brazier for keeping food hot at the table, similar to a fondue stand and pot combined, or for gentle heating to prevent curdling of sauces or such). For ordinary people, the cooking fire remained the central hearth of the hall, and over the embers which were kept warm to kindle the next day's fire was placed a pottery *couvre-feu*, or curfew, literally a fire cover. This stopped smouldering embers escaping from the hearth and setting alight to the straw and strewn herbs which often carpeted a floor.

Throughout houses and buildings of all sorts the only evening light was provided by naked flames. Candles were expensive and generally were the preserve of the wealthier elements in society so early candlesticks tend to be rare finds on archaeological sites, often in materials more expensive than pottery. Rush-lights might be held in wall-mounted iron brackets. In the early medieval period most common are lamps, often small pottery pedestals with a flared bowl rim. Alongside these were cresset lamps, a heavy, flat-bottomed ceramic block which was made for stability and could be stood on any flat surface without fear of being knocked over. A number of examples are found from Coventry in the J.B. Shelton Collection at the Herbert Art Gallery and Museum although one is arguably thought to be a ceramic mortar. Some held more than one reservoir for the fuel, usually olive oil, thus allowing the benefit of multiple candlepower! Since the centre of the household remained the hearth, most non-natural light was provided by the cooking fire in the hall so lamps might only be needed elsewhere in the home, or after the hearth had been allowed to burn low.

Ceramic lamps and cressets were often replaced later in the medieval period by wall-mounted glass oil lamps, which worked on exactly the same principle as their pottery precursors but their capacity for wall mounting (out of harm's way) meant they could spread their light further around the room, since the flame shone down through the glass as well as upwards. Unlike rush-lights they had the added advantage of not producing hot drips or embers which might be a fire hazard. Thus the unstable table-top lamp and the cresset of doorstop proportions were gradually phased out.

During the later medieval period there came a revolution in drinking fashions. From the later fourteenth century pottery cups become widespread where previously there had been very few. Drinking was restricted, presumably to beakers in treen (wood), leather or occasionally horn or (by comparison) expensive metals or glass. In a distinctive apple-green glazed white fabric appears the multi-lobed cup from whiteware potteries in Surrey (known generally as Tudor Green), not uncommon in Coventry by 1400. Within two generations the Tudor Green had given way to many other drinking vessels in a range of pottery fabrics.

In the third quarter of the fifteenth century the first vessels appear in Coventry's archaeological record in what is known as Cistercian Ware (although the long standing name-association with the Cistercians is erroneous and misleading). Its distinctive thin walls and shiny black glaze are said to have been deliberately reminiscent of tarnished silver or pewter. This assertion, however, seems redolent of that which made the bronze patina connection with green glazes in the thirteenth century. It presupposes that all who bought such wares were deliberately aping more expensive types and thus appealed to the aspirant masses. In fact when viewed, Cistercian Ware is clearly nothing like its metal cousins and the range of types quickly expanded beyond the drinking vessel alone to forms which were clearly not paralleled in silver or pewter. Cistercian Ware was simply innovative and had no peers. It simply set new heights of fashion and its distinctive shapes and slender forms (with an inherent fragility) meant that it stayed up front as tableware in a range of forms which were to be associated primarily with consumption, not preparation or storage.

The origin of all the local Cistercian types is unknown. Some are clearly fabrics from the flourishing Nuneaton industry but there are other Cistercian fabrics present in Coventry which may have come from other local kilns or further afield, possibly Wednesbury in the West Midlands.

At the same time there began to be an influx of imported foreign types which flooded the national market and can be found on many urban sites. Most were stoneware drinking mugs or flasks for use at the table and their technologically-advanced potting and glazing caught on quickly (54). They came initially from Raeren, Limburg and Siegburg, on what is now the border country between Germany and Holland, being imported through the international ports of

54 Fifteenth-century German drinking mugs *c.*20cm high. *Photographed by kind permission of the Herbert Art Gallery and Museum*

Amsterdam and Rotterdam in particular. These types can be seen in both of Dutchman Peter Breughel the Elder's 1568 paintings 'The Peasant Wedding' and 'The Peasant Dance' (both now hang in Vienna). Here these types are depicted being used in profusion in an alehouse setting. In a detail of the latter (significant for the archaeologist) the handle of one mug lies broken on the ground amidst nutshells and general detitrus of a street cafe.

The same ships which brought this material to these shores also brought new cooking types, particularly glazed red earthenwares from Holland and fired a wish to emulate the continental methods of manufacture and glaze technology. While not recognised by contemporaries as such, stonewares were already known in Coventry, such as the local Midland purple wares and a few kilns producing near-stoneware or proto-stoneware arguably approached the quality of the continental imports for their durability, if not their grace and beauty. Their overall finish was achieved by the increasing use of coal as a fuel and thus the attainment of kiln temperatures far higher (*c.*1300°C) than could be managed by most English kilns, which were still for the most part wood- or charcoal-fired. To this they added the glaze, salt; lead would vaporise at these high temperatures. Some of the resultant clear, shiny freckle effects imitated successful German types. The only drawback with employing salt-glaze is that it glazes the interior of a kiln. As a result the kiln could never again be used for anything else other than salt-glazed pottery.

The range of forms of all types of pottery continued to diversify during the fifteenth century. Specialised types appeared, some connected with the table, such as a four footed apple-baker in a yellow-glazed earthenware. There was a sudden profusion of chafing dishes in many fabrics; in a survey, in 1992, Coventry's Herbert Art Gallery and Museum held 41 examples in its collections from city excavations, at that time more than the British Museum. Chafing dishes were relatively highly valued; they were apparently used to keep food warm or provide gentle heat and reflected a growing sophistication in the way food was served at table in ordinary households. Their importance can be seen in a 1532 inventory of the goods of Robert Goodman, who lived next to Hill Street Gate, one of the least sought-after parts of the city at that time, beset with problems of derelict properties and in amongst the city's tanners:

First four candilstikes
Item a ewer of latten (*an alloy of tin and zinc*)
Item a littil pott of latten
Item a pynt pott of pewter
Item two plates, two saucers
Item a chaffinge dish
Item a litill brasse pott
Item an old…, two little pannes
Item a littill skewer

Highly decorated ceramics also came to be used in new (wealthy) household situations. Long used to make tiles for the floor, the roof and occasionally the wall, in the early sixteenth century specialised tiles could be used to decorate stoves, to heat rooms or, in exceptional circumstances, to insulate and make watertight plunge-baths. One such tile was found in Dissolution levels at St Anne's Charterhouse in 1987 with a contemporary topical theme. It was decorated with two figurines, possibly depicting a fox in a set of stocks, stood over by a victorious goose, in a reversal of the satirical medieval depiction of a voracious fox as a Friar, preaching to his edible flock, the geese. More recently in 2000 a number of possible architectural salt-glazed stove tiles were found at St Mary's Priory. Stove tiles remain relatively rare since stoves for either heating rooms or water remained the preserve of the very wealthy for quite some time. Tile-stoves or tile-ovens were a simple form of central heating and in post-medieval Scandinavia and parts of eastern Europe were to become the principal form of heating; there the style remained in common use into the twentieth century.

TILES AND THE STOKE TILING INDUSTRIES

Lying just to the east of medieval Coventry and now firmly within the modern city lies the parish of Stoke. Originally made up of a variety of small hamlets, namely Hill Stoke, Stoke–Biggin (also known as just Biggin), Stoke–Aldermoor (also known as just Aldermoor) and Upper and Lower Stoke, the parish stretched from Gosford Green at the west to Binley Bridge at the east, Barras Heath in the north to Pinley in the south. The southern boundary with Shortley and Pinley was fluid and both of the latter were often said to lie in Stoke parish, although strictly they comprised parts of the city's St Michael's parish.

The proximity of Stoke meant that it was caught up in the influence of the city and its main contribution besides its farms was its mineral wealth, particularly clay. Spread throughout the parish were numerous kilns which, by the fourteenth century, had established a reputation for the production of fine quality decorated floor tiles, a repertoire later improved by the addition of roof tiles. The industry seems to have flourished in different parts of the parish and on its periphery until at least the middle of the seventeenth century, when brick overtook tiles as the principal product.

Industry regulation

The tiling industry in Stoke was sufficiently important for it to acquire parts in a named trading guild, that of the Millers, Wrights and Tilers, (with, at some time, the Pinners too; there never was one for the potters). Benefiting from all the worst excesses of the day, most notably price fixing and protectionism, the tilers attracted regular attention from the city authorities who sought to regulate all the trades, and further protect their output. In 1421 the City Leet Book set the wages. For a master tiler 4d per day; for his mate 2d daily. This was on a par with a thatcher, labourer, dauber and a palyer (fencer), but less than a master carpenter (5d). In 1553, amidst years of rampant inflation and little new building this was increased to 7d per day for the master and 5d for the mate.

The authorities were keen to ensure high quality products and in 1448 they decreed that no one was to lay semi–tiles or cracked/broken tiles; neither were they to set anyone on who did not have a proven track record. Only six years later it appears that their efforts had not been wholly successful since the Leet was forced to have brought before them the Tilers' guild wardens and the tilers in order for them to swear not to lay or sell semi–tiles. In 1474 the industry received a massive boost since the Leet forbade the use of new thatch in Coventry; in addition all existing thatched roofs were to be re-roofed in tile. This was clearly a health and safety measure; fire was the bane of all medieval cities, and medieval Coventry was predominantly a city built of timber. In that year, with the country, and particularly the Midlands, in the grip of the Wars of the Roses, siege, and with it fire, was a constant danger. Coventry suffered numerous civil riots, which increased the risk of fire breaking out. Even without such disturbances concern was ever-present. Disastrous domestic fires eventually destroyed large portions of the old medieval towns and cities of Norwich (1507), Northampton (1675), Warwick (1694) and, most famously, London (1666). By way of illustration to this might be added the enemy blitz on Coventry in November 1940. It was, after all, mainly the buildings of the medieval and later timbered city which burned so fiercely that the glow in the sky was seen from south of Banbury.

Quality-control remained an issue and it is clear that in the early sixteenth century the home market was trying to combat fierce external competition. The size of roof tiles was regulated in 1478. The Leet in 1518 had to enforce quality controls on brick and tile imports into the city. Whether this was a matter of trade-protectionism or consumer-protection is difficult to say. Both may have been considerations. In 1529 the Leet laid down an ordinance that no one was to carry on the dual roles of plumber and tiler together, although both may have been needed for the same roof. Perhaps at first ineffectual, the same requirement was repeated in the following year. This may reflect the rapidly spiralling economic decline of Coventry.

With the Guilds and Chantries Act of 1545, the last act of the Dissolution under Edward VI, the country's trading guilds were dissolved. Thus, ratified by order of the Leet, the emasculated Guild of Millers, Wrights and Tilers was formally disbanded in 1551.

The tiles and the floors

The exceptional local artist Dr Nathaniel Troughton drew a number of Stoke tiles when they were pulled out of the River Sherbourne during culverting work in the 1850s. However at that time there was no clue as to their origin. The first recognised indication of the remains of the tiling industry was found in 1911 during the construction of what was then known as the Victoria Park housing estate. This lies around the area of Harefield Road, between Walsgrave Road and Binley Road. A large tile kiln was discovered just east of Harefield Road along with a number of the tiles it produced. Although only a few examples were kept, they were passed to the British Museum and have ever since formed the basic fabric to which all Coventry tiles of the fourteenth and fifteenth centuries can be compared. The kiln was rediscovered and its scant results published by the local archaeologist Philip Chatwin in an early study of all Warwickshire tiles then known in 1936. Since then, thousands of floor tiles (and roof tiles) have been found in excavations in Coventry, of which perhaps 99 per cent are Stoke products. A second kiln site was found in 1940 adjacent to the Walsgrave Road

55 Fifteenth-century floor of Stoke tiles in Wormleighton Church, Warwickshire

during the construction of an air-raid shelter. Otherwise the nearest other kiln sites known are in Polesworth, Warwick (excavated in 2003) and Nuneaton (1960s).

Good *in situ* medieval tile floors are rare. Around Coventry such floors still exist, such as adjacent to the Beauchamp Chapel, Warwick and at Wormleighton Church (55). Excavated examples are rare, but Coventry has seen a wealth of them. At St Mary's Cathedral in 2000 two tile floors were found *in situ*, the heavily worn fourteenth-century church nave floor and the north-range refectory floor of *c.*1360 with repeating geometric patterns (*colour plates 4 and 20*). Another, relaid example was found at Whitefriars in 1977, while from the Charterhouse in 1987, dispersed patches of surviving *in situ* tiles betokened a later fifteenth-century repeating chequerboard of green and yellow plain tiles; these followed a more austere approach to patterns seen also at the Beauchamp Chapel, Warwick and Maxstoke Priory, near Solihull. Both at the Charterhouse and at the Cathedral the patterns, laid in bands or zones, could be altered to demarcate different uses of the space, such as processional routes or private chantry-chapel space.

At the south range of Cheylesmore Manor were found the scattered remains of a restrained geometrical floor, probably lost when the range was extensively remodelled as the town wall punched through it in the 1380s (*56*).

The durability and capacity for reuse means that tiles, often individually or in small groups, survived the dispersal of the floor for alterations, particularly intramural graves. However the patterns rarely survived. A specialist paver was rarely used to make repairs, the work seemingly being done by monks or at least someone with little aesthetic feeling for the floor, to judge by the bodges excavated above graves! In 1473 repairs to the paved floor in the hall and parlour of St Mary's Guildhall warranted an account of their own but cost a mere 3d. It is often from patches alone, between the later insertions, that the original, intended pattern can be discerned. Additionally, in the case of long-lived floors, the patterns of wear and use, valuable in archaeological terms for understanding uses of buildings and postulating door, window and furniture positions where structural evidence is lacking, can obliterate whole sections of a pattern.

56 Cheylesmore Manor south (hall) range, decorated tiled floor pattern, fourteenth century

The tilers

The documentary evidence for the industry is now known to be considerable, relating to numerous kilns and tilers over 300 years.

Within the city and in most of Warwickshire area they had a virtual monopoly and their fame spread far and wide. Stoke tiles, or their derivative copy designs have been found at Dudley Castle and Priory, Chastleton church (Oxfordshire) and even in Wales. They appear to have been sought by wealthy patrons whose arms make up a small but significant proportion of the decorated examples. They were not without local rivals, however, as a fourteenth-century kiln from Warwick shows.

The documentary history of the industry begins in the late thirteenth century. In 1299 Robert of Stoke (Lord of the Manor) and his wife acquired a marlpit near their manor house. Such Stoke marlpits become increasingly common in documents of the fourteenth century. In 1363 Richard le Fleccher (possibly either a flesher [butcher] or an arrow-maker [fletcher]) passed two houses and about 20 acres in Stoke to John de Coughton of Stoke, described as a tiler. This was held of the lord of Caludon so it may have lain at the north edge of Stoke. Coughton was indicted in 1368 for failing to deliver an order of 8,000 tiles. Another tiler, William Collyn, of Stoke Biggin, appears in Cheylesmore Court rolls in 1374 and was accused of theft in 1378, while a colleague, Richard Walssh, aided and abetted by hiding the miscreant thief. In 1389 a mercer, Robert Blatherwyck passed to John Thryft of Stoke a house with outbuilding, dovecote and a tile kiln. The gift included an access road and another right of way to a quarry. In that same year one John Tylere of Stoke was a witness in a coroner's court, having found someone dead in a pond in Stoke, possibly an old clay pit. Ten years later the manor of Stoke changed hands, including a field called Tylhurst, apparently described as being in Sowe (Walsgrave). Tilers might also be found closer to the city. In 1410 one such, John Hall, Tiler, was recorded as having recently lived on the north side of Gosford Street. Another, John Greene or Grove, described as a Tiler, held Earl's Mill at the north end of what is now Cox Street in 1410. In 1438 Richard Kerde, Tiler, held a house in Cross Cheaping on a twenty year lease., and as late as c.1600 Robert Swan, Tiler, was to be found living in West Orchard. It is not clear whether either of them had any kilns in the close confines of such urban locations.

In the fifteenth century the records become more straightforward and contain more detail. In a document of 1416 some idea can be gleaned of the environmental damage caused by the industry. In that year the manor changed hands. Thomas de Stoke granted to Thomas and Agnes Clement the lease together with woods, underwood (scrub) and tile-quarries, allowing them to use the trees for firewood and enclosures. They also gained the rights for taking wood to build houses and straw for thatching. In addition they were given 30 acres and three enclosed fields, Longcroft, Pekerscroft and Lewyncroft specifically for tiling at an annual rent of 40 shillings, with the rights to the shredding of trees there. Similarly in 1458 the Stoke close called Cleycroft changed hands, together with bitumen for tilemaking in a 50 year lease at an annual rent of 6s 8d. Once more was given the right to fell trees, inevitable in order to fire the kilns. The de Stoke family may have enjoyed wider dealings in tiles since they also had a residence at Polesworth in North Warwickshire, where there was at least one tile kiln also.

An indication of the distances purchasers of Stoke tiles might travel can be gauged by a transaction of 1415. In the accounts of the Cistercian Nunnery of Catesby (Northamptonshire) is the record of a purchase in that year of 700 tiles at Coventry, costing 4s 6d. This also indicates a cost of three tiles for a farthing, cheaper than pottery. It is not known for sure whether this purchase was for floor or roof tiles; the former seems more likely since there are numerous sources of good roof tiles much closer in Northamptonshire, where hewn limestone tiles were also common.

In the period 1455-66 are found the best documents for the industry's output. In 1455 Nicholas Dilcock of Biggin and Thomas Hatton of Stoke, tilemakers were bound to Richard Wade, a grocer from Coventry to the sum of £2 unless he received from them 1,000 tiles at Michaelmas for each of the next 10 years. Evidently he had paid up front at a rate of just over four tiles per farthing. Seemingly the costs had fallen in the 40 years since the 1415 purchase, probably as a result of competition. In that same year Nicholas Dilcock agreed to deliver before Pentecost (six weeks after Easter) to Robert Newell, a Coventry baker a total of 7,000 tiles as measured in Stoke, and furthermore to deliver to him each year at that time six quarter dry weight by gold and not by kiln. This last proviso is presumably to stop weighing of quantities before firing (he would receive less tiles if the clay was weighed wet, straight from the ground, since firing removed the water from the fabric of the clay). This may be to avoid genuine misunderstanding over weights but may also hint at concern over sharp practices, which were a constant problem for the authorities who tried to oversee Weights and Measures from an official Steelyard in the town. Officially marked steelyard weights are an occasional find in excavation.

Nicholas Dilcock seems to have made a success of his venture since in 1466 he was able to grant a 14 year lease on a Stoke cottage to Thomas Holas or Holyes, Tilemaker, with an option on a further six years. He also was able to pass to John Hickes Claypittes Close in Biggin and a wood in Biggin Grove. That the two went hand-in-hand indicates that here was another tiling concern.

The tiling community at the end of the fifteenth century almost disappears from view in documents, compared with what had gone before; the industry was in rapid decline. A William Nyx was described as being a tilemaker in 1510–11 and William Ruyley was recorded at his tile-house in 1516 with an assistant named Alice; there he died in that year, killed when another colleague, William Besworth, threw a lump of tiling clay at him. Later, in 1653, one Harry Crowder is mentioned as just previously living in a house in Stoke Biggin which had a tile kiln attached. In 1655 the manor of Aldermoor (Stoke Aldermoor) which had been carved out of Pinley was sold by the Lord of the Manor Edward Hill of Tixall. The sale expressly mentioned his tile kiln on Stoke Aldermoor.

Thus there is now probably more known about the history of the Stoke tile industry than any other of the medieval industries of Coventry. The industry was probably responsible for a degree of environmental blight since it dug enormous pits to extract clay, it deforested the parish for its fuel, it clouded the skies with smoke and it would have waterlogged the clay soils due to the loss of the trees. It also made Stoke rich. By the end of the fifteenth century it was becoming a place where rich men of Coventry began to build villas and retreats. In the mid-seventeenth century the county historian Sir William Dugdale remarked upon the fine residences built there, clustered around Stoke Row (probably well away from the claypits). The old clay-related names survived into the seventeenth century and a 1650s description of Biggin Hall made great play of every building on the site being fully tiled. But by the eighteenth century the industry had largely gone. The clay pits began to be filled in and turned into farmland. The new clay industry was brickmaking and for this new clay sources were found, north of Bishop Street (Pudding Pits) and Gulson Road (Brick Kiln Lane). Eventually almost every other field north of the ancient Far Gosford Street suburb would become a brick-field. Hillfields was built entirely of brick made from clay excavated on its doorstep. Today the traveller from Binley Road to Barras Green invariably passes by Stoke Row along the lane which still bears an evocative name, Clay Lane.

12

Moats and manors

'They resembled more fortresses than peaceful buildings for agricultural use.'
F. Goblet (1927) on the Cistercian Grange

In many of the surrounding villages and hamlets lie a number of sites of manor houses and moated sites, some coinciding, others not. They were constructed by a variety of groups: monastic, noble and mercantile middle class. Only a few of them have any visible trace above ground since many have been redeveloped or incorporated into the modern suburbs. However, enough survives of most to warrant discussion of the type in a local context. Coventry contained a large number of sixteenth- to seventeenth-century great houses, which were the centre of large post-medieval gentrified estates, sharing the sites of their medieval manorial predecessors. While these in many cases have been included in the list below, the redevelopment they represent means that they are best suited for the study of both the medieval and the immediate post-medieval and post-Dissolution city and its environs, rather than just the medieval. Theirs is a story of continuity with a particular comparative value since they were a long term success story. The concentration of such foci derives partly from the pull of the city, which from 1451 lay within its own county, the County of the City of Coventry. Those which were abandoned or dwindled away became derelict for a reason, be it economic, fashion or the long term unsuitability of their location.

THE SITES

The known medieval moated sites and manor houses in modern Coventry comprise:

Allesley Castle and Manor (Baronial: Lord Hastings)

Bell Green Manor House (minor local gentry)

Biggin Hall, Stoke (Benedictine Grange – St Mary's Priory, moated)

Binley Grange (Cistercian Grange – Coombe Abbey)

Caludon Castle and separate moat (Baronial: Lord de Seagrave/Mowbray Earls of Norfolk)

Cheylesmore Manor, moated (Baronial/Royal: Earls of Chester/Crown)

Crow Moat, Spon End (?minor local gentry)

Ernesford Grange, moated (Cistercian Grange – Coombe Abbey)

Fletchamstead Manor, Canley (Hermitage/Knights Templar/Knights Hospitaller)

Foleshill Hall (minor local gentry)

Harnall Moat, Primrose Hill, Hillfields (Benedictine grange – St Mary's Priory)

Hawkesbury Grange, moated (Benedictine Grange – St Mary's Priory)

Henley Green Moat (Seagrave of Caludon/ St Mary's Priory)

Horewell Grange (Cistercian Grange – Stoneleigh Abbey)

Keresley Castle, moated (?minor local gentry)

Magpie Hall, Walsgrave (minor local gentry)

Moreall Manor, Canley, moated (Bagot, minor local gentry)

New House, Radford, moated (John Hales, Clerk to the Hanaper – a post-Dissolution redevelopment of Whitmore Grange, below).

New Lands Manor, Exhall (Benedictine Grange – St Mary's Priory)

Pinley Manor, moated (Langley – minor local gentry)

Shortley Manor, moated (Langley – minor local gentry)

Stivichall Grange (Helenhull or Kingshill), Stivichall, moated (Cistercian Grange – Stoneleigh Abbey)

Stoke Manor (de Stoke – minor local gentry)

Walsgrave Hall (minor local gentry)

Walsgrave Moat (minor local gentry)

Whitmore Grange, Radford (Benedictine Grange – St Mary's Priory)

Whoberley Hall (minor local gentry)

Willenhall Hall (Benedictine Grange – St Mary's Priory)

Woodway Grange (Attoxhale, Erneys Piece, later Deane's Farm), Henley Green, moated (Erneys family from 1279, later Benedictine Grange – St Mary's Priory)

Some of these sites have been chosen for further discussion in this chapter since they have been the subject of specific archaeological research or excavation up to this point (see below). It serves however to compare the various moats which can be characterised from records or visible remains.

57 Caludon Castle. The remaining north wall of the fourteenth-century Great Hall

Occasionally there are the merest glimpses of the manor houses which lay scattered around Coventry. Unlike many other counties in the medieval period, the great noble families of England did not dominate the landscape with vast estates, but the landscape of this county was peppered with many smaller holdings of what might be termed minor local gentry. While this may have ensured that none became too powerful, it also meant that the rate of attrition was particularly high. Some fell victim, however briefly, to debilitating confiscations, such as Allesley castle, when Henry de Hastings backed the rebel Montfortian cause against Henry III and was captured at the battle of Evesham in 1265, alongside his equally ill-starred neighbour Stephen de Seagrave of Caludon Castle (*57*).

Thomas Mowbray, Duke of Norfolk's abortive and ill-advised duel against Henry, Earl of Derby, at Gosford Green in 1398, meant that Caludon once more was deprived of its overlord, who died of plague in Venice within a year; he was a broken man. While on both occasions, the Caludon lands were restored to the family, as they were too at Allesley, the effects of royal confiscations were to freeze the assets, appoint overseers, scrutinise the accounts, and exact a heavy toll. Such estates rarely had the opportunity to flourish thereafter. In a survey of Allesley in 1387 the Seagrave seat was clearly in a parlous state:

> And there is within the site of the manor a hall with two chambers annexed, one in front and the other in the rear, the one covered with shingle and the other with tiles. Also within the bounds there is one large chamber with two other chambers covered with shingle and a small chapel annexed covered with lead and altogether ruinous. Beyond the bounds are one long bakehouse covered with tiles and a grange covered with shingles and ruinous.

Here, as elsewhere, decay might have been a result of the Black Death or other plague; the effects locally could be dramatic. The Black Death was the most famous plague of them all, visiting England disastrously on numerous occasions from 1349. According to the City annals, the city was hit in 1349, 1359 and 1368. However, Coventry is known to have been badly hit by pestilence on at least two other occasions. The medieval travel-writer William Worcestre recorded in 1480 that his grandmother Agnes was the daughter of Adam Botoner, gentleman of Coventry (the Botoners built St Michael's tower and endowed the Charterhouse). While that link is perhaps unremarkable he also records that Botoner died in 'the great plague of Coventry in 1386'. His infant grandmother was in Bristol and escaped. Later a post-medieval chronicle records that Coventry was hit by plague in 1478-9, with a death-toll of 4,450 (this figure seems implausibly high and may relate to a wider area). Thus while for the country as a whole the Black Death is seen as the nadir of a disastrous half-century in national fortunes, for Coventry the difficulties were longer-lived and plague was a regular, unwelcome visitor.

Plague might well have accounted for Moreall Manor in modern Canley. Latterly known as Canley Moat, the Manerium de la Mor (Manor of the Moor) was recorded in the Stoneleigh Ledger Book in the fourteenth century. However, when Thomas Burton of Canley took over in 1585 his main holding was the moated site, where he found no house. He had to build a new More Hall, as it became known, from scratch.

In cases where key family members died, the succession in title would be unclear and many manors became a bitter battleground over which rival claimants fought. This happened spectacularly at Shortley in Coventry. Here, however, it was not because of plague but because of different interpretations of how the manor was held, by whom and from whom.

In 1358, on the death of the Dowager Queen Isabella, Edward the Black Prince in his own register made it clear that he

> considered the manor and town of Coventry his by right and ordered Sir Hugh de Hopwas to seize it on his behalf.

This is perhaps overweening speech, requiring not so much a seizure as a declaration of intent. By the 1380s the dependent manor of Shortley was a matter of dispute between rival claimants. On the one side lay Baldwin Freville II of Tamworth, whose father (Baldwin I) had been companion and bodyguard to Edward the Black Prince (and Lord of Wyken) and who had been paid £40 a year out of Cheylesmore Manor. The Prince's death had deprived the Frevilles of power and prestige, plus their place in the Coventry scheme. On the other side was the Langley family who had held the dual manors of Shortley and Pinley for generations but whose place in the former was at the will (or whim) of the Lord of Cheylesmore (formerly the Black Prince, who ratified their position in 1364; after 1377 Richard II as Earl of Chester was Lord).

Matters were complicated when Frevilles and Langleys both pressed claims to be identified as founders of St Anne's Charterhouse in the period 1381-5 along with competing junior lines of the same families. Freville even gave permission for the land to be given to the Carthusians despite his own claim being under scrutiny. In a society where claims were often backed up the addition of dependent claims, however spurious, with enforcement carried out by violent trespass and takeover of land, the ultimate arbiter would always be the Crown. It took a whole generation to settle the Shortley question. In the end John Langley of Atherstone on Stour was victorious through litigation and in early 1417 he regained the manor lost 30 years before. It had changed hands six times between 1381 and 1400. So relieved must Langley have been that a magnificent wall-painting of that year, commemorating the completion of the Charterhouse refectory, depicts the newly returned Lord of the Manor, John, as the centurion Longinus, pointing at the crucified Christ and uttering the words of the Gospels (in Latin) 'Surely this man was the Son of God'. However the results of the protracted struggle were a Charterhouse which languished for a generation, lacking proper funding. Their endowment remained insufficient as late as 1421 when Henry V further endowed the house 'on account of their poverty'. Even under Henry VI there was still concern. Furthermore, the result for the manor itself was unmitigated disaster. An Inquisition Post-Mortem taken on a Langley family member in 1489 stated that he had owned 100 acres of pasture in Shortley and 6 acres of moor and pasture in Stoke. It went on to recount that:

> There once lay there a certain manor house, then called the Manor of Shortley. The manor house is a complete ruin and lies waste.

It had surely been a Pyrrhic victory for the Langleys. The location of the ill-fated Shortley manor house is probably that of St Anne's Chapel, over the river from Charterhouse, where the 1393 endowment grant of lands to the new Holy

Trinity Guild records that the chapel stood 'with house, garden and land of a pond running around them, lying next to Langley Grove'. Holy Trinity Guild rentals for the late fifteenth century continue to mention the chapel which was in regular use, but of the manor house, the contemporary sources agree on its demise by their very silence.

The violent trespass mentioned above was all too common. From the Exchequer Receipts for 1336 comes evidence that no one was unaffected by such things, nor was anyone too exalted to stoop to such bullying tactics. In the Warwick Bag Roll is the complaint of the Prior of St Mary's that his manors at Newlands (Exhall), Sowe and Hawkesbury had been sacked by his neighbours Sir Thomas and William Erneys of Attoxhall. The Erneys were certainly in a long running dispute with the Priory but they seem to have been acting with the open connivance of Queen Isabella, whose own relationship with the Priory was rocky. She had apparently also destroyed all the Priory's hay at Fyntford (now a deserted hamlet where the River Avon is crossed by the A45) and had also engaged in cattle rustling and seizure or slaughter of the Priory's horses.

Close to the modern suburb and medieval hamlet of Canley, lay the hamlets of Horewell and Fletchamstead. Originally sparsely populated, the two were dominated by the Cistercian and Knights Templar/Hospitaller monastic orders. Cheek-by-jowl stood the Stoneleigh Abbey grange of Horewell, close to Canley Road and the independent hermitage of Fletchamstead. In the middle of the twelfth century there is evidence that Fletchhamstead was being considered as a possible site for what became Stoneleigh Abbey. At around that time there stood a hermitage there, founded under Henry I (1100-35) run by a hermit named Gerard. With Stoneleigh's interest moving elsewhere, Gerard spent his remaining years in isolation, in his complex which comprised a chapel and other buildings, just south of what is now Torrington Avenue and north of the railway line. He died and was buried there. His replacement was one Brian Lomsey, who was subsequently manipulated into going on a diplomatic mission to Ireland by his brother Peter, a Templar Knight. Brian died on the mission and his hermitage was transformed into a Templar manor, a state confirmed under Henry II (1154-89). To what extent they rebuilt the manor is not known, but the hermitage chapel remained, as the centre of a 360-acre estate, run by a Knight-Priest and a small staff. When the Templars were disbanded by the Crown in the early fourteenth century, the property came into the hands of their rival, acquisitive military order, the Knights Hospitaller, with whom it remained until the Dissolution in 1539. Observation of service trench-digging near Torrington Avenue has suggested that stone structural remains lie up to two metres below the modern ground surface which may derive from the manor, and if so, this is a rare Templar/Hospitaller survival. Although the manor was later rebuilt on

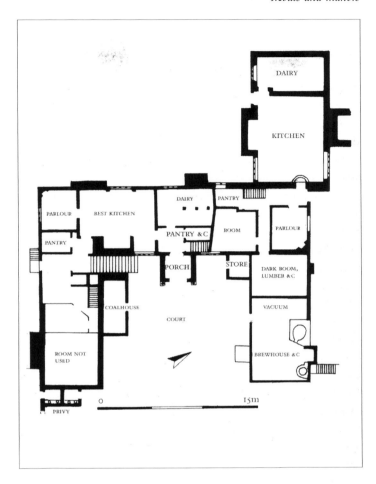

58 The first
Fletchamstead Hall
(formerly Templar/
Hospitaller Manor).
Demolished by
1766; redrawn from
a document in the
Shakespeare Birthplace
Trust

another, nearby site and became known as Fletchamstead Hall, the buildings
and fish ponds on the earlier site, just to the south, lingered long enough to be
mapped in 1597 and a seventeenth-century plan drawn of them, before they can
be seen to have disappeared from another map of 1766 (*58*).

Even apparently successful manors can over the years become effectively lost.
In the fourteenth and fifteenth centuries there were repeated references to the
manor of the de Stoke family. Unsurprisingly this was Stoke Manor. It appears to
have been a quite grand affair as a number of brief descriptions of 1349 show:

> Grant by John de Stoke to his son Robert and his wife Margaret … two chambers and a
> garden in Stoke Manor with free access, one chamber called 'le Knytteschambr', the other is
> built over the entrance gate, whilst the garden lies between the wine-store [another version
> also has a pond on this side] and Stoke Chapel's graveyard.

Clearly the manor lay somewhere close to St Michael's church in Stoke. Its exact location has yet to be pinpointed. Not all such manors continue to elude archaeologists and historians, however, as will be seen from the following high-profile examples.

BIGGIN HALL

Biggin Hall stood in the area which today lies south of Coventry and North Warwickshire Cricket Ground below the Crescent which still bears its name. It is today covered in houses of the period 1900-1930 but its estate can still be made out in the modern property boundaries. It benefits from excellent documentation, having been originally a moated grange of St Mary's Benedictine Priory; after the Dissolution of the monasteries in 1539 it came into the hands of the Drapers Company and thereafter was purchased by the City Council. Thus a full sequence of detailed deeds, leases and topographical descriptions exist for it from the fourteenth to the nineteenth centuries. It has also been mapped in 1759, 1841, 1852 and 1887. If that were not enough its buildings were both drawn and painted in the late eighteenth and early nineteenth centuries.

The first inkling of the extent of the former grange is gained in a lease of 1653, recalling an earlier one of 1611. The lease describes the buildings of the property of Biggin Hall. This was a former grange of exceptional size and quality:

> The Hall, comprising twenty tiled bays with a lean-to porch door, with an interior courtyard, a one-bay gatehouse with a pair of gates, a foldyard, a two-bay barn with hogsty, a four-bay barn to the north with an adjoining shore used as an oxhouse, a three-bay adjacent barn with a two-bay shore, a gatehouse with two arches. Old Orchard, New Orchard wherein stands a dovehouse, a grass pleck (between the fish ponds and the house) paled along the pond side to the house side, another adjacent little pleck (four yards long by ten yards broad), another grass pleck upon the western side of the house, a tiled house of office (toilet), Sanpit Close, Woodcroft, Cley Close, the adjacent Dove House Close.

Only one year later leave was granted for the new leaseholder to demolish within two years 16 bays of the Hall buildings, described as a 'vast olde building and much out of repayre'. He was also to build five new bays to join the remaining three old ones to make the complex fit for habitation. The new work was to be in timber.

By 1667 there seems to have been more activity there since the immediate area was more intensively farmed. A third fish pond was described and a hopyard had been established near the house. In 1687 a lease described the orchard as containing apples, pears, cherries, plums and wardens.

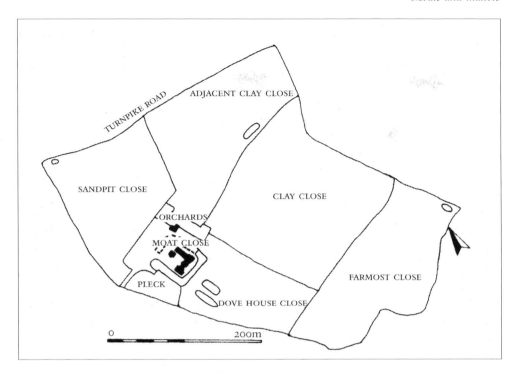

59 Biggin Hall; the former Grange estate. The names show it was little changed from 1611 and probably earlier. Composite from maps and documents, 1611-1759

Until 1756 the leases then record no change to the hall until, in that year, permission is given to replace a brewhouse chimney and leave given to demolish a small building at the end of the stable. By 1800 the hopyard had gone and the orchards had become gardens. In 1814 the field names had for the most part changed (a common occurrence in the eighteenth century), but the changeover can be traced field for field. During this time the estate was mapped (1759) (*59*) and the Hall's remains drawn (1804; 1820) (*60*). It was mapped again in 1841 for the tithing of Stoke and the final map was the Ordnance Survey of 1888, which finally put the whole area into a standard scale, just before the estate was subsumed under modern housing.

The seventeenth-century descriptions and, in particular, the late eighteenth-century antiquarian view from the west (*60*) can be put into the mapped context to create a typical late medieval manor house, comprising four sides of a rectangle arranged around a courtyard, the whole surrounded by a water-filled moat. The south-west wing was a two-storey structure of stone surmounted by timber framing and a tiled roof. This was probably the remaining three bays

60 Biggin Hall(Benedictine Grange); pencil and grey wash *c*.1804. *Birmingham City Archives, Aylesford Collection; Volume 1: Country Seats and Castles, fol 72*

of the medieval structure, left after the 1653-5 alterations and a double lancet window at ground floor level is clearly of medieval origin. Behind that lay the main south range, the domestic part of the manor. It had a porch projecting into the courtyard and a flanking south-east wing balancing that on the south-west. These, however, were uniformly rendered as if of one finish, perhaps the 15 new bays of 1653-5. An outbuilding is shown protruding into the left foreground at a position not repeated on the early maps.

The drawing of 1820 shows what is probably the same range but considerably dilapidated from its former glory. It may have been rebuilt once more, but with considerably less vision and little eye to the fast diminishing glory of the complex. Briefly the hall became the subject of antiquarian interest in the nineteenth century. The seminal Coventry antiquarian, Thomas Sharpe wrote of it in 1835. Unfortunately he accorded it only the briefest of descriptions, clearly at a loss to understand its place in the landscape. Rev Blythe in his *History of Stoke* (1897) could add little, although he was intrigued by the number and quality of historic remains which the hamlet of Biggin and neighbouring Pinley were held to contain.

Between 1841 and 1888 the fish ponds were filled in and the moat suffered the same fate in preparation for the construction of housing after 1888. It retains a tremendous archaeological potential since such moats and water-filled features rarely dry out and are deep enough to have survived the type of buildings which supplanted it. Parts of the hall were clearly cellared, on the evidence of the 1820 drawing. Also there is a good chance that a pre-moat manor survives beneath the platform which, as was seen in excavations at Ernesford Grange, would have been created by the upcast from the first digging of the moat.

ERNESFORD GRANGE

Archaeological excavations took place at Ernesford Grange in 1971-3. However, it remains one of the most puzzling of the city's moated sites since it represents (comparatively) the complete economic failure of a site. It is today a Scheduled Ancient Monument off Princethorpe Way, close to a school which bears its name.

Ernesford was probably taken into the lands of the Cistercian Abbey at Coombe between 1250 and 1279, when Henry de Erneford, already the private owner of the site, entered the Cistercian order as a monk. By 1291 the site had achieved the full status of a Grange when it was described as such in the Great Church Taxation by Pope Nicholas IV.

The excavations of 1971-3 showed that the moated platform was created by the upcast of digging the moat. That upcast sealed the flattened remains of an earlier layout of buildings which probably comprised the original de Erneford manor, that of Henry's father, Robert, who left it to Henry in his will of *c*.1250. Ironically Robert was sufficiently anti-monastic in his sentiments to introduce the proviso that Henry should not leave it to a monastic house. Coombe was already showing an interest and the Abbot had acquired hunting rights there by 1257. The independent-spirited Henry subsequently took holy orders by 1279, circumventing the whole issue; his goods and lands passed to Coombe upon his profession as a Cistercian.

If the change of ownership proved the undoing of the former de Erneford manor, it gave rise to grand new quarters which were in the finest Cistercian Grange tradition and of sumptuous proportions, true to the statement by the Belgian historian F. Goblet (above).

Built upon the moat upcast, which continued to preserve the earlier manor site, a range of stone and timber buildings was constructed at Ernesford which comprised a hall range and a separate kitchen range (*61*). To the former was attached an enormous garderobe pit. Entrance was gained by a causeway and stone and timber bridge over the eastern side of the moat. The platform outside the buildings was gravelled or cobbled. The complex was put up in two distinct

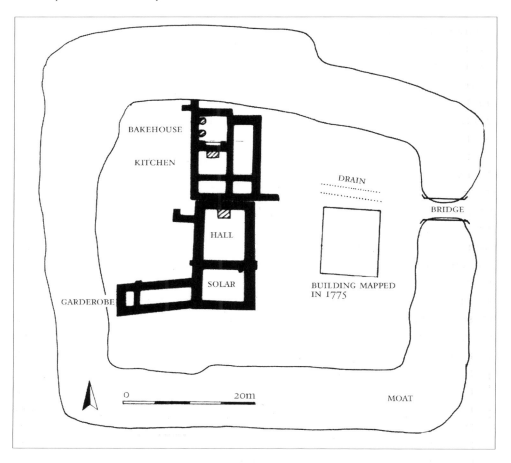

61 Ernesford Grange(Cistercian) from excavations, 1971-3

episodes, with the hall range probably the earlier, the kitchen later squeezed into the limited space available between hall and moat. The positions of the two ranges, when both standing, left a portion of the remaining platform, perhaps 20 per cent of the area, largely inaccessible except through the buildings. Unless there was some specific reason for ensuring the privacy of this small area to the west of the buildings (and no one can be sure there was not), such planning might be seen as a rather inept use of the limited platform space. A third range may have been present, since there is a building shown just inside the causeway entrance on a map of 1775-8. However, it is not known whether this was a post-medieval construction or a medieval survival, whether in use or ruined. It did not survive to the end of the nineteenth century and its site was not included in the excavations of 1971-3.

The most curious aspect of Ernesford Grange is the rather abrupt end to the evidence for occupation. After a clear period of use there exists no evidence for occupation of the buildings after *c*.1350. As if to emphasise the finality of the episode, the large garderobe pit was deliberately filled in. Within it was a primary dump of pottery which included both ceramics of late thirteenth or early fourteenth century, along with a twelfth-century vessel which was certainly an antique by that stage. While this date is of course nationally significant, since 1349 marks the first (and worst) visit of the Black Death to England, this alone seems too bland and simplistic a reason to which to attribute the abandonment of a complex of high-quality buildings when the same plague affected the whole area, particularly the cities. To date there has been no purely archaeological evidence for similar contemporary derelictions hereabouts although it is abundantly clear from documents that the city and its outlying villages were appallingly affected.

A contributory cause of difficulty seems to lie in the financial management of the Grange's mother house, Coombe Abbey. When the abbey was taxed in the great ecclesiastical taxation of Pope Nicholas IV in 1291, it was the richest house of any order in Warwickshire (St Mary's Priory, the natural front-runner, was only just emerging from decades of poverty brought about by damaging litigation). However within one generation the abbey was petitioning the Crown for financial help in 1322. The reason given for this dire state of affairs was 'defective rule'.

Study of the 1291 ecclesiastical taxation indicates that Ernesford Grange had attached to it a wholly inadequate estate, and was by far the smallest of the Coombe granges. In itself this is not significant but it is also the lowest valued land of any of the Coombe granges, less than half the yearly value per acre of its nearest neighbour, Binley Grange (which was twice its area). Regardless of the amount of this land which was given over to pasture, Ernesford was assessed as having the highest ratio of stock to land of any of the granges, more than twice the amount, and three times the density of the two largest, home granges (near Coombe) and 60 per cent greater than at nearby Binley (the highest valued land of all the granges). It may be significant that when mapped for its post-medieval landlord, the Earl of Craven, in 1775-8 the grange, still distinct from the Parish of Binley out of which it had been carved, was surrounded by its distinctively-shaped estate nestling on the Sowe valley, jutting out into the neighbouring parishes to Binley's west. The farm was a mere 82 acres (*62*).

It seems that Ernesford Grange may have suffered from a simple form of financial mismanagement: overgrazing. It carried with it simply too small a land holding to be viable in the long term. Its agricultural functions could easily be transferred to Binley and with no farm to oversee, the buildings could be abandoned. Curiously, in neighbouring Willenhall, the hamlet of Newton,

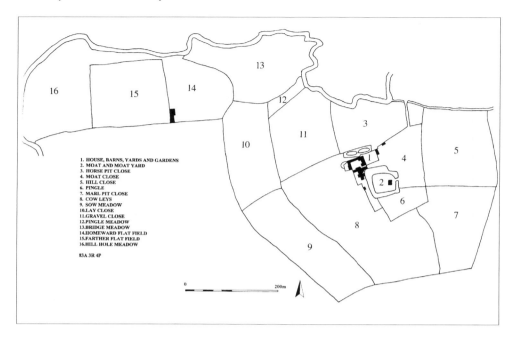

1. HOUSE, BARNS, YARDS AND GARDENS
2. MOAT AND MOAT YARD
3. HORSE PIT CLOSE
4. MOAT CLOSE
5. HILL CLOSE
6. PINGLE
7. MARL PIT CLOSE
8. COW LEYS
9. SOW MEADOW
10. LAY CLOSE
11. GRAVEL CLOSE
12. PINGLE MEADOW
13. BRIDGE MEADOW
14. HOMEWARD FLAT FIELD
15. FARTHER FLAT FIELD
16. HILL HOLE MEADOW

83A 3R 4P

0   200m

*62 Ernesford Grange: the former Grange estate. Redrawn from the Craven Estate Maps 1775-8.
Warwickshire Record Office*

adjacent to the modern London Road, had also been largely abandoned
probably at about this time, despite being the home of one of the Benedictine
Priory's great Tithe Barns, off St James' Lane. The ramifications of the loss of
Coombe's stabilising presence in the area may have been a contributory factor
in an age when crop-failures and resultant famine were rife (*c*.1310-20) and the
plague (1349-*c*.1375) and the great plague of Coventry (1386) struck repeatedly
with indiscriminate frenzy. One late reference may inadvertently make a canting
allusion to the demise of Ernesford Grange. The Benedictine Priory's own
Cartulary referred in 1410-11 to its Binley rental and its local neighbours:

> Manor in Erneford within Binley parish from which Abbot and Convent of Combe and
> successors will take all tithes etc of the manor if they hold in their own hands or set to farm.
> Abbot and convent and predecessors held the manor in gift.

The key word is 'if'. The status of the erstwhile grange, here called a manor, was
clearly an equivocal issue, perhaps neither grange nor tenant farm; in fact the
archaeological record suggests it had already been abandoned.

CHEYLESMORE MANOR

The only manor house which stood within the actual walls of the late medieval city of Coventry was that of Cheylesmore, commanding the large Cheylesmore Park. The north range gate-house survives today and constitutes the city's modern Register Office (*colour plate 21*). The east range almost survived to the present, being demolished in *c*.1955. Contemporary photographs show that within a nineteenth-century skin of brick, elements of the medieval range remained, particularly a distinctive crown post roof of the fourteenth century. However a great deal more has been learnt about the manor as a result of extensive excavations in 1992 which concentrated on the east and south ranges (*colour plate 22*).

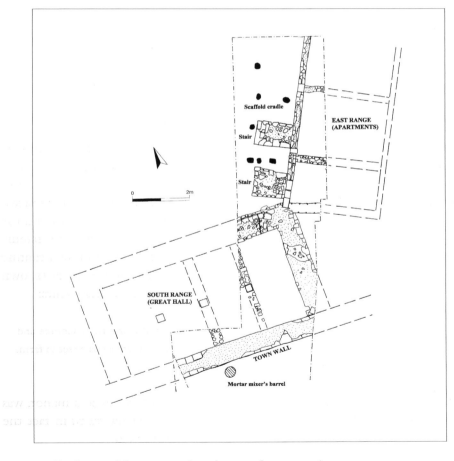

63 Cheylesmore Manor: east and south ranges from excavations, 1992

Cheylesmore Manor was inextricably linked to the town as it grew, and so close did it lie physically, that it was taken in at Crown request when the walls were built in the fourteenth century. However, it was also to be regarded as a separate entity, since this was to become the true *camera principis* in Coventry, the seat of royal power and home to princes, kings and queens.

From its earliest mention in documentary sources the manor was always presented along with its park: high quality land stocked with raw materials and game. However, it was also surrounded by a ditch, to demark the distinct jurisdictions of manor, town and friary (Greyfriars). Proximity to and association with the newly arrived Franciscan Friars in the 1230s cemented the urban link and it was near enough to the city to command adequate labour. Originally the manor was established by the Earls of Chester, probably the last of the direct family line, Ranulf de Blondeville, whose seat was moved there from the fortified but ill-suited Coventry Castle in the town centre in the early thirteenth century. The Earldom of Chester was one of the highest ranked titles in the country and was for many years seen as a foil for the equally powerful neighbour, the Earldom of Leicester. The rivalry between the two achieved a certain notorious equilibrium. When the Chester line died out in 1232 the estate passed to the last Earl's nephew and thence by 1243 to the de Montalt family, not nobility but one time stewards of the Earl of Chester, perhaps high-ranking civil servants in modern terms. In the Post Mortem Inquisition of Robert de Montalt in 1275, Cheylesmore was described as a 'Capital Messuage'. By the time it is mentioned in a Fine of 1327, it has been termed 'Manor'.

In archaeological terms the earliest manor buildings appear to have been laid out in the late twelfth or early thirteenth century over levelled ridge-and-furrow agriculture and isolated rubbish pits. The south range comprised a massively constructed stone hall-keep measuring 18m (60ft) x 9m (30ft) and containing four bays at 4.5m (15ft) centres. The walls were 2.6m (8ft 6in) thick, pierced by arrow-loops at ground level, as indicated by the sill of one which survived. At ground level the hall was subdivided into four rooms at the bay divisions by secondary walls, suggesting that the hall space, for entertaining, was on the first floor. The ceiling or floor of that hall, was supported upon an axial row of timbers set upon stone pads (*63*).

The first east range, although contemporary, was far flimsier, and possibly all timber-framed, comprising stone post-settings with sole-plates between, marking bays of 3m (9 ft) width. The longevity of this early east range is unknown but it appears to have been replaced, probably in the fourteenth century, by a successor on almost the same footprint. This was squeezed into the available space and its south-west corner was actually built into the north-east corner of the adjacent hall-keep. Parallel with the new range lay a line of post-holes marking the site of the builders' scaffolding used to erect the structure. The new range comprised sandstone dwarf walls 0.6m (2ft) thick which supported timber framing. In total the range measured 22m (72ft) x 7m (23ft). At ground floor level it was subsequently and unequally divided into separate rooms, again by stone dwarf walls (63). In each room the floor level was slightly lower than the courtyard, producing the effect of a semi-basement. Curiously, there was no means of access into the building from the courtyard at ground level. However, this apparent shortfall can be explained by the presence of two massive stone bases against the courtyard-facing wall. These were all that remained of two stair bases which gave access to the first floor. It is unclear whether they were contemporary or whether one had replaced the other.

Numerous masons' marks decorated the exterior dwarf wall and the quality of stonework far exceeded that of the older south range. The roof of the new range, glimpsed in 1955 when the last vestiges of the superstructure were demolished, was clearly of high-quality crown-post construction. These were new apartments of great architectural merit and were probably fit for royalty.

In 1327-8, with the last of the Montalt Earls of Chester dying without an heir, the manor reverted to the new king, the young Edward III and his brother John of Eltham. They gave it to their mother, Queen Isabella, the widow of Edward II as her dower house. Subsequently on her death the gift of the manor was conferred upon Edward III's son, Edward the Black Prince, newly created Duke of Cornwall and Earl of Chester. His untimely death in 1376, a year before his father, in time brought the manor into the hands of the Crown in the form of his son, the young Richard II in 1377.

The immense construction programme of the town wall, begun in the 1350s, soon reached the area of the manor. With a royal grant of unlimited stone from the park, the king ensured that his manor was encompassed within the city. Its economy was tied to that of the booming city, although at the expense of its physical separation from the park. It is possible that from this time the original king's park ditch began to be filled in out of necessity now that the manor had become a true part of the town.

Excavation has shown that this building work took place at the expense of elements of the manor. The fortified south range was partly dismantled, losing its south wall, and (necessarily) its roof. This line was now occupied by the town wall which was built with a remarkable precision, so far encountered nowhere else in the two and a quarter mile circuit of the wall. It seems likely that the range was then re-roofed and became effectively a lean-to structure, utilising the new defensive capability of the town wall. The repair needed may be hinted at in a reference in the state Patent Rolls in 1385 to sell wood from the park and 'apply the proceeds to the repair of the park pales and of the manor house'. Ironically, in terms of defensive potential, the remaining walls of the old south range were actually thicker than the new town wall itself.

Repair of such a major building complex was, however, a regular requirement. A reference in the Black Prince's Register in 1360 and corroborated in the State Papers records:

> to the auditors of the account of Nicholas Michel, the Prince's Receiver of Coventry, to allow the said Nicholas, on his account, certain expenses which he has acquired ... about the repair of a chamber within the Prince's Manor of Cheilesmore.

The manor may not have been a regular or preferred port of call for the young King Richard II since in 1398, the night before he attended the infamous lists at Gosford Green, he stayed with Sir William Bagot at Baginton Castle, despite stopping off to hear three masses at the Charterhouse on the way to the tournament. Both Charterhouse and Gosford Green are less than a mile from Cheylesmore Manor.

Later in 1421, the King (then Henry V) gave licence in the Patent Rolls for:

> Robert Castell, steward of the Manor of Chailesmore, to receive twelve oaks within the park of Chailesmore for the repair of the manor and also to cut down underwood for sale to the value of 40 marks (£27 6s 8d) and apply that sum to the repair by the advice and supervision of Adam Deyster of the town of Coventry; as the King understands from his information that the Manor is ruinous and has great need of repair.

Clearly Henry had not visited the manor in some time, relying on his stewards and local officials to keep him informed.

Wheels of government grind exceedingly slowly and it was only in the following year that the state Charter Rolls issued orders for the oaks to be felled. In the Bailiff's Accounts of the Duchy of Cornwall are references to ongoing repairs to parts of the manor. In 1431-2 *le Gatehous* is mentioned, as are the *Magne Aula* or Great Hall (the south range), the camerae (apartments), stables and 'le foryerd' (an outer court), while repairs detailed in the same accounts in 1473-4 indicate a level of privacy from the town in mentioning repairs to '*divers plaunchers* [planks] *of le drawbridge*', clearly indicating the presence of a ditch around at least the approach to the manor. In that same year the roof was repaired since the bailiffs had to pay a *tegulator* or tiler.

How effective such repairs were is difficult to say with certainty since when the great traveller John Leland passed through Coventry in the 1530s, he described the Manor as 'a palace ... now somewhat in ruin'. Similarly, Henry VIII's commissioners, when they came to suppress the nearby Franciscan Friary in 1539, found 'an old manor of the king's called Chyldesmore'. They added 'the hall is down'.

The south range, the hall, clearly ruinous by the mid-sixteenth century, did not survive the slighting of the City walls in 1662. The King wrote to the earl of Northampton to complain that part of his house had been destroyed when the wall was taken down and ordering that it be rebuilt. This was only part of the story, however, since a commonwealth survey of the manor in 1659 summed up the remains as

> all that capital messuage or mansion house called Cheylesmore Manor House with the barns, stables, outhouses, orchards, yards and backsides etc. consisting of about ten bays of old decayed building.

The archaeological evidence indicates that the rebuilding of the south range never did take place. The east range was subjected to numerous repairs, reframed and encased in brick. The Victorian Coventry historian, Benjamin Poole, wrote in 1847 in his book *Coventry: its history and antiquities*:

> The buildings on the eastern side are in many parts raised upon stone walls of great strength (he had no idea of the south range since they were below ground), but a close investigation is necessary to discover the few traces of its former importance.

Later, when he reprinted in 1870, Poole added:

> Little or nothing now remains to show what this estate was in the ancient times … the land still exists; but its grand features and old furnishings are all gone…. The principal dwelling, and the gateway now standing in Cheylesmore, may supply some idea of the general outline of the manor house, but nothing more. Some vestiges of ancient stone walls are to be traced but rebuildings, repairs, and fallings away, have entirely destroyed the character of the original.

Such has been the value of modern archaeological investigation, even 40 years after the last of the buildings had been demolished, that Poole's lament has been proved unfounded. In addition to recovering and understanding the layout of some of the buildings, the finds from the excavations have given a rich insight into the workings of this royal manor, part of – yet distinct from – the city as a whole, as will be seen elsewhere in this volume. The site is now built over by apartments but the east and south ranges are protected under a specially-formulated foundation layout and design, sympathetic to the buried structures and deposits.

13

Feeding the city

'Whitmore Manor, wood, grove, park and fields, brought together from gifts and purchases. Edward III gave permission to enclose and let out 433 acres of waste and wood in the manor and to impark it.' St Mary's Priory 1411

DIET AND ENVIRONMENT

As the size of the city grew, so also the challenges of trade increased in the most basic commodities. With space at a premium, there was less room for food production. While any town or village relies on its hinterland for the provision of food, this reliance is especially acute where population is at its most concentrated.

In Coventry excavations have revealed a variety of sites on which mammal, bird and fish bones, seeds and other environmental products have indicated the nature of foodstuff provisions together with biases and preferences which betray distinct levels of wealth, patterns which can be compared at other towns and cities.

Excavations in Coventry (1960-2004) have produced remains of the following edible species dating between the thirteenth and the sixteenth centuries:

Mammals: cow, sheep, goat, pig, red deer, roe deer, rabbit and brown hare

Birds: domestic fowl, domestic goose, teal, pheasant, woodcock, mute swan, grey heron, dove, black grouse, woodcock, partridge, wood pigeon and mallard

Freshwater fish: sturgeon, salmon, perch, eel, pike, dace, roach and tench

Sea fish: cod, herring, conger eel, haddock, plaice, ling, thornback ray and whiting

Molluscs: oyster, mussel, winkle, cockle and whelk

In addition are the remains of many species of, if not inedible, then not-normally-eaten species which both indicate the inevitable working animals and pets and also, more particularly, provide a great insight into the health and biodiversity of the landscape within and just outside the city walls, including vermin. The Latin name for most of the mollusc species is given in the absence of a common English name. The first three are variations of the common garden snail; most of the rest live in ponds and wet areas and come principally from the town ditch.

Mammal: dog, cat, horse, donkey, badger, black rat, house mouse, water shrew, common shrew, field vole

Birds: tufted duck, buzzard, godwit, great northern diver, hawk, crow, jackdaw, thrush, magpie, blackbird

Molluscs: *helix aspersa, helix hortensis, helix nemoralis,* wandering pond snail, *planorbarius corneus, gyraulus albus, anisus leucostoma, anisus vortex, bathyomphalos contortus, hippeutis complanatus, lymnaea peregra, succinea sp.*

Amphibian: frog

The majority of urban archaeological excavations produce a preponderance of the large mammal meat-bones which tend to survive better than their avian or fish counterparts due to their robustness, both in terms of surviving butchery and their longevity in the ground. In addition the recovery of all very small animal bones relies to some extent on appropriate and consistent recovery strategies, including sieving, being deployed with some degree of uniformity. Archaeology is anything but an exact science; archaeologists have rarely witnessed such broad-based strategies, and certainly not over a whole generation. As a consequence no two assemblages can be compared at every level with total confidence, since no two sites are the same. Care has to be taken when comparing any aspect of any two sites since the consumer is never exactly the same.

Excavations at the Cathedral and Benedictine Priory of St Mary provide valuable comparative assemblages in that the animal bone remains from specific rooms around the cloister derive from the diet of the monastic community while those from the nave of the Cathedral church come from the immediate post-Dissolution phase of the site's history; a site which is known to have become a dumping ground for the city's butchers in the nearby Butcher Rows. Their tipping incurred civic wrath at the turn of the sixteenth to seventeenth centuries. As illustration of the difficulties of comparing two assemblages, their waste from 1539 is totally different from that of the monks in 1538, despite occupying the same site.

Cattle in medieval towns were considered the meat of choice, partly because the animals took longer to rear and many of Coventry's cattle came overland with drovers from North Wales, possibly to be folded in the numerous barns and large open plots which characterised the area of Hill Street and Barras Lane. One large barn complex on that street even became known as The Welsh Inn. Fairs rather than markets were the centre of cattle trading, the two biggest fairs being at Coventry and nearby Birmingham. These were held only once or twice a year and were particularly celebrated occasions. Most cattle sold were beef animals; dairy herds were a poor investment, since medieval cows only lactated about 150 days a year, following calving. The remaining part of the year was mainly gestation. An illustration of the trade done at Coventry is a 1415 note on a purchase by the Cistercian Nuns from Catesby (Northamptonshire) who travelled 25 miles to the city to buy four cows at a total price of 31s 4d. The standard price of their other bovine purchases that year was 10s so it may be that their Coventry purchase included a bargain. Elsewhere in their accounts it can be seen that of nine calves born on their home grange that year, five went to the kitchen. There must have been very specific reasons to travel to Coventry to buy cattle when they clearly already had a herd of their own. It may have been to buy particular breeding animals or to replace those lost in one of numerous murrains or diseases which could and did decimate stock.

Towards the end of the fifteenth century there began an enclosure movement which increasingly turned former arable land over to sheep farming, effectively fossilising large areas of the distinctive earthworks of the former ridge-and-furrow cultivation regime which survive today. In some cases this involved forcible depopulation such as happened at the end of the fifteenth century at both Fletchamstead (by Henry Smyth, MP for Coventry) and Ryton-on-Dunsmore (by the Knights Hospitaller), where numerous families were ejected, losing their land and livelihoods. In some ways this echoed the widespread Cistercian practice of depopulating villages to begin sheep farming in the twelfth century, such as had been perpetrated by the monks of Coombe Abbey at the nearby villages of Upper and Lower Smite, near Ansty. Sheep were generally eaten only as old mutton, when they could no longer produce profitable fleeces.

Such a policy must have resulted in many dying either of old age or infirmity out in the fields or of cold over the winter. At such times their meat would have been suspect, even if someone retrieved the carcass before it became food for wild animals and carrion.

Since they needed less space than either cattle or sheep, pigs were kept in the woods, back yards and outhouses, they were kept as much for waste disposal, their diet supplemented by the likes of autumnal acorns, as for meat production and it is possible that it was the young of a large litter which were the first to be eaten, but only when the waste disposal provision outgrew the waste supply.

Dovecotes or pigeon-houses were common. The Prior of St Mary's owned two such buildings in Radford and off Dog Lane while the Prior of Kenilworth owned another off Greyfriars Lane. Most monasteries would have had one as would most manor houses. They continued to provide winter meat, at a time when most flocks of four-footed animals were being prepared for breeding.

While the loss of the monasteries in general meant that after centuries of reliance, many people lost their livelihoods, the redistribution of monastic lands in the early 1540s carried with it a risk that the new owners would choose to stock their lands and distribute the produce differently. Thus there was no guarantee that the farms which had supplied the monastery pre-1539, would continue to supply the city after 1539. Rampant inflation during the period also meant ordinary people's living standards were eroded.

MONASTIC FARMING

The strength of the assemblages from medieval sites such as monasteries is in their reliance on their own supply chains for their provisions. These supply chains can be demonstrated by historical precedents and documentary evidence. They were, by dint of their monastic rules, separate from the ordinary marketplace which facilitates a comparison with the consumption of ordinary people. Their farms were run to service the monastery, to the exclusion of all others. Although their administration certainly changed between the twelfth and sixteenth centuries, particularly in the fourteenth century when famine and plague forced a rethink on the way in which the manor farms or Granges were run, their *raison d'être* did not. It is clear from the early medieval period that the benefits of direct access to land and the fruits of the land, which were enjoyed by the monasteries, were shared by few others, perhaps only royal and baronial estates.

There is considerable evidence for monastic farms around Coventry, dominated by those of the three big monastic houses, Coombe and Stoneleigh (Cistercian Abbeys) and St Mary's (Benedictine Priory). However they were not alone and the lesser orders were also represented. At Fletchamstead lay the manor or *Camera* of the military monastic orders, first the Knights Templar (*c.*1150-1322), thereafter of the Knights Hospitaller (1322-1539). This covered 145ha (360 acres) and was answerable to the nearby Preceptory at Temple Balsall. It was staffed by a chaplain and a bailiff; the rest were tenant farm workers. On the other side of the city lay another Templar/Hospitaller manor at Ryton-on-Dunsmore, covering a further 121ha (300 acres). Closer to the city lay the principal lands of the Benedictine Hospital of St John the Baptist, a dependent house of St Mary's Priory but separately staffed and run. The site of the manor house remains unclear but the estate centred on the area around the Swanswell, formerly Potters Harnall and eventually to become Hillfields.

Many farms were major land-holding units, not all necessarily well-run. However not all could justifiably lay claim to the ubiquitous term of 'Grange', strictly speaking a Cistercian term for a farm within a day's journey of the mother house. Some were well-appointed; others often no more than a barn. Some were moated; others not. Almost all changed dramatically in the fourteenth century when plague and an exodus of tied workers from the countryside into the towns and cities meant they had to be increasingly farmed out to secular tenant farmers, rather than staffed by monks who oversaw landless peasants. Most were viable entities under either regime and many survived to become successful secular farms in the post-Dissolution world of the late sixteenth century. Some of the most spectacular are separately dealt with above (see Chapter 12). They all represent neat land parcels with intense pockets of surviving archaeology benefiting from good early descriptions (occasionally with surviving buildings, such as at Newlands Farm, Exhall). Their estates are often still traceable in the landscape and as a result their continued place as a subject of historical and archaeological study is justified by the influence they continue to exert in the changing face of the suburban and rural landscape.

Newlands Manor in Exhall had been a gift to the Priory by the Earl of Chester in the twelfth or thirteenth century. By 1291 the estate had probably coalesced into a single farming unit since it appeared by name '*Nova terra*' in a Papal taxation of the church in that year. State papers make it clear that in 1369 it was augmented by the enclosure of 100ha (246 acres) there. It subsequently figured strongly in the 1410-1 Priory Cartulary. It was visited by the bailiffs of the Court of Augmentations in 1547, trying to clear up the last of the former monastic assets not accounted for by the Crown. Let by the Priory just before the Dissolution (in a probable panic lease) to Michael Cameswell, brother of St Mary's last Prior, the Bailiffs found that the monks had reserved for themselves rights to:

the hall and chambers of the said mansion house, chapel, buttery, kitchen and stable, whenever it shall please them to sojourn there and they shall have liberty of fishing in the waters there and herbage for their horses within the park of Newlands.

This was probably the kind of package they had enjoyed for centuries, but it was the first time they had felt the need to commit such terms to paper. Events beyond their control ended their sojourns at Newlands, just as they did for all the orders at all the former granges and monastic manors across the country from 1536-9.

Some prospered under new ownership, such as St Mary's Benedictine Priory's estate at Henley Green, the moated site originally known as Attoxhale and later Erneys Piece. Documented in 1279 as dating back to the Norman Conquest, it was owned by the Erneys family from the 1270s before becoming a monastic holding. In 1581, a generation after the Dissolution, it was surveyed by the City Corporation under a new name, Deane's farm:

> There is the mansion house within the moat containing eight bays of building and four barns, all tiled, and one barn thatched. There is an orchard and a garden within the compass of the same moat wherein grow seven ashes. There is outside the moat a large court, wherein grow three ashes and in the same court stands one barn of four bays of building, tiled, another low barn of four bays, tiled and one other barn of two bays, thatched.

Clearly the monastic foundations were for the most part strong and the complete change of regime had hardly touched this farm, which continued to supply a hungry city up until the 1960s. Today the site is Woodway Grange where more modern buildings have recently been demolished; it remains one of the most important monastic granges in Coventry.

FISH PONDS, RIVERS AND THE SEA

Most monasteries, regardless of their order, included the provision of fish amongst their necessities, not least because their rules usually required its consumption on Fridays and during Lent, instead of meat. The Carthusians at the Charterhouse went one further and were vegetarian (but not a strict interpretation) so fish was even more important for them.

Monastic and ecclesiastical fish ponds are known in Coventry at many sites. The Benedictines had them at Pool Meadow (St Mary's precinct), Biggin Hall, Whitmore Grange and Newlands (they also had the tithes of all fish caught in the floodgates at Stivichall); the Cistercians at Coombe Abbey (home grange) and Ernesford Grange (two ponds); the Carthusians had seven ponds in the Charterhouse precinct; the Franciscans had one in their Greyfriars precinct while the Bishop enjoyed two ponds at his Palace. In addition most mills had fish stocks in their mill ponds, an unsatisfactory practice since a mill pond could be emptied totally to run the mill-wheel.

At the Charterhouse, animal bone remains were found in all periods of the site's occupation (despite the fact that the church might be expected to be kept scrupulously clean). Most, however, derive from the immediate pre- and post-Dissolution phase. Here too a relatively robust diet is indicated, although the presence of sea-fish alone seems at odds with the fact that the monastery had its own fish ponds within the priory precinct. The proximity of the then filthy River Sherbourne just downstream of the city may be an issue in understanding this trend, or the rapid exhaustion of pond stocks by the poor and the band of commissioners come to dissolve the house.

The supply of sea-fish to the city was very considerable. There must have been a sustained demand judging by the entrepreneurial spirit shown by some of the city's fishmongers. This included in the mid-fifteenth century the likes of Thomas Napton, who obtained crown licence to charter a ship out of Sandwich and trawl off Iceland (the licence was necessary since the fishing grounds were disputed with Norway and Denmark and ships, cargoes and even lives were forfeit for unlicenced trade). The trade of a Norfolk fisherman, Richard of Yarmouth, was sufficiently valued for he and his wife to be made members of Holy Trinity Guild. In the late 1430s cloth bound from Coventry for Norway was seized by the Crown at Boston. The same ship would probably have returned with fish. The papers were not in order and the requisite licence had clearly not been obtained; the cargo was seized and the voyage cancelled. To the fishmonger, however, any number of ports were open for trade and even if a whole ship could not be chartered, catches were brought in regularly while the weather was suitable. From Sandwich to Hull a dozen ports were available, and then Bristol too landed large quantities. As early as the thirteenth century Bergen in Norway was said to resemble a frontier town, a cosmopolitan place inhabited by almost every nationality in Europe including English, principally fishermen and traders who waited through the inclement winter months for the weather to abate.

Clearly Coventry's distance from the sea made no difference to her demand and she remained throughout the medieval period a ready market for marine fish. The species found in excavation seem to indicate a wide variety of taste, not too different from today. Cod and herring predominate in the archaeological record, but the occasional conger eel and thorn-back ray clearly betray an additional, more exotic taste, although these fish were probably occasional, incidental catches in the nets, not staple fare. During the siege of nearby Kenilworth castle

in 1266 a whale was brought to the King from Hull by his Serjeant John de
la Linde. Only a year later John had a whole fortified town named after him
(Lalinde in Dordogne, France). Fittingly that town had become known for the
quality of its fishing. Clearly anything could be had for a price. Most marine fish
were probably smoked as soon as they were landed, in quayside smoking houses
to preserve them on the overland journey (they may already have been in the
trawler's hold for quite some days or even weeks before they made port). Any
potential for what might pass as a sort of refrigeration was, of course, entirely
reliant on winter weather conditions and no more.

HUNTING PARKS

At Cheylesmore Manor, the royal manor site was a dominant landmark from
the thirteenth century. Built as the Earl of Chester's successor to his defunct
town-centre castle, it lay at the urban end of its distinctively oval-shaped park,
which was a self-contained estate of 209ha (516 acres). Throughout its life it was
renowned for the quantities of game it contained. Strict hunting laws introduced
earlier under Norman control ensured, however, that its bounty was largely
restricted to its baronial and later its royal lords. Archaeologically the range of
meat available at table may be seen as a general guide to a measure of true wealth,
that of open access to land ownership and its fruits. Cheylesmore remained
renowned for its venison as late as the seventeenth century, long after the feudal
lords had relaxed their grip and the estate had long been rented out by the
Crown. However, lying so close to the city, Cheylesmore must have presented
an inviting prize to any poacher who wished to procure a wider than average
range of meats either for his family or to pass on at a profit, though the penalties
for his being caught could be severe. Most telling are two documents which hint
at the bounty which the park produced. In 1249, Henry III ratified the grant of
the park by the last hereditary Earl of Chester in 1243 to his former steward and
heir Roger de Montalt:

> with free liberty to [him] and his heirs, whensoever they should come in person to
> Coventre, for hunting and hawking, within the precincts of the mannour.

On the death of the last de Montalt in 1328 the manor was settled on the dowager
Queen Isabella, widow of the murdered Edward II (1307-27) and mother of the
King Edward III (1327-77). During her son's reign, Isabella and her grandson,
Edward the Black Prince, were frequent visitors to the manor, her dower house
(although like all medieval nobles they constantly progressed from one property

to another). It remained the property of Edward III and his brother John of Eltham. After Isabella's death the manor passed in 1337 to the Black Prince, newly designated Duke of Cornwall and Earl of Chester, rightfully marked out as heir apparent, who would become the national hero of the battle of Crecy (1346) and adopted favourite of the City of Coventry. He continued to take a keen interest in the city and in his new investment. The Benedictine Priory Cartulary indicates that Cheylesmore park was, from the first, enclosed with a hedge. It was only in the mid-fourteenth century that greater permanence (and presumably greater security for the stock) was achieved when the Black Prince had fencing made using timber from Barnacle and Ansty Parks, employing a lath maker from Binley and a carpenter from Styvechale. To avoid waste, their wages were paid by his stewards, Richard Stoke and Robert Fowler, out of the sale of the old, grubbed-up hedges, presumably for firewood.

The nature of the Prince's investment can then be gauged in the work of this same steward, Robert Fowler, whose name recurs repeatedly in the 1350s and 1360s. In January 1358 he supplied 24 coneys (rabbits), which were judged to be so good that the Prince promptly ordered 24 more to be sent on to him at the next stop on his itinerary. Later in 1364 his register recorded:

> Grant for life to Robert Fowler [a significant surname] the prince's ferreter, for good service of the keeping of the Prince's manor and park of Cheylesmore, to wit, of the wild game there and the coneys [rabbits] and other game within and without the park ... 3d per day for his wages.

The location of the Cheylesmore rabbit warrens is today not known but a document of 1664 may give a clue in that it mentions 'the mounds' belonging to the great park. These may be the rabbit warrens and are mentioned in connection with other landmarks close to the city near Greyfriars gate.

The park always enjoyed the stewardship of an official Parker. Clearly he was accompanied by other specialist countrymen, whose skills were appreciated, and who probably were able to live almost rent free within the confines of the park. The extension of his rights beyond the park is an interesting allusion to the fact corroborated in many early documents, that some areas to the east, principally in Pinley and Shortley, were thought of as within the purview of the park. Doubtless the lord's officials ate well.

The excavations at Cheylesmore Manor, perhaps unsurprisingly, given the documentary record, have produced the largest single group of deer (10 per cent of the sites mammal assemblage of 1,355 bones) and rabbit bones (6 per cent) in the city, together with domestic fowl (38 per cent of the bird bone assemblage of 252 bones), goose (30 per cent), pheasant (11 per cent), partridge

(10 per cent), mallard (6 per cent), wood pidgeon (2 per cent) and heron (2 per cent). The domestic fowl, ubiquitous on every medieval urban site, were here of a large bantam size, much smaller than their modern counterparts, but were mainly female. At another excavation of a comparatively rich tenement in the sixteenth-century city (24 Bayley Lane, 1991), a large group of chicken bone indicated a stock ratio of one cock to three hens, stongly indicating a domestic flock kept primarily for egg production. They were eaten only when they could no longer lay.

Perhaps a guide to the relative wealth of the Cheylesmore Manor is the discovery in excavation of two semi-butchered carcasses just outside the east range buildings in the fifteenth or early sixteenth century. A whole cow and half a pig indicate that on occasions consumption did not match the supply and meat could, on occasion, be allowed to decay and be rejected as unfit for consumption, a level of waste not so far seen in the city where all parts of every animal were used (*colour plate 23*). Even at the comparatively rich manor, such waste cannot have been common, but is likely to be the result of slaughter patterns dictated by the needs of a skeleton staff, eating only what was necessary while the lord and his court were away on progress, at another of the lord's many properties.

The restricted species of deer and rabbit are far more prevalent than at any other site in the city where such might be represented by less than 1 per cent of the mammal bones, despite there being managed warrens or 'coneygrees' in Harnall Grange and at Pinley (and rabbits are notoriously difficult to pen in). The bird bone too is much more evenly spread across a range of species. By contrast a non-royal, ordinary Coventry site produces a preponderance of domestic fowl. This is even so at the Cathedral Priory where the Benedictine monks enjoyed access to the produce of their own private land and where noble visitors could be expected to dine regularly, including kings when parliament convened at Coventry, as it often did, headed by the King. In fact for the whole of 1460-61 the government of Edward IV was based at Coventry.

The Benedictines owned Whitmore Park, a large cattle-farming grange of 281ha (694 acres), from at least the mid-fourteenth century; perhaps not with quite the hunting provision enjoyed at Cheylesmore but probably equally restricted. Less is known about Whitmore Park since the priory land was broken up after the Dissolution and all that is known of the medieval manor is its location, the component fields which made up the land of which 177ha (436 acres) comprised waste, an area known as Pomleigh. A licence to enclose this was granted in State Papers to St Mary's in 1369 but Whitmore was already in Priory hands by 1349 when it was recorded as valueless due to the Black Death. In addition the Priory attracted other bequests which helped supply their house. One major example was that of 1249 when the de Montalts, newly ensconced at Cheylesmore, granted them the right to roam in their Coventry manor lands, with freedom to select and fell timber for firewood and for fencing. Furthermore they were given a cartload of firewood every week for St John's Hospital.

At Fletchamstead (now part of Canley) from 1492 lay a private hunting park of the Smyth family, 256ha (632 acres) carved out of the former Fletchamstead hamlet, which was forcibly depopulated in the park's creation. Just to the west lay the 145ha (360 acre) manor of the same name, owned by the Knight's Templar (to the early fourteenth century) and later the Knights Hospitaller (until 1539).

A similar park lay almost adjacent to Fletchamstead at Allesley, owned by the Hastings family, Lords of that manor and benefactors of the Coventry Franciscans at the Greyfriars. It lay centred around the Norman motte and bailey castle at Allesley which was their principal local seat. It covered 170ha (421acres) and stretched south as far as Broad Lane.

Carved out of the parish of Wyken was Caludon Park, the home of the Lords Seagrave and subsequently the immensely powerful, but ill-fated, Mowbray family, Dukes of Norfolk. The latter family turned the manor into a veritable mansion (Caludon Castle) to which was attached a considerable park of 100+ha (247+ acres) bounded by the River Sowe on the south, east and north and by Stoke on the west. Recent excavation evidence suggests that this prestigious seat was not moated on all sides but instead looked north out onto a broad expanse of water, or *mere*, a feature which was all the rage in the fourteenth century. Doubtless it would have been well stocked with fish. Locally Kenilworth Castle may have provided the model in its own massive mere, which helped in considerable measure to defend it against the King in the famous siege of 1266. Caludon Park remained a local feature well beyond the medieval period but the castle decayed rapidly after the banishment of Thomas Mowbray by Richard II after his infamous, abortive duel with Henry Bolingbroke (Earl of Derby and the future Henry IV) on Gosford Green in 1397. He was banished to Prussia, Bohemia, Hungary or 'to the land of saracens and unbelievers'. After a pilgrimage to the Holy Land, he died in Venice within a year of plague and his family seat at Caludon began to decay.

Further afield in 1518 Sir Thomas Docwra, Grand Prior of the Order of Knights Hospitaller (and the most prominent member of a Coventry family), enclosed the Hospitaller manor at Ryton on Dunsmore, thus emparking a further 121ha (300 acres). This brought to an end the rash of park creation which left Coventry surrounded by no less than 1,282ha (3166 acres) of private hunting parks.

UNRESTRICTED LAND

For the ordinary people of Coventry, who mostly bought their produce in the city's markets (minus the restricted species) there was the Swanswell which, although surrounded by land owned by either St Mary's Priory or St John's Hospital (itself priory-owned), was more easily accessible for fishing and probably fowling also. The Swanswell as it survives is a more regular shape than was known to medieval Coventry. It once stretched further north according to Speed's map of 1610. However, it did not extend as far west as it does today, the extension, by the digging of a new pool in 1551, being related to the establishment of a mill on the site of what would eventually become White Street.

As late as 1893, the remarkable Coventry diarist and self-taught renaissance man Joseph Gutteridge (1816-99) recalled the Swanswell of his youth before it was tidied with the construction of Hillfields, the so-called New Town, after 1828:

> A rather large pool of water still (1893) remains, called Swanswell Pool, upon the borders of the old city and the New Town … this now thickly populated district was a wild and romantic place. The low ground immediately surrounding the pool was covered with extensive osier and reed beds. The place was the favourite resort and breeding place of several kinds of water fowl the wilds duck, the widgeon, the dipper, and the water hen were constant visitors, and the reeds and osier beds were enlivened by the songs of the warblers that abounded. The water itself teemed with fish, as it does to this day. Pike, perch, roach, tench and eels afforded fine sport for anglers. Before the new town of Hillfields encroached upon the pool (i.e. before the 1840s) it was a wild and weird place. The water was bordered by fine old pollard willows, and on two sides the ground gradually rose from the edge of the water into Hill fields. The view of the pool was almost obscured in the narrow causeway by the willows and clusters of tall elms, oaks, chestnuts and maples that surrounded it.

The work to tidy the Swanswell in the 1840s, which merged the original pool with the new pool of 1551 and took out an island which had stood in the middle, also deepened the existing expanse and took in the former reed and osier beds which had stood on the north. Whatever medieval archaeological refuse there may have been preserved in it must have been removed without trace, since a similar clearance to remove silts in the early 1990s dredged up only later nineteenth- and twentieth-century refuse, principally bottles and utilitarian pottery.

Of course there were always those who wanted a little extra for their efforts and poaching was widespread. In 1480 Prior Deram complained bitterly to the Corporation that he was losing his fish stocks to the city's poachers and the locals were washing their clothes in the ponds which were still not fully enclosed. He received little comfort from a slow and unenthusiastic reply from the mayor. He was not being singled out for poor service since the wall was everywhere progressing very slowly indeed, but its absence was keenly felt as the townsfolk could simply slip around the monastery precinct from either Cox Street or the newly-built Swanswell Gate and gain access from the edge of the city.

HORTICULTURE

The raising of vegetables for consumption and herbs for cooking and medicine was without doubt everyone's business. Mentions of gardens in the documentary record are everywhere, although there is rarely any detail as to what was being grown. One of the few is a late document of 1646 in which a workman claimed expenses from the city for work he had done in levelling ground outside Hill Street Gate and widening the town ditch, presumably as Civil War precautions. In the process he had damaged a number of allotments and was claiming expenses for the compensation he had laid out for damaged plots planted with onions, parsnips and carrots, suggesting the work was done in summer or early autumn, while the town ditch was at its driest. These ordinary gardens of the working man had been neatly set out as he also bought hurdles and thorns (quicksets) to make good the damaged fences and hedges.

Recent discoveries at 68-70 Whitefriars Street (2004) also indicate that where wealth permitted, flowers may have been grown for pleasure. Amongst the high-status rubbish backfilling fourteenth-century stone quarries behind Gosford Street (*48*) were parts of a lavishly decorated planter.

Excavation has found good evidence for gardening at the city's monasteries. Neatness was a hallmark of the monks' gardens at Charterhouse, where excavations in 1986 showed the cell nursery beds divided from paths by lines of roof tiles dug in on edge. Gardening for the Carthusian was a biblically-inspired pastime and an opportunity for work and contemplation together. Here too the light into the garden was maximised by limewashing the garden walls and the planting trenches were still discernible in the clayey subsoil, having been enriched with organic matter in the best tradition. They could not raise everything themselves, however, since in the 1539 Dissolution accounts was an unpaid debt for the January purchase of peas for the monastery guest house (presumably dried, since they were out of season). For the more communal life of the Benedictines, the monastery garden might also be a place of contemplation since a small patch of garden was excavated in 2000 just outside the north range refectory undercroft which was bounded by a shaded stone seat. Certain Coventry monks were described as 'gardener' from the thirteenth century. Pottery from the rich humic soil of this area showed it was in use right up until the Dissolution.

ARABLE LAND

Throughout the medieval period the market remained the place of trade for most ordinary people, especially for foodstuffs. The greatest period of market expansion was between 1250 and 1300 and usually they needed to be in a town or borough to survive. Markets usually had a radius of between five and ten miles and provided a magnet both for the vendors from surrounding areas and the hopeful consumers of goods they could not get at home. Some markets became very sophisticated, such as Coleshill which specialised in harness and tack, shoes, clothing, cooking utensils, spices and wines. In Coventry the range of goods on offer was so diverse that different streets would support a different type of market each day. Occasionally one street would come to dominate one market so that it became known by the goods in which it specialised. There are numerous examples in Coventry, Potter Row (off Cross Cheaping, or Chipping, meaning Market), Butcher Row (outside Holy Trinity), Fishmonger Row and Ironmonger Row. Some were specifically food-dominated, including spices. The range of spices sold locally may have extended to the full range seen coming in at the ports, such as pepper, cumin, saffron and, as indicated by the goods imported by the appropriately-named William Spicer of Southampton, dates, figs and almonds. The spicers would have traded for the most part out of Spicerstoke, at one end of Broadgate, which later became the home of goldsmiths. The most useful, and widely used such commodity was undoubtedly salt. While some probably came from the coast, at least some would have come from the salt-towns of Worcestershire, such as Droitwich where the Bendedictine Priory owned a salt-pan.

MILLS

The single biggest bulk commodity remained corn, since the very stability of an entire medieval society could hinge upon the availability of bread flour at a reasonable price. Bread was often the cause of civil disorder, and Coventry suffered regularly from damaging riots of one sort or another, such as in 1383, 1396, 1489 and 1525. Inflation could be a real enemy when it came to foodstuffs and the most basic commodity was corn. Between the eleventh and the thirteenth centuries, the price of corn rose from 2s to 6s per quarter. By the time it had been milled and baked, its price would have risen sufficiently for each loaf to reflect payments to landowner, farmer, carters, miller and baker. Warwickshire had no county grain network as such; the clergy handled large amounts which came in through tithes (one tenth of all produce) but the ordinary peasants in the country paid their dues to their overlord and from whatever was left consumed what they needed and if there was a surplus it was generally bought up by 'Baggers' or 'Badgers' who resold it as a monopoly at a higher price. As an example in nearby Warwick in 1417 only two men were dealing directly with cornmongers. By the late thirteenth century the average income for a rural peasant was about one pound a year. In modern terms this means very little but a household would spend between a quarter and a half of this income on food, a fact which is in stark contrast to modern lifestyles.

Mills were a valuable commodity throughout the medieval period and the tolls exacted for milling grain meant they remained sought after and the watercourses to power them jealously guarded. A very few water mills had been around since the Saxon period and later both the city and all of the villages which constitute today's suburbs contained at least one, their sites being known today, largely from the distinctive channels needed to divert and dam the courses of the rivers Sherbourne and Sowe to form the races.

In the city centre Priory Mill stood where Priory Place now lies (*colour plate 24*). Its site is today marked by a water feature. The fifteenth-century timbers of its wheel pit were excavated in 2001; Earls Mill stood at the bottom of Cox Street (formerly Mill Lane). A third mill once stood where Bond's Hospital was later built, on Hill Street, while yet another stood close to the Ram Bridge, adjacent to the Lower Precinct. Most had more recent successors on the same site, such as Foleshill and Walsgrave Mills, which continued milling well into the twentieth century. Perhaps the most densely packed stretch of river lay between Gulson Road and Whitley, where stood no less than six mills: Altegeder (bottom of Gulson Road), Bisseley (north of Charterhouse), Dilcock's (south of Charterhouse), Swift's, Alreneford (north of London Road bridge) and Whitley Mill. These were a contributory cause of the flooding which repeatedly affected the city and their demise during the first half of the twentieth century was greeted with much relief. Alreneford Mill (also called Alderford), together with the thirteenth-century Pinley Mill, between Allard Way and Willenhall, were never replaced by modern successors and remain sites of immense archaeological potential for the study of the technology which put bread on medieval tables.

Windmills began to appear in England as an unlicenced alternative to water mills in the thirteenth century. Comparatively easy to construct, these post-mills needed no water to power them and could be put up on most slopes which

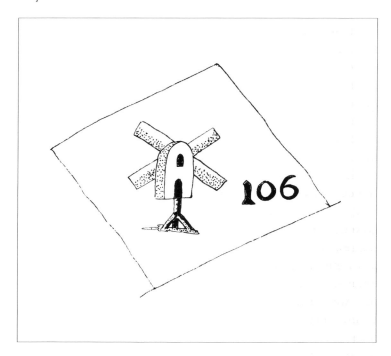

64 Medieval post-
mill: Windmill Road,
Foleshill.. Redrawn
from the 1774 Tithe
Map. *Coventry Archives*

faced the prevailing winds. The stranglehold of the mill-owning elite could be
loosened by a little entrepreneurial spirit. Thus the city was ringed by such mills,
some of which survived to be mapped or drawn into the eighteenth century.
The earliest known was documented at Coombe Abbey's Binley Grange in 1291.
In 1388 a post mill (and a horse mill) stood in Dog Lane, Harnall at the north-
western edge of what is now Coventry and Warwickshire Hospital, replaced
before 1800 by a brick tower mill, which survived just long enough to be drawn
in a map of that year. By 1851 it had been converted into a water tower. Post
mills stood west of Hill Street and west of London Road on the grassy approach
to the London Road cemetery. Another stood on the west side of Warwick
Road, above where the modern railway station lies. Yet another, Priory-owned
in 1410, lay at the western end of Spon Street. There were many more further
afield. Such mills stood in Radford (1410), west of Clifford Bridge Road in
Binley (its former mound mapped in 1746) and there were at least three in
Foleshill (one off the eponymous Windmill Road, mapped in 1774 (*64*), and one
either side of Deedmore Road, now in Wood End). So as not to be outdone,
even St Mary's Benedictine Priory owned both a windmill and a horse-mill in
Sowe (Walsgrave), an addition to their water mill there. These must have been
very common sights in the landscape, such that a typical post-mill is graphically
depicted in the fourteenth-century wall-painting of St Christopher carrying the

Christ-child in the church of St Mary Magdalene, Wyken (*colour plate 25*). From there, it is likely that the Deedmore Road mills would be visible.

While the mill sites are rarely excavated anywhere in the country, their products are – or at least those grains which were not ground up very successfully. However, not all archaeological sites entertain the right ground conditions for the preservation of seeds. Generally it needs to be waterlogged or the seeds to have been charred by fire. A few such consumer sites have been excavated in Coventry to provide a good cross-section of the arable land supplying the medieval city, while others indicate the nature of the flora which grew in or surrounded the walled city and found its way into the threshing grain as weeds.

The largest quantity of grain excavated was at the aptly named Castle Bakehouse next to St Mary's Hall on Bayley Lane. Although the name is suggestive – and it was called *Castelbachous* in a Priory rental of 1410 – it had in fact long ceased to be part of the castle by then. The remains of a building were excavated which contained two circular sandstone ovens, side by side. Although one was damaged by later building, the other contained the charred and finely comminuted remains of the last baking. Unsurprisingly it contained entirely bread wheats. Ironically, however, the ovens not only post-dated the destruction of the castle, they themselves had ceased to exist by the time the tenement was named *Castelbachous* in 1410, the bakehouse having been replaced by an unrelated, open-sided building which burnt down in 1642.

In this particular instance, the poorly preserved nature of the grain rendered it impossible to clearly identify all the species of wheats used in the oven of the so-called Castle Bakehouse. However, in circumstances where such species have been identified, such as at the Priory, a variety can be seen being used to supply the daily bread. Two types of wheat (bread-type and rivet-type) and rye had been grown together as maslin, producing a dark bread when ground. The mixture of types reduced the risk of crop failure, an ever present fear, particularly after a run of such disasters between 1310 and 1320; it also helped to smother weeds.

While the ears of corn were destined for the table in the form of bread, nothing else would be wasted and both rivet-type wheat and rye grow on long straw stems which are ideal for thatching. Although the fear of fire in any city was immense, and Coventry's answer to this was to back tiling as opposed to thatching as the preferred roofing method, nevertheless most rural buildings, right up to the city walls, and many ancillary structures within the city, would have been thatched right through the medieval period. Most such surviving local buildings have long since been re-roofed in tile or slate; a few retain their fully thatched character, however, such as Cherry and Broomstick Cottages in Walsgrave.

The Priory seeds also indicate that the Cathedral Priory was receiving its grain from a variety of sources. This is because the weeds which found their way as contaminants into the bread varieties derive from different soil environments. One, thorow-wax, lives on alkaline soils, the other, corn marigold, on acid soils. This is not surprising, given the variety and extent of the Priory's principal grange farms at Whitmore Park, Biggin and Harnall. There was also plenty of scope for suppliers to change the nature of their provision. In the early fifteenth century the Priory was negotiating with its principal tenants in Walsgrave, Barnacle and Ansty for large tracts of their pasture to be ploughed up for the first time and turned over to arable land.

Also from the Priory comes evidence of the environment of a short section of the River Sherbourne, from the wheel pit of Priory Mill. It was clear that the deposit had been laid down while the mill was in use (the wheel-pit timbers were tree-ring dated as being felled in 1432-56). Considerable amounts of wood were found, together with whole hazelnuts, acorn cups, holly and three-nerved sandwort. These appear to depict a river-bank-cum-mill-race with shady banks overhung with at least this variety of trees. Undergrowth was represented by species denoting disturbed ground and grassland, and others, such as Ragged Robin and Meadowsweet, suggest that livestock were denied access to the riverbank, since they would not have grown to produce seed, but instead, as delicious fodder, been eaten before they could mature. Other types indicated a free-flowing watercourse, with no evidence of stagnation. Indeed, the presence of flax and hemp seeds also suggest the same stretch of water was being used for production of fibres for rope and cloth. Flax-retting required lots of water and if time and money was being invested in this operation, this may explain why livestock could not get to the riverbank, thus allowing otherwise closely-cropped grazing species to produce their seed.

The wheel-pit and other Priory samples may be compared with those taken in the 1970s from a site on the town wall close to Cox Street. Specifically from the accompanying town ditch they indicate the nature of the watery banks and were taken from a position just downstream of another mill, Earl's Mill, itself a twelfth-century mill, but owned by the Earl of Chester, not the Priory. Pollen analysis here complemented that of the macroscopic remains and they suggest that cultivated fields extended right up to the town walls. However, just as a few hundred metres upstream at the Priory Mill, this site too produced flax and hemp, further evidence that this stretch of the River Sherbourne (at this point used to flood the ditch), was being used to produce rope and hempen cloth. Near to both sites, a long, thin piece of land adjacent to the town wall between Priory (Swanswell) Gate and Cook Street Gate was known as Rope Walk, for the twisting and stretching of fibres to make rope.

In an urban situation one of the problems with understanding archaeobotanical remains is the variety of sources from which they may have come before deposition. Natural deposition (the most likely event for most species in the above sites) is only one. Add to this the potential for remains to have passed through the human gut as faeces (since urban waste disposal was usually in pits) and there is a problem of sourcing the species present. Faecal waste tends to be distinguishable by the bias to naturally edible plants, particularly fruit stones and pips, although the non-nutritional and sometimes downright poisonous do occur, such as corn cockle in potentially dangerous proportions in bread–wheat threshing waste from Woolmonger Street, Northampton. Recognition of faecal waste, however, is not straightforward, since such an edibility bias may be masked by the fact that unpredictable proportions of seeds could have been ground up and finely comminuted beyond recognition simply by the process of chewing. At Bayley Lane in 1988, cesspit deposits were, however, distinguished beyond doubt by the presence in the pit of a medieval wooden toilet seat collapsed into the pit and copious quantities of moss, the medieval equivalent of toilet paper. Also of note is the practice of using a mixture of plants, straw, leaves and other dry organic materials to spread onto floors as a moveable carpet which could be swept up, scooped out and replaced by similar materials with a regularity which was a matter of household whim. John Gerard in *The Herball or Generall Historie of Plantes* (1633) wrote:

> The leaves and floures farr excell all other strowing herbes, for to decke up houses, to straw in chambers, halls and banqueting houses in the sommer time; for the smell thereof makes the heart merrie, delighteth the senses.

Clearly medieval urban environmental deposits must be approached with considerable circumspection, since any rubbish pit may contain (in perfect preservation conditions) waste from food storage, food preparation, toilet waste and the household rubbish. In such circumstances it can present a confused mass of data which is ill-suited to characterising the surrounding land by its vegetation. To ensure the best data, deposits need to be well-dated, discrete, well-sealed and closely related to a known building context; quite a set of requirements! To date, few suitable areas of waterlogged deposits and few suitable charred deposits have been identified in the city which meet all or most of these ideals. The acids of the Keuper marls on which much of the city lies makes preservation of organic, environmental material unlikely over wider areas. Thus it is to the watercourses of the Sherbourne, the Sowe and their tributaries that archaeologists must continue to turn (especially the mill sites). Otherwise the waterlogged sites are limited to certain stretches of the town ditch and deeper pits of a variety of uses. Since there still exists the best part of two and a quarter miles of town ditch, its course for the most part known, the potential sample for future study remains phenomenal.

As a guide to the former biodiversity of the city's immediate hinterland, there exists no better guide than the diarist Joseph Gutteridge, quoted above. Writing of his youth in the 1830s, he watched the creation of the first true modern suburbs at New Town (now Hillfields; from 1828) and Chapelfields (from *c.*1845). He wrote of the flora around the former place, where he roamed in his youth and where he later lived:

> Harnall Lane ends at the point where Coventry joins Stoke, the Stoke end being called Swan Lane. It was a rugged but beautiful place in bygone times, so narrow in parts that farmers' carts almost touched the fences on either side. In other parts there were broad stretches of waste land bordering the roadway, the furze and brambles upon which made them a veritable paradise in my eyes. Ferns grew in rich profusion in the more sheltered parts. There were the male fern, the female fern, the bird's nest fern, the polypody, the hart's tongue, with pretty specimens of smaller species in the hedge bottoms and on the banks. There we could find the primrose, the bluebell, many species of cranesbill, stellaria, St John's wort, alehoof, two or three species of epilobium, the large yellow toadflax, avens, the wild horehound, and wood sage, and many other plants that were used in the household for their medicinal properties.

Ironically, just by moving to Hillfields he contributed to the destruction of the place's former character and biodiversity, an observation all too common in twenty-first century England on a far grander scale.

14

Defending the city

'Coventry is a faire, famous, sweet and ancient city, so walled about with such strength and neatnesse, as no city in England may compare with it.' John Taylor 1639

EARLY DEFENCES

From the thirteenth century the growing town was probably defended to some degree. Despite many attempts since the issue of the wall was first addressed archaeologically in 1960, no conclusive evidence on the nature of any early defences has been forthcoming. While such a ditch may have been glimpsed in Lamb Street in 1960 and again at Cox Street (1976), its identification with early defences has become less secure since similarly dated, and very considerable ditches, appear in documents as the back-boundaries of plot rows, acting as drains, sewers and simple, but substantial, demarcation lines. The biggest of the town's ditches, however, is simply huge; whether in documents or excavation it is unmistakable.

From the early medieval period the Hyrsum ditch or, in translation, 'obedience' ditch was a quasi-defensive line which was drawn around at least part of the southern side of the town (*10*). On this side it appears to have divided the town from the early Cheylesmore Park, keeping Coventrians out. As such it may be construed as one part of the first park pale. While it prevented the town's encroachment onto the northern edge of the park, the Hyrsum ditch was itself in part breached, probably in order to strictly regulate encroachment and set out the burgage plots of Earl, Little Park and Much Park Streets as officially-sanctioned land units. The ditch continued to appear in documents, over much of its length described as the Red Ditch (so called probably because of the colour of the clay or the colour it turned the water which lies in the bottom of such ditches hereabouts). A northern 'tributary' was dug, to drain the spring at the eponymous Jordan Well. Its close association with the park continued, however, as a single set of Drapers' Company deeds for one property on the west side of Little Park Street refer to the same ditch as a boundary of that plot between 1313 and 1441 variously as 'the ditch of Robert de Montalt's park, Coventry park ditch, the red ditch, a ditch once Robert de Montalt's and Cheylesmore Park ditch'. That Hyrsum, Red and Park were one and the same, seems an inescapable conclusion. The Red Ditch has been located three times archaeologically, in 1970 and twice in the 1980s, on each occasion aligned east–west between Much and Little Park Streets. The open nature of this location retains great potential for further investigation as do two further sections which documents relate continued west (south of High Street from Little Park Street across to Greyfriars Lane) and east (along the rear plots of the south side of Gosford Street). The immense size of this ditch, 7.2m (23ft 8in) wide and 4m (13ft 2in) deep, means that whereas later, less substantial remains are affected by modern development, the ditch has escaped unscathed. Its later history was less salubrious, seemingly relegated to the role of town sewer and the name Town Ditch and Vill Ditch (for which read sewer and drain) became interchangeable in documents with Red Ditch along with the later defensive ditch (see below). In places it continued to be a documented feature, and presumably a topographical constraint, into the sixteenth century. However its identification in excavation is rare since it requires very deep excavation.

While a ditch of this size could be construed as having a defensive capability, the course of the ditch seems to point to its having more of a park-boundary role. This boundary, around the Cheylesmore Park, can still be seen in the steep escarpment which angles south from London Road cemetery across Whitley Common, describing an arc which was discernible on all the city maps until recent times. This escarpment would reflect the added slope formed by the combination of ditch and banked upcast on the inner, park side of the ditch. On the west of the park the boundary was aligned down the east side of Warwick Road and then along Leamington Road.

If ever the Hyrsum and Red ditches assumed any defensive function, perhaps even with a parallel bank, they must quickly have become liabilities in a growing town. The laying out of whole town centre streets such as Bayley and Hay Lanes whose early plots appear to knit seamlessly, after the demise of the castle in the later twelfth or early thirteenth century, meant that the economic and mercantile potential of the city centre was quickly realised. At roughly the same time, documents appear to suggest that streets as far out as St Nicholas to the north, Gosford to the east, Hill and Spon to the west and London Road and Warwick Row to the south gained acceptance in legal documentation almost simultaneously in the late twelfth and early thirteenth centuries. There was a sudden increase in surnames with rural connotations or village–origins indicating a massive influx of country folk in search of new wealth. The presence of creative planning of burgage plots suggests a high degree of desirability and a lack of serious constraint; in fact positive, mercantile planning seems to have been on the agenda. To try to draw, or continue to observe, any defensive line across the growing town would be economic suicide as the desirability of being inside any defences would exclude more and more newcomers who tagged onto the end of each suburban ribbon development. While Coventry stood in the centre of a realm at peace, such defences were superfluous anyway. Although the area was much affected by the baronial wars of the 1260s, Coventry was physically unscathed, but for the ill-advised choice of the Hastings family (Allesley) and the Segrave family (Caludon) to back the ill-starred Simon de Montfort the younger. Even the siege of Kenilworth in 1266 left the city relatively unaffected by the royal attention given to its near neighbour and its then near-impregnable castle.

At salient points around the city stood the bars, customs posts which could be chained up at night. Whether they were what would now be described as gates, barriers or simply chains, they enabled the city officials to stop inward and outward traffic at will for the purposes of levying duties on goods. It is doubtful if they had any defensive capability, other than perhaps forcing an approaching enemy off the road and into the roadside ditch. They stood far enough outside the defended area to make all goods subject to customs, even if destined for, or emanating from, suburban premises. Although they were operational from the early medieval period, they continued in use throughout the fourteenth, fifteenth and sixteenth centuries.

LICENCE TO CRENELLATE

With the passage of the fourteenth century came the decision, for mixed economic and military reasons, to build walls from scratch (*1* and *3*). Following the success of funding paving for the principal streets in 1285 and again in 1305 from market tolls, the city secured crown agreement and a murage grant in 1327–8 for the same toll system for a period of six years to enclose the city and build gates (there is at this stage no mention of a wall). However, a whole generation was to elapse before it became clear that this system was woefully inadequate for a programme on so large a scale. In 1363 Coventry received the official licence to crenellate *'muro de petra et calce includere, firmare et kernellare'* ('with a wall of stone and mortar to enclose, strengthen and fortify') from Edward III. This time, however, the licence allowed for the toll to be levied upon the people directly, with the exception of churchmen, a rather short-sighted approach given the magnitude of the church presence. With the city approaching the height of its prosperity (ranked fourth in England on the basis of taxation in 1377, after London, Bristol and York), the physical expansion of the city had slowed. Civic pride was about to take over in a construction programme which was startling because of how late it began and how long it took to complete. However, it left Coventry with the newest and some of the strongest defences in the realm.

The wall was begun at New Gate at the head of the London Road in the 1350s (before the royal licence), this first gate being sensibly named; its name was somewhat ironic when attacked in 1642, since it was by then the oldest. The wall was at one point being built in both directions at once, a short section per year. At one time the city took the murage levy very seriously indeed and in places no expense was spared. Around the royal manor house at Cheylesmore, excavations have revealed that the wall had no foundations per se, but the finest ashlar stones were cut with immense precision and carried right down to the base of the foundation trench with no loss of quality. When investigated in 1992, the excavators could not even fit a pointing trowel into the horizontal mortar joint between two courses. During the same excavations the base of a mortar-mixer's barrel was discovered next to the wall, set into the natural clay (*colour plate 26*). Within it lay a 10cm thick layer of lime putty, still soft and malleable after 600 years. The alkali of the lime had neutralised the acid of the clay and the water-holding properties of its setting had preserved the wood of the barrel perfectly. The putty was devoid of all visible impurities. The royal status of the site clearly meant that cost was not an issue. However at times in the later fifteenth century work was virtually at a standstill, there being little remaining appetite for so costly an enterprise and with no apparent end in sight.

With the building programme already two generations old, there is a brief glimpse in 1410-1 of the disruption the work caused. The Cartulary of St Mary's Benedictine Priory records that from 1403 the new wall and ditch scythed through their property on Spon Street, Well Street, Golding Lane, Bishop Street, Cook Street, Gosford Street, Priors Orchard and Dog Lane. In relation to the Priory holdings on these streets alone it destroyed 13 houses and in addition wrecked seven gardens with more given up as good as lost. Furthermore it condemned others to forever lie outside the city. What happened to the tenants is not recorded, nor is how many non-Priory properties were similarly affected

EXCAVATIONS

Since the first took place in 1960 there have been 16 separate excavations on Coventry's late medieval town wall and its accompanying ditch, arguably making this the most intensively excavated single structure in the city. However, since the wall took 180 years to construct and ran for 3.62km (2.25 miles) when complete, the total length excavated represents less than 6 per cent of the total circuit, despite the pressures of redevelopment since the Second World War. Knowledge of the wall is considerable, but the value of what still lies unexcavated remains massive.

Many of the excavations on the town wall have been small sections across its fabric, with only a few metres uncovered, recorded and re-covered to protect the remains under new development. In 1970 a section of some 60m length was excavated at the north-east corner of the medieval city along the former Godiva Street where the wall is believed to date between 1480 and 1534. The surviving stonework was subsequently conserved and is today a Scheduled Ancient Monument, standing in part above ground. Similar status and consequently statutory protection has been afforded to all other upstanding parts of the surviving wall.

In 1990-91 excavations took place which were arguably more instructive than any other about the wall so far. These were adjacent to The Cheylesmore and Friars Road, on the southern side of the city, a section of wall probably built in the period 1385-91.

This section stretched for some 45m and lay adjacent to an earlier (and much smaller) Friars Road section of 1990 (*colour plate 27*). At this point the wall was laid out to swing out south-west around the Cheylesmore Manor, at the behest of Richard II who wished his manor house to be included within the city. The wall hereabouts was set into a 3m (9ft 10in) wide construction trench cut 750mm (2ft 6in) deep into the natural clay. The foundation comprised clay-bonded roughly squared sandstone blocks, those on the inner and outer edges being considerably larger than those which formed the core. Typically the foundation was three courses deep.

Robbing of the wall in this area had been very extensive and in 45m only one proper ashlar survived of the wall above foundation level, much less than in other parts of its circuit. A shallow chamfer cut into the upper face of the foundation showed that the need for accurate coursing was taken very seriously. The single surviving ashlar and mortar bedding left behind by stone robbers show that the wall proper was 2.1m (6ft 10in) thick, on a par with the wall as excavated in 1987 at Fleet Street/Spon Street (built 1391-9), thinner than the 2.4m (7ft 10in) in 1991 at Gosford St (after 1430) but fractionally thicker than at other points in

65 Cook Street Gate from the
inward side. The wall to the side
stands to about three quarters
of its original height. The upper
rooms of most of the 12 gates
were used as homes

the city, such as in 1970 at Godiva St (1480-1534) where it was 1.8m (6ft) or in
1992 at the Cheylesmore Manor (also of 1385-91) where it was of an apparently
slender and presumably less defensible 1.4m (4ft 7in) thickness. The thickest
section excavated to date was in 1976 adjacent to Cox St, (1516-17) which was
2.8m (9ft 2in) thick, on a raft up to 3.6m (11ft 9in) wide; the excessive width was
probably to counteract the wet ground in that part of the city.

From the excavations at The Cheylesmore came evidence of the battlements.
A single, broken block of roll-moulding is all that survived of either a merlon or
crenel which finished off the crenellations of a parapet behind which a defender
might take cover. Observations of the surviving Cook Street and Swanswell
(Priory) Gates show that the walkway which ran all the way around the wall,
stood at a height of between 16-20ft (4.9-6.0m) (65 and 66). An early reference
to remains in 1814 states that in that year a section on the north side of Gulson

66 Priory Gate, also known as Swanswell Gate, from the inward side. Blocked in 1643, unblocked only a couple of years later, it was blocked once and for all in the nineteenth century

Road still stood to 18ft (5.4m), arguably its full height. It goes on to point out that it could only be demolished in that year with the aid of explosives.

Perhaps the most valuable result of the 1991 excavations on The Cheylesmore was the discovery of one of the 20 towers which punctuated the wall between the gates (*67; colour plate 28*). The foundation measured 8m x 8m (26ft x 26ft) in plan, although mortar remains set back from the edges of the foundation surface make it clear the tower proper measured 7.4m x 7.8m (24ft 3in x 25ft 7in). Within it lay a single room at ground floor level which was 7.4m square but had its outer corners smoothed off in a gentle curve, rendering the otherwise rectangular interior room apsidal, additionally making the walls at the corner considerably thicker and therefore a more reliable defensive prospect against battery. On the projecting three sides the tower wall was 1.4m (4ft 7in) thick while the fourth, rear wall was of course the town wall itself at 2.1m thickness.

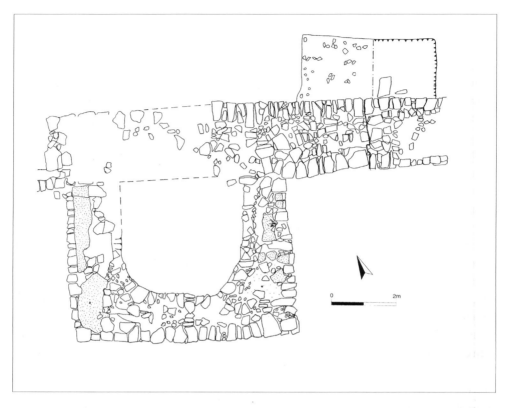

67 The excavated late fourteenth-century tower on the town wall at The Cheylesmore, 1991

However the thickness at the corners, across the arc of the apse, doubled the tower stonework to 2.8m (9ft 2in) and with it its ability to withstand impacts.

The archaeological evidence of this tower demonstrates the accuracy of both the 1610 map of Coventry by John Speed and the 1656 prospect of the city by Wenceslaus Hollar (68). Both show a tower in this location, suggesting a degree of reliability elsewhere around the circuit. In addition the City Annals hint at a tower in this area, an apparently rare factual observation in an otherwise untrustworthy document on topographical matters (since it indiscriminately relates matters of clear folklore with apparent historical fact, blurring its reliability).

Directly behind the wall at the rear and to one side of this tower lay the robbed base for a flight of stone stairs (67). By placing the stair to one side anyone who successfully broke into the tower and the first floor walkway on the wall would have to traverse a short, open length of that route, exposed to the defenders, before reaching the top of the stair which lay at the end furthest

68 Detail from the 1656 prospect of Coventry, originally engraved by Wenceslaus Hollar. The Cheylesmore town wall excavations in 1991 showed his view to be broadly accurate, only six years before the walls were slighted. By far the better of only two early contemporary views of the city. From an engraving printed in 1870

from the tower. They then had to turn and expose their generally unshielded right-hand side in order to descend into the city. Since the stair base was 4.6m (15ft) long and treads and risers are normally of a depth : height ratio of about 5:4, a walkway height is suggested at this point of *c.*3.68m (12ft). The crenels of the parapet would add a further 6ft to the overall wall height. This is entirely in keeping with the evidence from the two surviving gates and there seems to have been little variation in the intended height of the wall anywhere around the city, even if build quality and thickness were somewhat variable throughout the 180 years it took to complete the wall. The towers must have contributed greatly to the tremendous impression made on a young subaltern, Nehemiah Wharton in 1642, and he mentions them specifically (see below). The excavated example depicted at this location in the 1656 prospect is shown some 20 per cent higher than the wall, thus reaching a potential 21-22ft.

The length of wall investigated at this location meant that a quirk of the building was observed which has not been seen elsewhere in the city. It is known from documentary evidence that major building projects had to cease at the onset of winter since frost and generally low temperatures prevented the lime mortar used from curing properly. At Kirby Muxloe Castle in Leicestershire in November 1481 the invaluable building accounts state that a worker was paid 'for covering ... 10 loads of stubble and four loads of le ffern upn le towres'. In relation to Coventry's town wall documents record that each year's murage levy paid for an annual quota, which was signed off, before the next year's was begun. It varied from year to year, as budgets dictated. At the start of each winter the work would have stopped, just as at Kirby Muxloe, or any similar project. With such a long, linear construction programme the stopped end would need to be stepped back to allow the new courses of the subsequent spring to be properly keyed in. Two such winter stops were present in this section of the town wall, marking a whole year's work between them (*colour plate 29*). Each represented a butt-end to the foundation which was 1m (3ft 3in) deep. The length between the two butt joints is almost 20m (66ft), indicating that the builders were using a 16.5ft perch for survey and measurement. Two perches per year is the accepted building rate for the wall in the years 1499–1534 (for which period most documentation survives). On the evidence the original planned building programme (using four perches annually) would have been 90 years duration.

A fall to two perches per year resulted in a construction programme of 180 years to complete the 3.62km circuit. Such a lack of urgency was hardly the mark of a city concerned primarily with its security and defence. Yet on occasions the city was indeed faced with a clear threat. In 1396 about a hundred local lords (including the Boteler and Bagot families) rose in rebellion and attempted to take the city, causing great alarm; they were subsequently placated. However, it was later on that the issue became graver, principally in the mid–fifteenth century when, despite an unwritten (and arguably rudderless) civic policy of paying off whichever belligerent was in the ascendancy, the turmoil of the Wars of the Roses threatened to engulf Coventry. The walls had to be manned.

COMPLEMENT

On occasions the city had to support very large numbers of troops indeed, which might contribute to its defence. In 1322 the whole royal field army of Edward II had over-wintered at Coventry, as a base to blockade Kenilworth Castle, which was being held against him during a period of severe unrest. The situation was grave and in March that year the musters were called in Coventry, the Prior being put in charge. Later, in 1397, King Richard II and his friend, the powerful Duke of Brittany, Jean de Montfort, were reputed to have been attended at the lists at Gosford Green by 10,000 troops (perhaps a number which is unreliably-rounded). While the king at this time was wallowing in his own serious difficulties, any show of strength at Coventry would not have gone amiss, quelling any remnant disquiet from the 1396 local rising. At such times the city's defence was not a problem, but these were rare occasions.

There were always soldiers or veterans in the city in small numbers since, like all other cities Coventry was expected to furnish the Crown with armed men in time of war, whether at home or abroad. If the need arose their numbers could be swelled by strong, fit, yet largely untrained men who together would form the citizen militia whose job it was to defend the city. They comprised archers, billmen and armoured troops, the last of these often mounted. In all, equally divided between each type of soldier, the force amounted in the excellent muster records of the 1520s, to about 600 men. In the electric atmosphere of the Civil War of the 1640s, this figure rose to 800.

In the weeks preceding Jack Cade's rebellion in 1450, the muster was called and Coventry was able to raise the militia for its defence, funded by its wealthy and prominent citizens, equipped with weapons and armour kept at the ready by the City Corporation. In addition the authorities bought four new brass cannon (then still an unpredictable and terrifying new weapon) from Bristol, home at that time to the best gunsmiths in England. The city had probably enjoyed a form of artillery protection for some time already as the Priory Cartulary records one Philip le Arblaster living in Broadgate in 1305. Based upon an old Roman design, an Arbalist was an artillery-sized crossbow used primarily for defensive purposes, which could hurl two metre-long arrows at attacking personnel. It could also be converted to fire small-bore stone shot of a few pounds in weight. However, in 1450 the new city walls were still woefully incomplete. Stout defence of the still unwalled portions (about half of the circuit) would have been an ultimately fruitless task. Cities, when challenged by an enemy, were expected to surrender since to shut their gates was to invite a siege. Thereafter, if a besieged city fell to an attacker after being given good initial opportunity to open up, mercy might be in short supply. At this period the militia may have had to function in the open as a small field force with the incentive of knowing they would be defending their own families and homes. The danger of Jack Cade's rebellion passed without local incident and the four brass cannon were not needed. Their subsequent history is not known, but eventually they were probably melted down somewhere in the city.

THE TOWN DITCH

Throughout its history the wall was accompanied by a defensive ditch just in front of it. This generally measured up to 10m (33ft) wide and up to 3m (10ft) deep, although ground conditions sometimes resulted in it being wider or deeper in places, while corner-cutting meant that at other times it did not reach these proportions.

Thus the ditch, like the wall, describes a circuit around the city of 3.62km (2.25 miles). It has received a similar amount of archaeological attention (about 6 per cent) and has faced roughly the same development pressures. With the ditch, however, come very divergent archaeological issues. Unlike the wall, which has a solid, physical presence, even if remaining only as a buried foundation, the ditch, although so much larger, is more vulnerable to development pressures for two reasons. Firstly, in its filled-in state it contains a buried environment with artefactual and environmental evidence within. Secondly, in terms of both area and volume, it crosses proportionately more land plots than the wall. Thus threats to its survival arise more often than to the line of the wall, which can more easily be avoided by new structures.

Most excavations on the wall have also needed to locate the accompanying ditch to monitor the near-parallel course of both. It has been investigated less often than the wall, since intervention into its fill is often both costly and logistically challenging, as it involves deep excavation. Its vulnerability to modern foundations, even at depth, means that understanding the preservative qualities of the buried ditch environment is crucial to making informed decisions to guarantee its continued stability.

Perhaps the foremost archaeological quality of the ditch is how varied is its size along its circuit and how different was the cleaning regime applied to the different lengths, from one gate to another and from one property to another. At times it was very poorly looked after and the City Leet Book records that it was often fouled with rubbish, requiring a Corporation order for its cleaning. In fact a city ordinance of 1421 makes it clear that all who lived next to the ditch were responsible for its cleaning. The benefit of this responsibility was recorded by the City Wardens in 1581 who noted that such tenants were thus exempted from rent. That such orders were inconsistently carried out is, however, to the archaeologist's benefit since the ditch, at times dug just as slowly as the wall was built, contains not only the rubbish from the date of construction onwards, but that rubbish also reflects each individual quarter or enclave of the city which was dumping into it from close by. On occasion individuals can be discerned using the ditch quite legally. In one case in 1518 the immensely rich merchant Richard Marler was given full use of the ditch between Hill Street and Well

Street Gates so long as he kept it wet but cleaned it out. He himself was by far the wealthiest landlord in the city and no doubt would not consider getting his hands dirty, but most of his tenants on these two streets were probably tanners, for whom a waterfront site was indispensable. Even if they had no direct access to the Radford Brook, all his tenants could work from the ditch side, fed by the brook.

Each length of the ditch is thus treated as a separate feature containing rubbish with a slightly different time span and range of finds from that next door in either direction, sometimes subjected to cleaning out, sometimes not, all eventually filled in (such as cobblers waste of the 1500s at Hill Street 2005). Some lengths of the ditch, usually low-lying, were wet. That is they were to all intents and purposes treated as a moat which could be flooded. This is primarily where streams flowing into the River Sherbourne entered the city across the ditch and under a sluice-gate and culvert or 'spayer' into the city, or where the river itself flowed close enough to the walls for the river course itself to be used, or diverted to use, in conjunction with the ditch to add an extra layer to the city's defence. The spayer across the Radford Brook, half way along Bond Street, was built beneath a defensive tower in 1451, perhaps in recognition of the alarm at Jack Cade's rebellion less than a year before.

Thus while excavations at Fleet Street (1987), Lady Herbert's Garden (2001) and Lamb Street (2002-3) have investigated a dry ditch, on relatively high or inclined ground; those at Cox Street (1976 and 1978), Friars Road (1990, and by implication The Cheylesmore adjacent in 1991), Manor House Drive (1992), Hill Street (2002, 2005) and Well Street (2007) found the ditch generally wet and in some cases waterlogged, the very best conditions for the successful preservation of all environmental data and organic material. At Gosford Street (1991), it was noted that the River Sherbourne ran parallel and so close to the wall that any ditch as such was dispensed with and the river itself served as the ditch-defence for a short distance along to Brick Kiln Lane (now Gulson Road). The historian F. Bliss Burbage, quoting the City Annals, described these arrangements as 'a strong outwork without Gosford Gate, compassed round with a river'. This has now been proven in excavations in 2006 at the site of what is now Callice Court, where, as documents record, a house and garden were wrecked at Gosford Street outside the gate 'for the city's safety during the civil war'.

Of particular note were the widely differing archaeological sections cut at Friars Road and at Cox Street. The former, cut in the late fourteenth century (as part of The Cheylesmore length of fortification – see above) lies on the more sparsely-populated south side of the medieval city, adjacent to the Cheylesmore Manor and Park. Between the wall and the ditch lay evidence of a medieval stone and timber foot-bridge abutment projecting south across the ditch, which was narrowed at this point. Pottery in the layers which constituted the approach to the bridge showed that it was probably built as part of the wall and ditch design and continued in use at least well into the sixteenth century. When the structure was found, the nearby section of the ditch chosen for excavation here lay directly under the line of the bridge since it would have been difficult to clean out and in any case dumping beneath it was physically improbable (rather than over either side). Consequently, in the waterlogged ditch-fill was evidence of former wide expanses of water and a thriving pond life but with little evidence of attempts to dump rubbish into it (reflecting the restricted nature of manor lands). This part of the ditch appears not to have been overtaken by dumping from the expanding city until as late as *c.*1800 when a primary (near complete and unscattered) group of pottery and other finds was tipped into the ditch from a nearby alehouse. The bridge had, it appears, been lost by this date, its relatively insubstantial timbers having rotted away. The continued seepage of large volumes of water made further excavation inadvisable and the very bottom of the ditch hereabouts remained untested. It is in excess of 2m deep (6ft 5in) below the medieval ground surface and a further 1.7m (5ft 5in) below the modern pavement.

By contrast the latter excavation at Cox Street (formerly mill Lane), constitutes a late section of wall, probably built in 1516-17 (dated from the murage accounts of the early sixteenth century with the benefit of evidence for the use of the 16.5ft perch). Here, however, the wall and the accompanying ditch replaced an older defensive work, comprising a ditch and an earthen rampart, made from the upcast of the ditch. All was wet throughout, adding organic preservation to an excellent sequence of dumping with a break in that sequence occurring around 1640, exactly coinciding with national alarm at the onset of civil strife. During this period the nature of layers changed increasingly to silting (as opposed to rubbish) from *c.*1520, probably since the new stone wall prevented the citizens living nearby from reaching the ditch edge without great difficulty. Distinctive, pre-rampart layers hereabouts, at the inner edge of the ditch, suggest that the ditch and its rampart were newly constructed in the mid-fifteenth century. The bank seems to have been allowed to slump soon after and each successive slump contained quantities of late fifteenth- to sixteenth-century pottery. It may be that this precursor to the wall and ditch was hastily thrown up as part of the city's response to the perceived threat of strife from Jack Cade's rebellion in 1450. The apparent lack of care in allowing the ditch to become the local community's rubbish tip reflects the complacent attitudes of a long period of relative peace and calm, when the business of building wall and digging ditch resumed its unhurried pace of two perches a year until completed 22 perches and 6ft (732ft/221m) to the east of the site of the Cox Street excavations in 1534.

Even before the wall was finished, some rebuilding had taken place. The Leet Book records that in 1421 Hill Street Gate had to be rebuilt. The reason is unclear, but that gate can hardly have been more than a generation old. It may be that its design was flawed, or the carriageway beneath proved too narrow. The truth may never be known since most of the gates still lie beneath modern roads, shredded by dozens of pipes, cables and sewers. Also in the 1420s the Carmelite Friars who, in common with all whose land abutted the town defences, took responsibility for their stretch, were required to embank behind the wall down Gulson Road, a move which strengthened the defences but in this case may have weakened its long-term stability by pushing it outwards.

Further generations of peace meant that just before the Civil War more extensive repairs had to be made, an ongoing issue which gave rise to regular mayoral inspection-walks in the early seventeenth century, designed to pick up on problems before they became too great. On Gulson Road (then Brick Kiln Lane) a section of some 30m collapsed in 1636, likely to be the same section embanked by the Whitefriars. The order went out for its total rebuilding reusing stone from the former Greyfriars. Such delapidations were not uncommon and comparison of John Speed's 1610 map of the city with others shows that Coventry's defences were at least relatively intact. Speed's maps of Northampton and Stafford show that both these midland towns were missing very large chunks of their defences at this date.

THE BIG TEST

On 30 August 1642, Nehemiah Wharton, a young subaltern in the army of the Earl of Essex, arrived at Coventry as part of an advance Parliamentarian force. He wrote home to his former employer of his impressions as a soldier:

> Coventry is invironed with a wall co-equal, if not exceedinge, that of London for breadth and height; the compasse of it is neare three miles, all of free stone. It hath four strong gates (actually twelve in total, he omits eight smaller ones, plus a single postern-gate), strong battlements stored with (twenty) towers, bulwarks, courts of guard and other necessaries.

Wharton arrived in Coventry with the city buzzing over a skirmish which began the Civil War (1642-9). Before the King had even raised his standard at Nottingham, he attacked Coventry, seeking the county's powder store which had been held in the city on the orders of the Privy Council since 1640, along with all the provisions and material needed for improving fortification in an emergency. Placing their artillery in the former Cheylesmore Park quarries (still to be seen in William Paxton's landscaping for the 1847 London Road cemetery), the Royalists bombarded New Gate at the head of the London Road, causing a breach in the wall adjacent. The attackers tried to storm the breach, which was evidently insufficiently wide, since they were beaten off by the citizen militia, who then stopped up the hole with furniture and mattresses.

Evidence of the attack has recently (2003) come to light on the west side of Whitefriars Street during the building of a sports centre for Coventry University. Although this street was not constructed until 1900, the area was from the medieval period laid out as gardens. They lie in a direct line of sight with the Cheylesmore quarries across the location of New Gate. Spread across the seventeenth-century garden surfaces lay a scatter of lead musket balls, not flattened by impact but complete, and amongst which was a lead ball (again not flattened) of 12oz (340g). This exact weight of ball was commonly used by a light cannon common in the sixteenth to seventeenth centuries called a Demi-culverin or Robinet. It was already obsolescent by the time of the Civil War; other, heavier calibres such as the three-pounder (firing an iron ball) being preferred. Few Robinets remained in service by the end of the century.

The scatter of these munitions have shown two things. Firstly that the attackers, whose musketeers and small-calibre artillery were presumably trying to snipe at the defending militia on the battlements some 16-20 (4.9-6.0m) feet up, were at least in part aiming too high – the target was 200m from the quarry and the overshoot with this high target is an additional 200m (219 yards). Secondly, on the basis of this spent shot, it may be surmised that the King's travelling artillery train was inadequate for siege-works at this early stage of hostilities.

However in 1642, with the walls complete, Coventry had made itself a sought-after military prize. Soon after the disgruntled Charles I left empty-handed, the city declared for Parliament, with whom the sympathies of most of its citizenry lay and the walls provided safe storage for arms, troops, powder and thousands of refugees who sought shelter behind its fortifications. With its own militia of 800 under arms the walls could sport, if necessary, one soldier every five yards along its crenellations, a density more than adequate for defence behind the battlements.

Defence remained the prime concern and, even with the militia in place, further works were carried out in 1643-5. A new multangular tower was constructed adjacent to New Gate, probably on Parkside. This contained the latest in gun-loops to cover the London Road approaches, still thought of as the most likely direction from which an attack might come, while in front of the four main gates (Gosford, Bishop, Spon and Greyfriars) deep trenches were dug, called half-moons (presumably reflecting their shape). A bill for works carried out in 1644-6 indicates that the town ditch was also widened next to Hill Street.

These civil war trenches were investigated at Far Gosford Street in 2006, where a 'half moon' was characterised as just that, a crescent-shaped ditch dug to prevent direct access to the gate and drawbridge.

These were short-lived elements to the city's defence as the Royalist threat receded following their crushing defeat at the battle of Naseby (1645). In the following year a letter from Parliament ordered that the 'City of Coventry bee a garrisoned and the new worke slighted' on the orders of the Committee for Warwickshire. This probably refers to the half-moons, which may have hindered normal traffic in and out of the city. In addition the existing stocks of powder were to be dispersed among other sites, partly a safety measure as the city was brimming with refugees, but also to remove the prime reason for the city becoming a target once more. With the population at bursting point, it was in no shape to weather a lengthy siege, let alone the civilian carnage which would result from a full-scale attack.

The constant use of the now aged fortifications took its toll. In 1648 the constant round of inspection and repair which had pertained for much of the first half of the seventeenth century came to a head when it was recorded that Greyfriars, Cheylesmore, Hill Street, Well Street, Cook Street, Bastille and Priory gates 'are in grate decay and unfavourable'. A licence was granted for their extensive refurbishment, together with the recycling of existing building materials (itself perhaps a penny-pinching exercise betraying a lack of enthusiasm).

THE PRICE OF REBELLION

The demolition of Coventry's walls following the Restoration of the Monarchy was not an isolated act of pique on the part of the new monarch, Charles II. Other defended towns, such as Northampton, suffered the same fate, marked out only by the fact that they had backed the (eventual) losing faction and the king had no wish for lingering bands of disgruntled would-be rebels to seize a heavily fortified city against him.

In 1662, at the King's command, the Earl of Northampton issued a warrant to take down the walls, encouraging Coventrians to join in, allowing 'to every person the stone or such part of the walls as he or they shall wholly pull downe at their own expense'. Their zeal at this task was great since soon after Charles II was forced to write indignantly to the Earl, Sir Robert Townsend:

> in demolishing the walls of our City of Coventry part thereof, being a mound or fence to
> our Manor of Chillismore and parke thereunto adjoining, the pulling down thereof hath
> throwne downe part of the said house … we grant to Sir Robert all the stone of the said

walls that is upon our ground there towards the re-edifying of the said house and making up the mounds.

This was seen in the demolition of the south range of Cheylesmore Manor, excavated in 1992. The wall of the 1380s had replaced the south wall of the manor hall, which then lingered as a glorified lean-to. A Crown description indicates that it was 'down', possibly roofless, by the 1530s. Demolition of the town wall accounted for what was left. However, Charles' wishes seem not to have been followed up. The archaeology indicated that the range, seemingly already a wreck, was never rebuilt after 1662. The town wall, symbol of medieval Coventry's civic pride, was gone for good. It continued to provide stone, free of charge, for all who lived alongside it, well into the following century. The ditch too, for so long an illicit rubbish tip, now became infilled wherever anyone wished it. Long sections, especially wet ones, survived into the eighteenth century and are visible on early maps but few survived into the nineteenth, when development began to spread out over the city's former main line of resistance. The city had no further need of defence. At least not until 1940 and then it would suffer a different kind of siege.

Epilogue

'Everything in Coventry looks small and insignificant compared to what it used to. The only buildings which seem anything like what I remember are the churches.'
W.A. Andrews, 31 December 1861

Alderman, William Andrews expressed these sentiments in a city which in his short lifetime (at that time he was only about 30) had actually changed little to the eye. He had just spent 18 months on the continent and had had his horizons expanded. The generations which came after him saw the pace of change quicken and then run so fast, all that stayed the same was indeed the churches, helped of course by the Blitz and a level of economic growth previously unheard of.

Far from eschewing change, archaeology stands back and records it after the event, mostly long after. It should neither pine for what is lost nor should it automatically embrace the new. Somehow archaeologists stand back and monitor the change from afar, theoretically dispassionate, aware that each change of today forms the archaeology of the future.

In some ways Coventry has a split personality. Thanks to the Second World War it is both an ancient city and a twentieth-century reinvention of itself. The devastating Blitz of November 1940 and its follow up of April 1941, did far more than affect the generation alive at that time. Although the damage pales when compared to that later meted out to German cities such as Berlin, Hamburg or Dresden day and night for weeks on end, Coventry's destruction at the start of the war was far worse than the contemporary public's worst fears. The Nazi propaganda machine invented the verb 'to coventrate' to describe the utter destruction of a city. For Coventrians emerging sleepless from their air-raid shelters as the all-clear sounded on 15 November 1940, the world they knew had gone (69).

A much-debated pre-war regeneration programme had already accounted for the loss of three medieval streets, Great and Little Butcher Row and a large part of Cross Cheaping. The Blitz created a momentum and a reason for the continued regeneration of the city, which paved the way for the boom town of

69 View of the ruins of St Michael's Cathedral *c*.1948, from the spire. Bombed-out ruins at the corner of Bayley Lane and Priory Street lie behind. *W.F.Soden*

the post-war era. Every generation of Coventrians since then has benefited from a 'brave new world' attitude which, in looking steadfastly forward, cast only the merest glance back to what had gone before. The city centre was re-planned (*70*). An American-style shopping precinct was opened in 1948, the first of its kind in Britain. The Ring Road was on the drawing board in 1942, 20 years before the motor car began to enjoy its modern mass appeal. In 1962 the magnificent New Cathedral was consecrated (*colour plate 30*). Although some areas were adversely affected, much of what lay below ground, the archaeology, remained untouched. The biggest casualty was what had survived of the 'old' city above ground. While there was always protest, it was largely muted, and protestors were in the minority. Nowadays the last murmurs sometimes tend toward nostalgia, buoyed up on a national myth of a pre-war England, untouched by the world, safely cradled in the bosom of a benificent empire.

The nostalgic, however, should remember that for the generation or so until 1940, Coventry was a powerhouse, an urban captain of industry, producing tanks, arms, aeroplanes, engines and ammunition. The names ring down the generations: Alvis, Armstrong Whitworth, Hotchkiss, Morris, Royal Ordnance.... The city was at the heart of Britain's military output from before World War I,

70 Broadgate *c*.1948, from St Michael's spire. What had survived of medieval Smithford Street beyond was soon to be replaced with Britain's first purpose-built shopping centre. *W.F.Soden*

and proud of it. It had arrived there due to centuries of effort by generations of industrious and adventurous people who had already changed every inch of the city's face countless times.

The city lost on 14/15 November 1940 was not the medieval one, but the faintest echo of that which had survived sieges, the Black Death and the economic demands of numerous civil wars. Broken and beset by civil riots by 1525, it had dusted itself off only to have its heart ripped out by the Dissolution of the monasteries which closed its schools, its theological college, turned land-ownership on its head and made no recompense for the losses. Although assailed by economic stagnation, its still-proud walls made it a prize in 1642 and within two years it offered shelter to a war-weary stream of refugees. When peace offered its reward of renewed vigour and a growing economy, the Crown tore its walls down, reducing the city almost to a backwater.

Medieval England was magnificent, noisy, smelly, brutal and colourful; Coventry lay at its very heart and was all these things in good measure. Beneath the modern streets lies much of the city I have excavated for 30 years. It bears little relation to that of 14 November 1940, since only a tiny fraction of it was visible that fateful last day before the Blitz.

Medieval Coventry remains a palimpsest of layers, one on top of another, the buried physical remains of countless lives, hopes and fears, all aspiring to make the city what it remains today, an enduring success. It was not always pretty; it was sometimes downright ugly. It was sometimes corrupt. Beset by disasters, whole generations were wiped out. All that happens in Coventry has happened here before. The archaeology shows that.

Despite it all, the medieval urban experiment of Coventry continues. It won't go away. Its archaeology remains at the core of its identity as medieval new town, boom town. It is a story of industry, of culture, of spirituality, of perseverance and every hope and aspiration new Coventrians share with each generation which has gone before.

Further reading

This book has been many years in gestation. Many archives and other unpublished materials have been gleaned for salient points and facts relating to or having a bearing upon aspects of Coventry's Archaeology, as have lectures, seminars and day-schools I have either attended or delivered since 1984. It is not the purpose of this book to reference everything but to point the reader to the best and (comparatively) most accessible sources.

Of the unpublished records, it serves to bring to the researcher's attention the following:

Coventry Archives: the Borough Archive (BA) and Private Accessions (PA). These are wonderfully indexed and each year more become searchable on computer and through A2A on the Internet (Access to Archives). Birmingham City Archives also holds valuable documentation.

Of the pictorial views of the city's medieval buildings, Coventry Archives holds the antiquarian drawings of Nathaniel Troughton, while Birmingham City Archives holds the Aylesford Collection.

National Archives (formerly the PRO): particularly E164/21 (The Cartulary of St Mary's Priory, 1410-11). There is also a microform copy in Coventry Archives but the Latin and the court-hand are a bar to all but the trained. A translation is due to appear shortly as *Coventry Priory Register*, edited by Joan C. Lancaster and prepared for publication by Peter and Angela Coss (Dugdale Society Main Series). A small portion has previously been published by Arthur and Eileen Gooder as *The Pittancer's Rental*. Also in the National Archives are the records of the 1539 Dissolution of the Monasteries and the 1545 Chantries Act, and such documents as the Coroners' Rolls, Gaol Delivery Rolls and the Warwickshire Bag Roll. Again, their Latin and court-hand will put many off.

National Archives: PROB (Wills proved in the Prerogative Court of Canterbury). Some Latin, some English.

State Papers (Calendared in most Record Offices): Patent Rolls, Close Rolls, Charter Rolls, Inquisitions Post Mortem, Black Prince's Register.

Archaeological Archives and finds are held principally by the Herbert Art Gallery and Museum, Jordan Well, Coventry, with some significant Coventry items held by the British Museum, the Victoria and Albert Museum and a few items in the Burrell Collection.

Since the early 1970s it as been the practice to place a short note on fieldwork in the annual journal of the regional Group 8 of the CBA, *West Midlands Archaeology*. Most excavations can be briefly referenced there, however large or small. The entries do not, for the most part contain detail, however. Copies of most excavation reports can be found as archive documents in the Coventry Historic Environment Record.

The following are invaluable, although many are either out of print or attainable only as reference works. Many contain valuable bibliographies in their own right. Those known to be still available (2005) are marked ★:

Alcock N (1984) Coventry Streets: West Orchard and the Sherbourne, in *Transactions of the Birmingham and Warwickshire Archaeological Society (hereafter TBWAS) 91, 84-116*

Alcock N (1990) The Catesbys in Coventry; a medieval estate and its archives, in *Midland History 15, 1-36*

Bassett S (2000) Anglo-Saxon Coventry and its churches, *Dugdale Society Occasional Paper 41*

Bateman J and Redknap M (1986) *Coventry: Excavations on the town wall 1976-78*, Coventry Museums Monograph

Carpenter C (1990) *Locality and Polity: a study of Warwickshire landed society 1401-99*, CUP

Carus-Wilson E M (1954) *Medieval Merchant Venturers*, London

Chatwin P B (1936) The medieval patterned tiles of Warwickshire, *TBWAS 60, 1-40*

Coleman O (1960-1) *The Brokage Books of Southampton 1443-4*, Southampton Records Series vols iv, vi.

Coppack G and Aston M (2002) *Christ's Poor Men: The Carthusians in England*, Tempus★

Coss P (1986) *The documents of Early Medieval Coventry*

Coss P (1980) *The Langley Cartulary*

Coventry Museum guidebook (1986) *Whitefriars Story*, Coventry City Council★

Demidowicz G (1994) *Coventry's First Cathedral*★

Demidowicz G (2000) *A history of the Blue Coat school and the Lych Gate cottages, Coventry,* Coventry City Council★

Demidowicz G (2003) *The Buildings of Coventry,* Tempus★

Demidowicz G (2003) The Hyrsum Ditch, Birmingham and Coventry: a local topographical term, in *TBWAS 106, 143-50*★

Demidowicz G and Singlehurst M (2000) F*ar Gosford Street: historical notes,* Coventry City Council★

Dobson R B (1990) Urban decline in late medieval England, in Holt R and Rosser G, *The Medieval Town 1200-1540,* Leics University Press

Dormer–Harris M (1907–13) *The Coventry Leet Book*

Dugdale Sir W (1656) *Antiquities of Warwickshire*

Eames E (1980) *Catalogue of Lead-glazed Earthenware Tiles in the British Museum,* 2 vols

Fretton W G (1870) Memorials of the Whitefriars, *TBWAS (no volume number)*

Fretton W G (1874) Memorials of the Charterhouse, *TBWAS (no volume number)*

Fretton W G, (1879) Memorials of the Franciscans, *TBWAS (no volume number)*

Gooder E (1966, 1971) *The walls of Coventry*

Gooder E, Woodfield C and Chaplin R E (1966) The walls of Coventry, *TBWAS 81, 88-138*

Greatrex J (1995) *Biographical Register of the English Cathedral Priories of the Province of Canterbury 1066-1540*

Hilton R H (1950) *The Stoneleigh Ledger Book,* Dugdale Society

Hobley B (1971) Excavations at the Cathedral and Benedictine Priory of St Mary, Coventry, *TBWAS 84, 45-139.*

Hulton M (1995) *Coventry and its people in the 1520s,* Dugdale Society★

Hulton M (2000) *True as Coventry Blue,* City and County Heritage Publication 21★

Lancaster J (1975) *The Historic Towns Atlas II*

Lilley K (2000) Mapping the medieval city: plan analysis and urban history, *Urban History 27,* Cambridge University Press

Little A G (1917) *Studies in Franciscan History*

Locock M (2000) Animal bones and the urban economy: 30 years of archaeozoology in Coventry, in Anderson S (ed) *Current and recent research in osteoarchaeology 2*

Martin A R (1937) *Franciscan Architecture*

Monckton L, and Morris R K, (ed) 2011 Coventry: Medieval art architecture and archaeology in the city and its vicinity, *British Archaeological Assoication 33.*

Poole B (1870) *Antiquities of Coventry*

Pythian Adams C 1979 *Desolation of a city: Coventry and the urban crisis of the late middle ages,* Cambridge University Press

Ruddock A A (1951) *Italian merchants and shipping in Southampton 1270-1600*, University College Southampton

Rylatt M (1977, 1981) *Coventry: Archaeology and Redevelopment*, Coventry Museums Monograph

Rylatt M and Mason P (2003) *The archaeology of the medieval cathedral and priory of St Mary, Coventry*, Coventry City Council/Phoenix Initiative/Millennium Commission★

Rylatt M and Stokes M (1996) *Excavations on Broadgate East 1974-5*, Coventry Museum Monograph★

Sharpe T (1807) *Antiquities of Coventry*

Sharpe T (1835) *Epitome of the County of Warwick, containing a brief historical and descriptive account of the towns, villages and parishes with their hamlets*

Smet J (1975–85) *The Carmelites: a history of the Brothers of Our Lady of Mt Carmel*, 4 vols

Soden I (1985) *Coventry: Excavations at Ernesford Grange 1971-3*, Coventry Museum Monograph

Soden I (1994) Propaganda of monastic benefaction: statement and implication in the art of St Anne's Charterhouse, Coventry, in Locock M *Meaningful Architecture: social interpretations of buildings* , Worldwide Archaeology Series 9, 147-66, Avebury

Soden I (1995) *Coventry: Excavations at St Anne's Charterhouse 1968-87*, Coventry Museums Monograph★

Soden I (ed) (2002) *True as Coventry Blue: Papers presented to Margaret Rylatt*

Soden I (2002) The planning of a Carthusian Church, in Aston M, Keevill G and Hall T *Monastic Archaeology*, Oxbow★

Soden I (2003) The conversion of former monastic buildings to secular use: the case of Coventry, in Gaimster D and Gilchrist R, *The Archaeology of Reformation 1480-1580*, 280-9, Maney★

Soden I (2009) *Ranulf de Blondeville, the first English hero*, Amberley

Various (1960) *Victoria County History: Warwickshir*, volumes 2 & 8

Woodfield C C (1981) Finds from the Free Grammar School at the Whitefriars, Coventry *c.*1545-1557/8, *Post-Medieval Archaeology 15, 81-159*

Wright S (1988) Much Park Street, Coventry: the development of a medieval street; excavations 1970-74, *TBWAS 92, 1-133*

Zimmerman Fr Benedict (1899) The Carmelite Monastery at Coventry: Historical sketch with illustration *Carmelite Review 3* (Feb 1899), 43-6 and *4* (Mar 1899), 73-5.

Zimmerman Fr Benedict (1904) L'ancien couvent des Carmes de Coventry, Angleterre, *Chroniques du Carmel* XVI, 149-51

Index

If you are interested in purchasing other books published by The History Press, or in case you have difficulty finding any of our books in your local bookshop, you can also place orders directly through our website

www.thehistorypress.co.uk